ns. 0305 - 40/-

£11.50.

THE ENCHANTED ISLE

An Island History

by

C. W. R. Winter

PHOTOGRAPHS BY PAT WINTER

The title of this book is taken from a letter from Benjamin Disraeli, Lord Beaconsfield, to Queen Victoria, thanking her for some primroses she had sent him from Osborne.

He said — "They are the harbingers of Spring, and show that Your Majesty's sceptre has touched the Enchanted Isle"

CROSS PUBLISHING

*"The Enchanted Isle" is dedicated to all
those who, like the author, love the Isle of Wight,
and find it fascinating, intriguing, infuriating,
surprising and irrestible.
It is also dedicated to those who, like the author,
found history a deadly dull and boring subject
when they were taught it at school.*

Acknowledgements

The information contained in this book has been culled from a variety of sources and authorities, the help of all of which the author wishes to acknowledge with gratitude. The photographs have all been taken by Pat Winter, with the following exceptions, the sources of which are gratefully acknowledged. For the pictures on pages 65 and 222 the National Portrait Gallery, page 66 Montagu Motor Museum, page 70 National Maritime Museum, page 82 K. W. Terry, pages 146 and 165 Nunwell Symphony, pages 153 and 226 Department of the Environment, page 153 the Rt. Hon. Earl of Harewood. Maps and Charts have been drawn by Derek Smith. Copyright in the pictures on pages 88 and 225 is reserved, they are reproduced by gracious permission of Her Majesty the Queen.

First published in 1990 by Cross Publishing Ltd.
ISBN 1 873295 00 6 (hardback), 1 873295 01 4 (paperback)

Text © C. W. R. Winter 1990, Photographs © P. Winter 1990

Graphics by Derek Smith
Photoset by Quarr-T, Binstead, Isle of Wight
Printed by Crossprint, Newport, Isle of Wight

Other published works by the same author include —

The Ancient Town of Yarmouth

The Manor Houses of the Isle of Wight.
    (With photography by Michael Rainey)

The 'Queen Mary': Her Early Years Recalled.

The Run of the Tide.
    (With photography by Pat Winter and
    line drawings by Anthony Winter).

Village Churches of the Isle of Wight.
    (With photography by Pat Winter)

Front Cover: Back Cover:
The Causeway, Freshwater   *Primroses at Osborne*

Contents

SECTION II (continued)

There are four Time Charts with this book, to help relate local events to national events, and to the Kings and Queens of England. They each bear a prefix "C.C.", which stands for Chinese Chart. Why? Because you read them vertically, starting at the bottom. It is easier that way.

There are also a couple of family trees, three maps and a sketch, as follows:

Foreword

Dr. J. D. Jones, M.A., Ph.D.

The title of this book appositely picks up Disraeli's theme of enchantment. The Isle of Wight — for such a relatively small land area — seems always to have had that enchanted quality, that 'spirit of the place', which has given an unusual richness to its historical pageant, here so fully set out by our local historian, Ron Winter. This book shows the changing patterns, over the centuries, of Island society and administration, set within the broader canvas of national and European history. It shows too the real people who were and are the flesh and blood of this social framework. Above all it reflects the author's real love of the Island and its history. He has caught, and can communicate, its enchantment!

Jack Jones

TIME SCALE — CC1

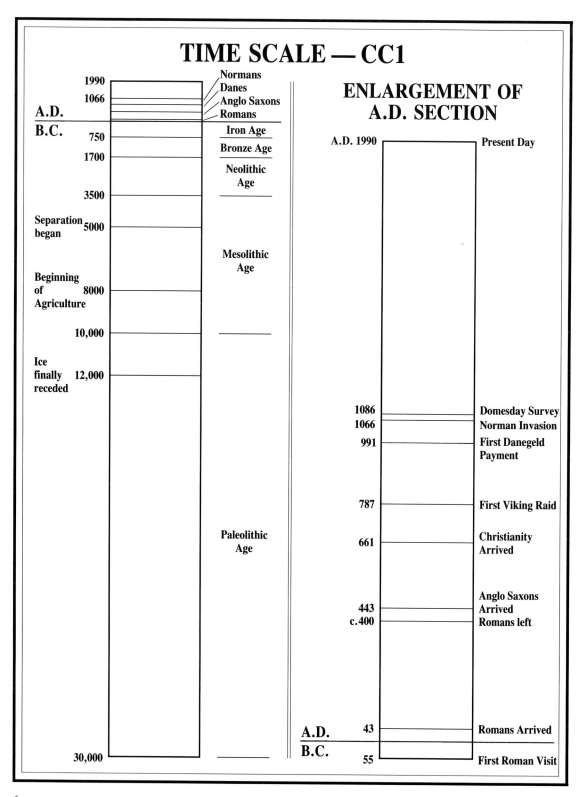

A.D.		
1990		Normans
1066		Danes
		Anglo Saxons
		Romans

B.C.

750	Iron Age
1700	Bronze Age
	Neolithic Age
3500	
Separation began	5000
	Mesolithic Age
Beginning of Agriculture	8000
	10,000
Ice finally receded	12,000
	Paleolithic Age
30,000	

ENLARGEMENT OF A.D. SECTION

A.D. 1990	Present Day
1086	Domesday Survey
1066	Norman Invasion
991	First Danegeld Payment
787	First Viking Raid
661	Christianity Arrived
443	Anglo Saxons Arrived
c.400	Romans left
A.D. 43	Romans Arrived
B.C. 55	First Roman Visit

I — In the Beginning

The Longstone at Mottistone, all that remains of a Neolithic Barrow, possibly 5000 years old.

In the world today it is customary and convenient to measure time from the birth of Jesus Christ, but the 2000 years (almost) that have elapsed since that world shaping event are a very minor and insignificant part of the several thousand million years of the world's history. What has happened during this vast period of time is the province of scientists, of astronomers, geologists and archaeologists, and it is not until comparatively recent times — say 30,000 years B.C. — that lesser mortals can begin to comprehend and relate to our own lives.

We are told that 30,000 years B.C. the whole of northern Europe was covered in ice, and that it was not until about 20,000 years B.C. that the ice began to melt and land appear from under it. At this time the Isle of Wight had still not been formed, it was part of what is now the English mainland which itself, together with the whole of the British Islands system, was still joined to the continent of Europe. There was no Solent, no English Channel, no Irish Sea, and indeed the level of the sea that lapped the edge of this great land mass was at least 600 feet lower than it is today.

As the ice melted and retreated northwards towards what are today the north polar regions, great rivers were formed to carry away to the sea the enormous volume of water generated, and gradually, though very slowly, the sea level rose. By the year 12,000 B.C. it is believed that the ice had finally receded and that northern Europe was beginning to develop.

Imperceptibly, over several thousand years, the land settled, dried out, and became stabilised. The four seasons had been established, vegetation began to appear, and much of the land became covered with trees. The forests so created gave shelter to wild animals, the rivers gradually became populated with fish, and once this had happened it was not long before man appeared on the scene.

These first men who pushed northwards from Europe into the country we now know as the Isle of Wight were hunters, nomadic people who did not settle down in any one place, and who lived on the animals they could kill, and the fish they could catch. By our standards today they lived a very simple, primitive life, dressed in animal skins and using for their tools and weapons the hardest substance they knew, namely flint.

These early people have left traces of their presence behind them, a good example being a flint axe head discovered some years ago in Great Budbridge. This axe head was found not far from the present house which is built in a U-bend of the eastern River Yar, the site being typical of those selected by these nomadic tribes as a temporary resting place, the river providing protection from attack on three sides. Attack, incidentally, not from men but from wild animals.

Round about 8,000 B.C. the world saw the dawning of agriculture, with men beginning to settle down and live in village settlements, learning slowly how to clear spaces in the forests, to grow crops, and domesticate animals. This process began in the Mediterranean area, the very name of which indicates that this was the centre of civilisation, and gradually, over many centuries, these new found skills and developments crept northward until they reached our own latitudes.

In the meantime major topographical changes were taking place here. In about 5,000 B.C., due to geological changes in the land, and the continual rising of sea levels, the separation of Britain from the continent began. The major rivers in this area at this time were, firstly, one that probably rose in what is now Somerset and flowed eastwards along the line of the Solent, where it joined another and greater east flowing river along what is now the English Channel. These combined rivers then joined with the Thames and the Rhine to fall into the sea as one huge stream off the coast of Holland, (so aptly named the Netherlands or the Low Countries). At some point the Atlantic Ocean broke through into these river valleys, Ireland and England became islands, and so did the Isle of Wight. Nature was well on its way to fashioning the geographical layout of this part of the world that we still have today in the 20th century A.D.

While all this was going on, and the Isle of Wight was being formed, it is perhaps worth pausing for a moment to see what was happening in the

Top. *For thousands of years, throughout the Neolithic and Bronze Ages, Afton Down was a favourite burial ground.*

Bottom. *A Bronze Age round barrow on Afton Down.*

8

Mediterranean area. While life here in England was still very primitive, civilisation in the Middle East was making tremendous progress, particularly in Egypt. In that country by 5,000 B.C., both in the arts and sciences, as well as in medicine, a quite sophisticated culture was developing, a culture which even today in many aspects we cannot match. By the year 4,200 B.C. the Egyptians had established a calendar which is the basis of the one we use today. They divided the year up into 12 months of 30 days each, but realised that the 360 days this gave them for the year was not quite correct, so they added on at the end 5 extra days which were given up to feasting and celebration. Four thousand years later the Romans, who had discovered that even 365 days was not quite enough, added an extra day once every four years, and this Julian Calendar — so called after Julius Caesar — is still in use today, in slightly modified form.

Developments in civilisation went ahead in the Mediterranean basin at a quicker rate than here in northern Europe, and by 1,500 B.C. the Egyptians had built up an empire that was the envy of surrounding countries. In the Isle of Wight at this time we were entering what we now call the Bronze Age, a period in which man had learned how to make fire hot enough to refine the ores of copper, tin, and other non-ferrous metals, and to make tools and weapons in bronze. Many Bronze Age relics have been found in this Island, as for example a bronze bracelet discovered at Stenbury where there had been a Bronze Age settlement.

750 years later men had learned how to make a hotter flame still, one that would melt iron, and this heralded the beginning of the Iron Age. With the development of iron weapons and tools the speed of civilisation increased, and modern history may be said to have begun.

Bronze Age and Iron Age men have left their mark on the Isle of Wight, principally in their burial mounds and hill forts, and archaeologists have established the existence of several settlements, though the total population of the Island at this time was probably not more than a hundred or two. Even in these remote days the Isle of Wight was subject to periodical invasion from the continental mainland of people looking for land on which to settle, though necessarily the numbers were small. As early as 1900 B.C. settlers known as the Beaker people — a name subsequently given to them on account of the distinctive pottery they have left behind — arrived from Europe and settled in the Island, but later they were supplanted by other immigrants, and from about 500 B.C. wave upon wave of Celtic invaders from northern France reached these shores.

One of the foremost and fiercest of these Celtic tribes was the Belgae who brought with them new ideas and a different way of life, and they established themselves not only in the Isle of Wight but also on the mainland of England. But the biggest gift they brought to these Islands was publicity, for the Belgae were enthusiastic traders with the Roman Empire, and it may have been through them that Caesar was persuaded to conquer Gaul and later England.

And the Roman invasion of Britain was by far the most important event to date in the history of the Isle of Wight.

II — *The Roman Island*

In Brighstone Forest, an ancient trackway through the woods which was already old when the Romans came to the Island.

The arrival of the Romans in Britain in A.D.43 was indeed a momentous affair and one that struck terror and rage into the hearts of the Celtic population, for though they resisted the invasion with the utmost bravery they were no match for the disciplined and better armed Roman Legions. On two previous occasions, in B.C.55 and B.C.54, the Britons had beaten off Roman attempts to establish themselves in Kent, but in A.D.43 the invaders were in greater strength and were determined to stay. The odds were heavily in favour of the Romans, who besides being uniformed, equipped, and trained to a high military standard, had behind them the confidence of having already conquered much of Europe.

Against these, the world's finest and most successful troops, the Britons were half naked, clad in animal skins, undisciplined, poorly armed, and possessing only their indomitable and ferocious courage. So that the issue was never long in doubt. Pockets of resistance held out for some considerable time, and various local chieftains — Caractacus being foremost among them — mounted counter attack after counter attack, but the Romans inevitably steam-rollered their way to victory.

In the Isle of Wight, which the Romans called Vectis, and where the total population was perhaps no more than 250, the question of resistance probably did not arise. The 5,000 strong 2nd Legion, under its 34 year old leader Vespasian, took over the Island in the name of Rome and was probably greeted with astonishment by the inhabitants who would never before have seen anything like these helmeted and kilted warriors.

For the Romans were different to any invaders the Island had experienced before, or for that matter, since. For they were civilised and cultured as well as militarily disciplined, and in their sophistication were hun-

11

dreds of years in advance of the native population. It must have been with bewilderment that the Islanders discovered that their conquerors did not wish to destroy, neither to rape nor to pillage, and it could not have been long before these new masters were accepted and life returned to normal.

How much of the peaceful capture of the Isle of Wight was due to the Roman commander, Vespasian, and how much was just simply standard Roman practice is not now known, but it is known that Vespasian was a good, plain soldier, frugal and temperate in his habits, sensible and affable, with a good sense of humour. Later in A.D.69 he became Emperor, having served in all parts of the Empire, and he reigned for about 10 years. At the end of his life, when he knew that death was near, he had a whim to die standing up, supported by his favourite slaves, and his very last words were in the nature of a joke, for he murmured to them "Have a care — I am about to become a God!"

For nearly 400 years the Romans occupied Britain, and these were years of peace during which the Celtic population did not have to bear arms and could lead their own lives without fear. Four hundred years is a long time, as long as from our own days back to the time of Shakespeare, and during this period some of the Roman civilisation and culture inevitably rubbed off on to the British inhabitants.

In the Isle of Wight a number of Roman farms were created, each with its own villa, and the remains of two of these — at Brading and Newport — have been expertly excavated and are now open to the public. Little is known about the people who owned these farms, they may have been high ranking army officers, or senior civilian administrators, or even men who had retired, in fact it is possible that these villas were in the nature of second homes, and that the Island was experiencing its first taste of being a holiday island. Traces of eight villas have so far been found, and there may be others still to be discovered.

The Brading villa, which was built towards the end of the second century A.D. must have belonged to someone of importance. It contained twelve rooms for living purposes, all on the western side of a large courtyard. The northern and southern sides contained buildings connected with the running of the farm, and also staff quarters, while the eastern side was open to a view of the sea, which in those days would have been closer to the villa than it now is. The west wing also contained a bathroom suite, and many of the living rooms had ducted hot air central heating. The latter was fairly common in better class Roman dwellings, and it is a sad comment on our own civilisation that when the Romans left Britain in the 5th century the practice of centrally heating houses left with them, and did not return for fifteen hundred years.

Six of the twelve living rooms in the Brading villa were fitted with elaborate mosaic floors, each one depicting a different classical or mythological scene. The entrance hall's mosaic was a particularly fine one, and the plastered walls were richly decorated with painted pictures, one of which showed a green basket with purple plums. In short, this was a villa of some considerable elegance and taste, a far cry from the primitive huts

Top Right. Mosaic showing a cock-headed man, Brading Roman Villa.

Bottom Right. Mosaic floor at Brading.

Left. The Medusa Mosaic at Brading.

Remains of corn dryer at Newport Villa.

in which the Celtic islanders were living.

The Newport villa is smaller than the above, and was built on a north-east facing slope descending to the River Medina. The living quarters are not so well preserved as at Brading, with the exception of the bathroom suite, enough of which has survived to show clearly how it worked and how sophisticated it was. It contained five basic rooms, starting with a changing room which was followed by three rooms of differing temperatures — namely, a frigidarium (cold room), a tepidarium (warm room), and a caldarium (hot room) — and finally a room for massage. The whole was heated by a hypocaust system which led hot air under the floors from an exterior wood burning boiler. All this in the 2nd century A.D. — a more elaborate and sophisticated bathroom set-up than in any house in the Island today.

Besides living in comfort the Roman inhabitants of the Isle of Wight kept up the life style to which they had been accustomed in Italy, farming the sea as well as the land for their food. For example, the Romans introduced oysters into Britain, for this was a delicacy of which they were very fond, importing them through their port of Rutupiae (Richborough) in

Fireplace

Kent. Oyster production in this country was developed efficiently, the best beds being established at Colchester, Whitstable, and in the Medina River — all sites near to Roman settlements.

In addition to Brading and Newport the sites of the other six villas are at Rock (Brighstone), Clatterford, Carisbrooke, Combley, and Bowcombe. The sixth one was at Gurnard but within the last hundred years it has been completely destroyed by the action of the sea. The Rock, Clatterford and Carisbrooke sites all suffered an ineffectual semi-excavation in Victorian times, and much more work is needed to add to our knowledge of these important remains. Rock was partially re-excavated between 1974 and 1976.

Other traces of the Roman occupation are scattered throughout the Island, but offer tantalisingly little information about the people who lived here. Coins of various denominations and reigns have been found in Ventnor, Yarmouth, St. Lawrence, Niton, Shanklin, Wroxall, and other places. In Shanklin an amphora was discovered containing a hoard of 600 coins, and in Wroxall an urn with no fewer than 5,000. Both these latter finds were probably coins hidden when danger threatened from invaders, and which their owners hoped one day to return to. The sad fact that they did not, suggests that they failed to survive the anticipated danger, and of course we know that towards the end of the 4th century armed raids from Germany were becoming more frequent and serious.

As well as coins jewellery has been found, also pottery and roof tiles, and all these finds would seem to indicate a fairly wide occupation of the Island, but it is strange that with villas spread from one end of the Island to the other no trace of any Roman road has yet been found. Up on the Downs in several places there are stretches of very ancient highways which were probably in use long before the Romans came, but to date no excavation has unearthed any part of a traditional, well drained and engineered

Roman road. With one possible exception, this being a length of Roman drain unearthed by a farmer a few years ago near Watchingwell, though this could possibly have been a conventional field drain.

Helge Kokeritz in his *"Place Names of the Isle of Wight"* suggests the possibility of Roman roads in the vicinity of three places — Haven Street, Rew Street (near Cowes), and Street Place (near Calbourne), but only excavation will prove or disprove this theory, for ground levels rise over the centuries, and any Roman roads would now be several feet below present surface levels.

Kokeritz also mentions another intriguing possibility. The position of the Roman villa at Gurnard is known, and there is a theory that in those days it was possible at low tide to cross on foot to Lepe in Hampshire. The theory also maintains that the Romans conducted a regular trade in tin, which they brought from the mines in Cornwall to Lepe, crossed to Gurnard, thence across the Island to Puckaster on the south coast. From Puckaster it was shipped to France and then down to Marseilles whence it could be taken by boat to Rome.

There are definite remains of a Roman road at Lepe running in a north-westerly direction, so that if the theory is correct it would be logical to expect another Roman road from Gurnard down through the Isle of Wight to Puckaster. Whether the Romans did in fact conduct this 'tin' trade is an interesting possibility, and there is no doubt that the Romans were an industrious people and developed the natural resources of the country efficiently. Besides farming in the Isle of Wight they quarried stone at Binstead, exporting it to the mainland. Their castle at Portchester is believed to be built of Binstead stone.

But though they worked hard and brought prosperity to the British Isles it is doubtful whether the occupation was profitable to themselves. There were always so many other people — Picts from North Britain, Scots from Ireland, Jutes, Angles, and Saxons from Germany — all trying to get a foothold in Britain, that the Romans never had an easy time of it, and though they protected the civilian inhabitants from war and invasion for so long, they themselves were continually fighting. Towards the end of the 4th century their stay here was becoming increasingly difficult, life for all in these islands, Celts and Romans alike, was more insecure, and as Rome herself was under increasing threat from Huns, Goths, and Vandals, it was inevitable that ultimately the Legions would have to be withdrawn from Britain to defend their homeland.

In A.D.410 the Legions were finally pulled out to return to Rome, and suddenly, after nearly 400 years of peace and prosperity, the people of England and the Isle of Wight were alone, defenceless and bewildered. The so-called "Dark Ages" had begun.

Note: Anyone interested in the last days of the Roman occupation is recommended to read *"The Long Sunset"*, a play by R. C. Sherriff. This is a purely fictitious and romantic account of the impact of the withdrawal on a Roman farmer and his family in Richborough, Kent.

III — *Jutes, Angles and Saxons*

The departure of the Roman military forces had a devastating effect on these islands. After nearly 400 years of peaceful existence, without having to fight or even train to fight, the population were quite unable to defend themselves. Some civilian Romans, to whom England was home, stayed on and desperately tried to organise themselves into local defence groups, but they and the indigenous Celtic population were ineffectual, bewildered by the turn of events, and in no doubt as to the probable fate that awaited them. Some Roman soldiers too, who had served in Britain for years and had made their homes here, found it difficult to leave, and there were many heartbreaks. Kipling's *"The Roman Centurion's Song"* sums up the plight of the latter very neatly —

> "Legate, I had the news last night — my cohort ordered home
> By ship to Portus Itius and thence by road to Rome.
> I've marched the companies aboard, the arms are stowed below:
> Now let another take my sword. Command me not to go!

I've served in Britain forty years, from Vectis to the Wall.
I have no other home than this, nor any life at all.
Last night I did not understand, but, now the hour draws near
That calls me to my native land, I feel that land is here."

Once the Legions had gone it was not long before the awaiting savage hordes took advantage of the situation and swarmed in, hungry for loot and land. The Isle of Wight was not troubled by the northern invaders, Picts and Scots, but received plenty of attention from the German tribes. These latter were not interested in taking over and continuing the Roman culture. They hated the Romans, and the wealth that Rome had created, and were intent on destroying it. Also they were desperate for somewhere to live, and this need fuelled their ferocity. Their speciality was destruction, and death to anyone who stood in their way, and many inhabitants were slaughtered at this time. Some managed to escape and fled to the west and north, and the Roman togas that many of these civilians wore have survived as the tartan plaids in Scotland to this day.

Jutes, Angles, and Saxons all came from that part of north Germany that included the later state of Schleswig-Holstein and part of Denmark. The Jutes got their name from Jutland which was the original name for the Danish promontory; to the south of them were the Angles, occupying Schleswig-Holstein; and further south still was the larger territory of Saxony. The incentive that drove all these tribes to seek new lands in Britain was severe overcrowding at home.

The period during which they established themselves in England, the 5th, 6th and 7th centuries is well named "the Dark Ages" for the information that has survived about it is very scanty, and authorities today are not in total agreement about the sequence of events. It was a period of "every man for himself", when the invaders were not only fighting the Celtic and Roman inhabitants of these islands, but were also fighting amongst themselves. It was an extremely bloody period.

Left. Junction of two old tracks near the Blacksmith's Arms, the site of a Saxon burial ground.

It is probable that some Anglo-Saxon settlements were established on the south coast of England, and in the Isle of Wight, even before the Romans left, and it has been suggested that the Roman named "Saxon Shore", which they defended with seven forts built in the 4th century, recognised the fact that Saxon families were already settled there.

The Anglo Saxon Chronicle, which apart from the writings of the Venerable Bede is the oldest historical record of these times, describes how in the year 449 Vortigern, King of the Britons, having failed in his appeal to the Romans to return and help restore order, appealed to the Angli tribe. He offered them land in return for their help in fighting the Picts, and as a result a small force of Angles was sent over. The Chronicle reports events as follows —

"They then fought against the Picts and had victory wherever they came. Then they sent to Angel (their homeland) to send more aid and to be told of the worthlessness of the Britons and of the excellence of the land. They then at once sent hither a larger force to help the others. These men came from three nations of Germany: from the Old Saxons, from the Angles, and from the Jutes. From the Jutes came the people of Kent and the people of the Isle of Wight, that is the race which now dwells in the Isle of Wight."

The Jutes were not allowed to live in peace for very long in the Isle of Wight, for in the year 495 two new leaders turned up in the shape of Cerdic and his son Cynric, and these two were destined to have a profound effect on the Island. There would appear to be some doubt about their ancestry, for the Anglo Saxon Chronicle says they were descended from the same Anglian forbears as the original Anglian leaders, Hengist and Horsa, but other authorities say they were Saxons. It has also been suggested that their names are not Germanic at all, but are Celtic, in which case they may have come to the Isle of Wight, not from Germany but from Wales.

In passing, it may be worth mentioning that though the Saxons ultimately became the most powerful influence in the Isle of Wight and southern England, it was the Angles who gave their name to England, and to the language, English. The name of the Angles has of course also persisted through the centuries in "East Anglia", but the Saxons gave their name to Essex (the East Saxons), Middlesex (the Middle Saxons), Sussex (the South Saxons), and Wessex (the West Saxons).

Cerdic and Cynric captured the Isle of Wight in the year 530, and according to the Chronicle slew many men in a place later named Wihtgaraburh, and now identified as Carisbrooke. The men they slew were presumably the descendants of the original Jutish settlers, it being the custom in those days when you captured a territory to put the inhabitants to death.

Saxon archway between nave and tower. The original entrance to Arreton church.

Four years later Cerdic died and the Isle of Wight was given to two relations of his, Stuf and Wihtgar. This Wihtgar died in 544 and the place where he was buried was then called Wihtgaraburh. Scholars have tried hard to explain how Wihtgaraburh was turned into Carisbrooke, and there are several theories. One of the most interesting comes from Kokeritz who suggests that the first element of the name "Caris-" derives from the Welsh word "Carreg" meaning a rock, which could well refer to the hill on which Carisbrooke Castle is built. If this were true it would lend support to the theory that Cerdic and Cynric were Celtic and came from Wales. The "-brooke" in the name is of course the Lukely Brook which flows through Carisbrooke down to the River Medina.

To digress for a moment, it is interesting to note that two of the Sealink Ferries that ply between Yarmouth and Lymington have Celtic names. "Cenred" was a king of Wessex who was directly descended from Cerdic, and "Cenwulf" was Abbot of Peterborough in 972 and later Bishop of Winchester.

After the death of Wihtgar in 544 and for the next 120 years the records are full of the struggle for power in England, and describe the fighting and killing that accompanied this struggle. The Isle of Wight is not mentioned again until the year 661 when Wulfhere, King of Mercia, invaded the Island — "ravaged" being the word used.

The church of St. George, Arreton, still showing traces of its Saxon origin.

"Wulfhere, son of Penda, ravaged in the Isle of Wight, and gave the people of Wight to Athelwald, King of Sussex, because Wulfhere had stood sponsor for him at baptism. Eoppa, the priest, at the command of (bishop) Wilfrid and King Wulfhere, was the first to bring Christianity to the Isle of Wight."

The poor old Isle of Wight was thus subjected to more barbarism, and in the name of Christianity too! But worse was to follow. Exactly 25 years later, in 686, the West Saxon King, Caedwalla, together with his brother Mul, "laid waste Kent and the Isle of Wight", and it rather looks as though they were recovering for Wessex the territories that Wulfhere of Mercia had previously captured. The official reason that was given for Caedwalla's invasion of the Isle of Wight was his anger at the idolatrous habits of the Islanders, which suggests that the Christianity brought in a quarter of a century earlier by Wulfhere had not proved very satisfactory. The Venerable Bede reports on this latest invasion in the following words —

"After Caedwalla had possessed himself of the kingdom of the Gewissae, he also took the Isle of Wight, which until then was entirely given over to idolatry, and by cruel slaughter endeavoured to destroy all the inhabitants thereof, and to place in their stead people from his own province: having bound himself by a vow, though he was not yet, as is reported, regenerated in Christ, to give the fourth part of the land, and

19

of the booty, to our Lord, if he took the island, which he performed by giving the same for our Lord to the use of Bishop Wilfrid, who happened at the time to have accidentally come thither out of his own nation.

The measure of that island, according to the computation of the English, is of 1200 families, and accordingly the Bishop had given him land of 300 families.

Thus, after all the provinces of the island of Britain had embraced the faith of Christ, the Isle of Wight also received the same . . . "

The Bishop Wilfrid mentioned above was not the same Wilfrid who lived in King Wulfhere's time, though they were both in their turn Bishops of York.

The following year after their conquest of the Isle of Wight Caedwalla and Mul had to return to Kent, and Mul lost his life there through being burned to death, along with twelve other men. No details are given as to how it happened, but it was obviously deliberate on the part of the Kentish men since seven years later they were forced to pay a fine of 7500 shillings in compensation. Caedwalla — which incidentally is another Celtic name — also went to Rome in 688 and was baptised by the Pope, but seven days later he suddenly died, still in his baptismal robes.

With the coming of Christianity to the Isle of Wight two things happened. Firstly, the periodical and wholesale slaughter of the inhabitants slackened off, certainly for the next 200 years. Until the coming of the Vikings towards the end of the 9th century, it would appear that only the kings, and sometimes the queens, continued to kill each other. The other development was that a peaceful and a Christian climate encouraged the building of churches, and some of the older village churches, notably at Arreton, Brading, and Freshwater, still exhibit traces of Saxon work. Naturally, over the centuries the majority of the Saxon buildings have decayed and have had to be rebuilt, and there have been several periods of reconstruction, culminating in the 19th century Victorian Gothic revival, which have inevitably covered up the original architecture.

The 400 years from the 5th century to the 9th were the most momentous in English history, since it was in this period that the nation was born. Jutes, Angles and Saxons established the English way of life, English customs and habits, and above all, the English character. Whereas the Romans had always been an occupying military power, and had never stamped a Latin personality and character on to the country, the Anglo-Saxons were the exact opposite, they became and were the English people. And whereas when the Romans departed from the Isle of Wight they left comparatively little trace behind, the Saxons never really left. They stayed and managed to absorb any other invaders who came along.

Some of their principal characteristics still shine through in the English character. In spite of their savage nature they were a nation of farmers and sailors, and as the latter they exulted in the challenge of rough winds and seas. They admired physical bravery above anything else, and were intensely loyal to one another. When danger threatened they united as one man, and they never gave in.

IV — *Terror from the North*

A 24-oared Danish longboat.

By the middle of the 8th century it really looked as though England was heading for an era of peace. The Anglo-Saxon Chronicle, while still reporting the deaths, and occasionally the murders of kings and bishops, concentrates more on peaceful items of news. Since the year 686, and the rather bloody conquest of the Isle of Wight by King Caedwalla, the Chronicle does not mention the Island for 200 years, and this must be regarded as a case of "no news is good news". It was not until 897 that the Isle of Wight was in serious trouble again.

On the mainland however it was a different story, and from the year 787 England was subjected to a series of attacks of unparalleled ferocity from Scandinavia. In that year, for the first time, three shiploads of Norwegians raided the English coast. The Chronicle calls them Norwegians, and in the next breath refers to them as Danes, and later as Vikings, and all three terms are often used. Though the Isle of Wight was not immediately involved with these raids it is necessary — in order that subsequent events

21

in the Island may be understood — to know a little about the wider history of England during this period.

The raiders came from all parts of southern Scandinavia including Jutland, which we now know as Denmark, and differed from the previous Jutes, Angles and Saxons in that they were professional fighters. They lived solely for warfare, and every spring from 787 onwards visited England for the rich pickings that were to be obtained. In 787 there were only 3 shiploads, but the numbers steadily increased. In 836 there were 25 ships, in 840 there were 33 ships, and in 851 there were 350.

The terror they brought with them was unimaginable. They destroyed houses, farms, churches, monasteries, anything that took their fancy, anything that would slake their blood lust. There is a record that one single Viking personally slew 84 monks in the Benedictine Abbey of Peterborough. Their atrocities were legion, and as the years went by they systematically destroyed the Christian Saxon kingdoms of Northumbria, Mercia and East Anglia. In East Anglia the Christian King Edmund fought valiantly but was captured and murdered. Later he was canonised, and in the Isle of Wight the old Saxon church of Wootton is dedicated to him.

In 851 the Vikings wintered in England (in Thanet) for the first time, and it should have been obvious then that they had come to stay. After subduing the North and Midlands they turned their attention to the kingdom of Wessex, and here they found resistance from a very doughty foe — King Alfred — who has well been called "the Great", for he not only fought and beat the Vikings but was instrumental in teaching them, reforming them, and ultimately integrating them into a more civilised community. King Alfred has connections with the Isle of Wight in that his mother, Osburh, is believed to have come from the Island, and he certainly owned the manor of Arreton, for in his Will he specifically leaves it to his younger son. Kokeritz also traces the derivation of the name Alverstone to "Alfred's Farm", so there may be another connection here.

King Alfred also figured in the first Island battle with the Vikings. The Anglo-Saxon Chronicle records the following for the year 897 —

> "This same year the (Viking) hosts in East Anglia and Northumbria greatly harrassed Wessex along the south coast with predatory bands. Then King Alfred ordered warships to be built to meet the Danish ships; they were almost twice as long as the others, some had sixty oars, some more; they were both swifter, steadier, and with more freeboard than the others. Then on one occasion the same year came six ships to the Isle of Wight and did much harm there . . . Then the King ordered nine of the new ships to put out, and they blockaded the entrance from the open sea against their escape . . . "

Thus the description of the encounter that is believed to have taken place in Brading Haven, although some historians claim that it happened in Poole Harbour. As the tide went down so all the ships, both English and Danish, went aground and the battle was fought on foot in the mud. The outcome was a victory for the English who lost 62 men killed, while the

Danish casualties numbered 120. Three Danish ships managed to escape, though they were badly damaged, and two of them got no further than Selsey Bill where they were wrecked on the Owers. The crews were captured and subsequently hanged.

Alfred died in 901 and was mourned throughout the kingdom of Wessex and in the Isle of Wight, particularly in his royal manor of Arreton. He was a great man, not only as a soldier but also as a scholar, and unfortunately some of the kings who came after him later were not of the same calibre. A measure of the regard in which he was held is that 40 years later the date of his death, 26th October, was still being remembered when his grandson, King Athelstan, died. Athelstan was followed by his son Edgar, another strong king who instigated the coronation service for Kings of England which is still used to this day.

Alfred's defeat of the Danes and the peace that ensued lasted for a hundred years. England settled down and prospered, its centre being the kingdom of Wessex, with its Royal Capital, Winchester. The Bishops of Winchester built their summer palace in the Isle of Wight, at Swainston, and traces of this building can still be seen in the basement of the present house, together with the building that was their private Oratory.

But this peace did not last for ever, and a succession of weak kings, culminating in the long reign of Ethelred (nicknamed the Unready) tempted the Vikings back again. Raids along the south coast re-commenced, and the Isle of Wight became the base from which they operated these summer raids, and their home in the winter. The actual site of their base in the Island is believed to have been Werrar on the west bank of the Medina

The old church at Wootton, dedicated to St. Edmund, once the King of East Anglia, murdered by the Danes.

23

River. To this day on this stretch of the river, just opposite the Folly Inn, there is a muddy creek which could well have been an ideal place for laying up the Danish longboats in the winter.

The Chronicle describes how, in the year 1001, the Danes sailed into the Exe estuary in Devon and overran the countryside, slaying and burning —

> ". . . and they brought much plunder with them to their ships, and sailed thence for the Isle of Wight, where they went about at will, encountering no resistance. No fleet by sea nor levies on land dared approach them however far inland they went. In every way it was a hard time, for they never ceased from their evil deeds."

King Ethelred was at his wits end, and finally resorted to paying the Danes to go away, a plan said to have been suggested to him by his Archbishop of Canterbury, Sigeric. This payment, the Danegeld, was a very ill-advised plan, for though it worked for a short time the Danes kept coming back for more. In 991 Ethelred paid them £10,000, a tidy sum for those days, but they were back again the following year, and each year the sum they demanded was larger. In 994 it was £16,000 and by 1002 it had reached £24,000. In this latter year Ethelred tried another and even more desperate ploy, for he gave orders that on St. Brice's Day, 13th November, all Danish people in England should be slaughtered. Not surprisingly, this merely exacerbated the problem.

In spite of the steadily worsening situation, fighting the Danes was still very much a seasonal occupation. The English armies were drawn from all parts of the kingdom, but returned to their homes during the winter. For example, in the year 1006 the Chronicle has this to say —

> "When it drew near to winter the levies went home and after Martinmas (11 November) the (Danish) host retired to its safe base in the Isle of Wight, procuring everywhere there whatever they had need of. At Christmas they proceeded out through Hampshire into Berkshire, to their well-stocked food depot at Reading."

Payments of the Danegeld continued, and in 1007 £30,000 was handed over. Fighting still continued however, and in August 1009 the Danes were again in the Isle of Wight, burning and harrying. In 1012 £48,000 is said to have been paid, and at the end of 1013 King Ethelred, after spending Christmas in the Isle of Wight, fled the country.

Actually he was not away for very long, and was back in England by Easter 1014, but by this time the Danes under their King Canute, were masters of the whole northern part of the country. Ethelred died in 1016 and was succeeded by his son Edmund Ironsides who continued to fight, but had to make a pact with Canute whereby Edmund retained the kingdom of Wessex, but Canute became King of Mercia. Edmund died shortly after, and in 1017 Canute became the first Danish King of all England. To make his position more secure he married Ethelred's widow, but felt able to exact tribute amounting to £72,000, plus an extra £11,000 from the citizens of London! But at least the fighting stopped.

The Chronicle records that in 1022 Canute "with all his ships" visited the Isle of Wight but it does not explain for what reason this show of force was made. Perhaps the Island was the last to accept his authority — as it had been the last to receive Christianity!

When Canute died in 1042 at the early age of 40 he was succeeded by Edward, a gentle and devout man who for his piety was known as the Confessor. When he in his turn died, in January 1066, Harold, Earl of Wessex, was elected as King. Unfortunately there were three other men who had an equally strong claim to the throne — one of these being William, Duke of Normandy.

V — The Normans

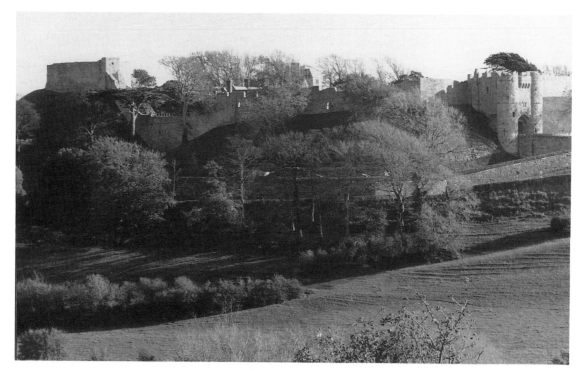

The great fortress of Carisbrooke, built in stone by Baldwin de Redvers. The Norman Keep on the left.

Harold, Earl of Wessex, who was elected King of England in 1066, can hardly be said to have had either a long or a pleasant reign. In fact it lasted only from January 5th, when Edward the Confessor died, to October 14th when Harold was defeated by William, Duke of Normandy, at Senlac near Hastings, and lost not only his kingdom but his life.

When Edward died there were three other men besides Earl Harold who had aspirations towards the throne of England. One was Harold Hardrada, King of Norway, who was looking for an opportunity to invade England and re-establish the kingdom that had been lost when Canute died, and who had been building up an army for this purpose. The second was William of Normandy, who though illegitimate felt he had as good a claim as any since he was the great nephew of the late King, and who was also preparing an invasion. The third was a son of Edmund Ironside, who possibly had the best claim of all, but whose chances were slim since he had no army at all at his disposal.

Earl Harold knew he was in for a difficult time, and that there were threats building up both from the north and the south. He decided that the threat from Normandy was the more imminent, so gathered his forces and established himself in the Isle of Wight waiting for events to develop. All through the summer he sat in the Island and nothing happened, and when harvest time came his men became restless and wanted to return home.

At this moment King Harold Hardrada of Norway, supported by Tostig, Earl Harold's own brother, decided to invade Yorkshire. Earl Harold and his army immediately set out and marched up the Great North Road, met the opposing Norwegian army at Stamford Bridge and defeated them, both Harold Hardrada and Tostig losing their lives.

While he was still celebrating his victory, messengers arrived to say that the Normans had landed at Pevensey, so Harold perforce had to march south again. It is hardly surprising that by the time they reached Sussex the English were in no fit state to fight a battle against the well-disciplined and fresher Norman troops.

So England fell to the Norman conquerors, and an important chapter in English history began. The man who had organised the Norman invasion was Duke William's cousin, William FitzOsbern, the Grand Seneschal of Normandy. He it was who had to decide how many ships were required, how many troops, how many horses, etc, and had to collect together all the thousand and one items needed by an invading army.

Consequently, when the invasion was such a success, and achieved its object at comparatively little cost, Duke William was most anxious to reward his cousin in a suitable manner. This he did by creating him Earl of Hereford and bestowing on him a large amount of land in that part of the world. But he also gave him much more than that; he gave him the Isle of Wight, with the title of Lord of the Island.

Right. *The massive entrance to Carisbrooke Castle.*

Far Right. *Another surviving example of Norman masonry, an early window in Arreton church.*

Both of these appointments were made with a very shrewd eye to the safety of his new kingdom, for Hereford on the River Wye was a good place from which to watch and control the Welsh, and the Isle of Wight was traditionally a bridgehead for would-be invaders of England. Indeed it is believed that the Normans themselves originally intended to sail into the quieter waters of the Solent and make their landing in Hampshire. In which case the history books would not have recorded the Battle of Hastings, but the battle of Southampton.

William FitzOsbern built a castle in Hereford overlooking the river, and he also strengthened the Saxon fort and defences he found at Carisbrooke in the Island. At this time both these strongholds would have been built of earth and timber; building in stone came later.

His title as Lord of the Isle of Wight gave him complete control of the Island, and the power of life and death over its inhabitants, and though he naturally owed allegiance to the King, he was, in the Island, his own boss. Just as the King had rewarded him by the gift of the Isle of Wight, so he rewarded his own supporters by giving them land, and this was done by ruthlessly dispossessing the existing English landowners. It must be said however that he did not throw them all out, and even 20 years later, when the Domesday Survey came to be carried out, there were still one or two Englishmen who were holding land in the Island.

Having satisfactorily rewarded his immediate followers who had assisted in the invasion, William FitzOsbern next made a very handsome gift to the Abbey of Lyre, in Normandy, which he had founded nearly 20 years previously in 1045. It was an established custom for these Norman war lords to build churches or to found Priories and Abbeys, and the practice may be regarded as a kind of insurance against the reception they were likely to receive in Heaven when they died. This was a cruel age, human life was cheap, and the killing or maiming of recalcitrant subjects was a common occurrence. As the man who had habitually practised these barbarities grew older it was natural that his conscience should begin to trouble him, and a favourite antidote that appealed to him was to found, say, an Abbey and install therein a number of monks whose task was to pray for his soul.

So William FitzOsbern decided to donate a small part of his new found wealth in the Isle of Wight to his Abbey of Lyre, and he did this by giving the Abbey six Island churches, together with their tithes and rents. At this time, after nearly 400 years of Christianity in the Island there were a number of prosperous churches. The Island had been divided into seven large parishes, each one running from north coast to south coast in strips with roughly parallel borders, this arrangement having been made with the object of providing each parish with a share of agricultural land (for their corn and cattle), downland (for their sheep) and water. The original seven parishes were Arreton, Brading, Calbourne, Carisbrooke, Freshwater, Newchurch, and Shalfleet, but within a short time Arreton parish was split and three new parishes were formed, namely Godshill, Niton, and Whippingham.

A map of 11th century parishes.

28

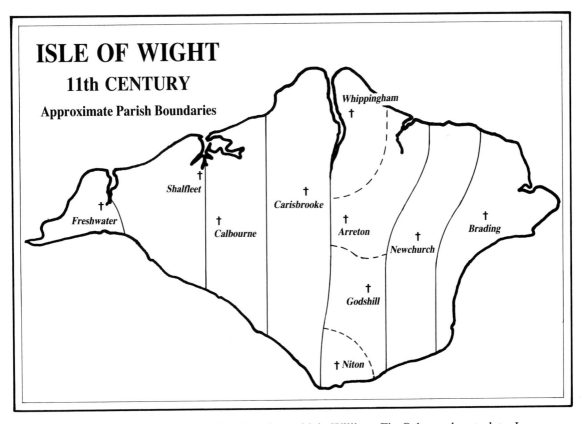

ISLE OF WIGHT
11th CENTURY
Approximate Parish Boundaries

Whippingham †

Shalfleet †

Freshwater †

Carisbrooke †

Calbourne †

Arreton †

Newchurch †

Brading †

Godshill †

† Niton

The six churches which William FitzOsbern donated to Lyre were Arreton, Freshwater, Godshill, Newchurch, Niton and Whippingham, and a glance at the map will show that these parishes covered almost 50% of the Island's surface, so that the gift was of some value. Tithes were payable on all agricultural produce, and every church had its great tithe barn where these "tenths" were collected. The Abbot must have been delighted with this addition to his income, and he only had one problem — he had to collect what was due to him — and the difficulties can be imagined. The Island churches were in a foreign and recently conquered country, where the population did not speak French, and were probably hostile, and there are inherent problems in collecting and transporting to France every tenth stook of corn, every tenth lamb, and piglet, not to mention every tenth swarm of bees.

Obviously a way round this had to be found, and the Abbot sent two of his monks over periodically to organise the business. Traditionally they are said to have landed in Bonchurch, and to this day the little bay there is known as Monks Bay. They are also said to have found the old Saxon church of St. Boniface in a state of disrepair, and as a thanksgiving for their safe arrival (their boat was probably small, the Channel was probably rough, and they were probably not very good sailors) they repaired it so that it could be used again. No doubt they also held their own service of praise there too before collecting their tithes.

The old church above Monks Bay in Bonchurch.

After the upheaval of the invasion had died down, life in the Isle of Wight settled down again to one governed by the steady and peaceful rhythm of nature, for besides bringing peace with them the Normans brought good administration and management, and though no doubt the English were more than irked at being conquered, yet there were compensations. For though Norman laws were harsh, at least men knew where they were. The system of administration — the Feudal System — was based solely on the concept of service, and land was only granted to a man on conditon that he gave service in return.

For instance, King William's "Tenants-in-Chief" — and there were less than 200 of them — had to swear to support the King and supply a specified number of armed and mounted knights as the King demanded. The commitment of each knight was a promise to take the field fully armed and equipped for up to 40 days in the year on every occasion his lord called on him. Other requirements included the payment of dues and attendance at courts of justice, a grant of land very often being accompanied by a grant

of jurisdiction. Thus every great tenant exercised civil and criminal jurisdiction over his own tenants, and similar rights were frequently granted to
abbeys and monasteries. But every landholder had to swear fealty to the
King over and above his allegiance to his local lord. This was a new condition brought in by King William, and it cleverly reduced the danger to him
of his barons becoming too powerful.

The system did of course have its disadvantages. It was unwieldly and
inefficient, and there were certain times in the year, e.g. at harvest time,
when men were most reluctant to leave home and serve the king. An army
composed of such men was often turbulent and unmanageable, and
because of this service was gradually replaced by a pecuniary payment
(known as 'Scutage' — from the Latin word 'scutum' meaning "a shield")
and the King was able to provide himself with an army of more efficient
mercenaries.

At the lower end of the social scale life continued to be hard and cruel.
The lowest form of human life was the serf who was simply a slave, treated
as a two-legged beast of burden and given enough food, clothing and shelter to keep him fit for work. Slightly better off was the villein who was not
a slave, neither was he a free man. He was given an interest in a small plot
of land by his lord, but he did not own it. He could not leave the lord's
estate, nor give up the land held by him, he was a servant for life, receiving
as wages the use of enough land to support himself and his family. If he left
his lord he could be recovered as a stray, unless he managed to live for a
year and a day in a privileged town or borough, in which case he received
his freedom. He could accumulate no property, for everything he possessed was his lord's.

The borderer, or bordar, had more freedom. He was a small farmer
tenant who was allowed to indulge in trade, that is, he could sell off the
surplus of anything he grew, and by this means he could accumulate property. But he still had to give service to the lord, usually in the form of mow-
ing or haymaking for three or four days in the year.

Norman laws were harsh and strictly enforced, punishment for trans-
gression being swift and terrible, and there is no doubt that under the
Normans the English peasants suffered more severely than they had done
under their own rulers. In Hampshire King William created the New
Forest, solely for his own pleasure, and his forest laws, designed to prevent
anyone killing his deer, were brutal in the extreme. Anyone caught killing
game was punished on the spot by having his eyes put out. Stealing, however minor, was punishable by cutting off the thief's hands, and this
certainly prevented him from ever stealing again. The fact that it also
stopped him from earning his living was just too bad, but the very nature
of this savage punishment virtually put an end to stealing. Fortunately the
Isle of Wight was spared many of the privations and oppressions which
were common on the other side of the Solent, but life for the poorer people
was bleak and bare.

Administratively the Normans preserved the old English divisions that
had been set up by Alfred the Great, and retained the system of Tythings

31

and Hundreds into which the land was divided. A Tything was a group of 10 families, and ten of these formed a Hundred. The families in a Tything were each bound to keep the peace and were responsible for each other, a leader or Tything Man being elected annually to preside. The Isle of Wight was originally divided into two Hundreds, the East Medine and the West Medine, though arithmetically the population soon exceeded these numbers, and in the Domesday Survey are listed "sub" Hundreds of Bowcombe, Calbourne, and "Hemreswel".

In 1071 William FitzOsbern was killed while fighting on the continent, and his English possessions came to his second son Roger de Breteuil, who became the second Earl of Hereford and Lord of the Isle of Wight. He enjoyed his position for a mere four years, as in 1075 he set up a feeble rebellion against the King, in partnership with the Earl of Norfolk. This was easily suppressed and ruthlessly punished by King William who stripped Roger of his titles and honours and imprisoned him. Roger spent the rest of his life, fifteen long weary years, in this Norman dungeon, a fate which it is painful even to contemplate, for the dungeon would have been unheated, unlit, with no sanitation or any creature comforts, and he would have been given just sufficient food to keep him alive. He must have been a very strong man to have survived so long, and there must have been innumerable occasions when he cursed himself for ever having thought of rebelling.

On Roger's imprisonment the Isle of Wight reverted to the Crown, and it remained in Royal hands for the next 27 years. During this period an event of the greatest importance took place, the compiling of the Domesday Survey, which was completed in 1086. This document has survived and provides the first complete record of the whole of the Isle of Wight, with details of all landowners and their holdings.

The Survey was a detailed register of all the lands of England, giving the quantity and value of each land holding, and was prompted by the fear of a Danish invasion and the need of the King to assess the amount of money he could raise for defence purposes, and also the help he could expect if there were such an invasion. A secondary object was to protect small land holders from encroachment by the big proprietors, and in general to help check evasion of paying taxes. Its importance can be judged by the fact that it was used as the basis of tax assessments until 1552, when a new survey was made.

In the Isle of Wight a total of 126 properties, or manors, were listed, of which 43 belonged to the King, these being the ones previously owned personally by Roger de Breteuil, 21 belonged to William FitzStur, 24 to William FitzAzor, 11 to the latter's younger brother, Gozelin FitzAzor, and 24 to various of the King's thegns. *(Footnote: Thegn or Thane. A rank lower than an earl but higher than an ordinary free man)*. Of the three remaining ones the manor of Watchingwell belonged to the Abbey of St. Mary at Wilton, Shalcombe belonged to the Church of St. Nicholas-in-the-Castle, and Swainston, the largest and most valuable in the whole Island, to the Bishops of Winchester.

32

The Survey was nicknamed rather gloomily the "Domesday" by the English, who saw in it the inevitability of Norman rule and the tightening of their grasp on the country. Also, against it there was no appeal.

Only a year after the Domesday Survey was carried out King William died. As he grew older he had become very corpulent, and he died through an injury caused to his belly by his horse rearing and plunging. Many of his English subjects were glad to see him go, for he had lived a harsh and cruel life, bringing tragedy and misery to countless families. On his deathbed he confessed and regretted —

> "... the barbarous murder of many thousands, both young and old, of that fine race of people."

But history has acclaimed him as a great king who disciplined and united the English nation, formulating hard but just laws and suppressing much evil doing. But he was also a human being, and like the rest of us had his weaknesses. For one thing he was a bad loser, and a charming story is told about him playing chess one day with the Dauphin of France. At this time Normandy had an uneasy relationship with the next door kingdom, France. it was not a vassal state, but nevertheless it was important to keep on good terms with the son of the French King. However, the game of chess was going against him, and as the Dauphin gradually forced him into a corner William's irritation rose until he could stand no more. Whereupon he lost his temper, picked up the chessboard, and beat his opponent over the head with it.

Perhaps William of Normandy's finest obituary notice is contained in the Anglo-Saxon Chronicle, written by a monk at the great Abbey of St. Peter in Peterborough:

> "Alas how deceitful and transitory is the prosperity of this world. He who was once a mighty king, and lord of many a land, was left of all the land with nothing save seven feet of ground: and he who was once decked with jewels lay then covered over with earth.
>
> If anyone desires to know what kind of man he was or in what honour he was held or how many lands he was lord of, then shall we write of him as we have known him, who have ourselves seen him and at one time dwelt in his court. King William, of whom we speak, was a man of great wisdom and power, and surpassed in honour and strength all those who had gone before him. Though stern beyond measure to those who opposed his will, he was kind to those good men who loved God.
>
> He was so stern and relentless a man that no one dared do aught against his will. Earls who resisted his will he held in bondage. Bishops he deprived of their Sees and Abbots their Abbacies, while rebellious thanes he cast into prison, and finally his own brother he did not spare. Among other things we must not forget the good order he kept in the land, so that a man of any substance could travel unmolested throughout the country with his bosom full of gold. No man dared to slay another, no matter what evil the other might have done him. If a man lay with a woman against her will, he was forthwith condemned to forfeit those members with which he had disported himself."

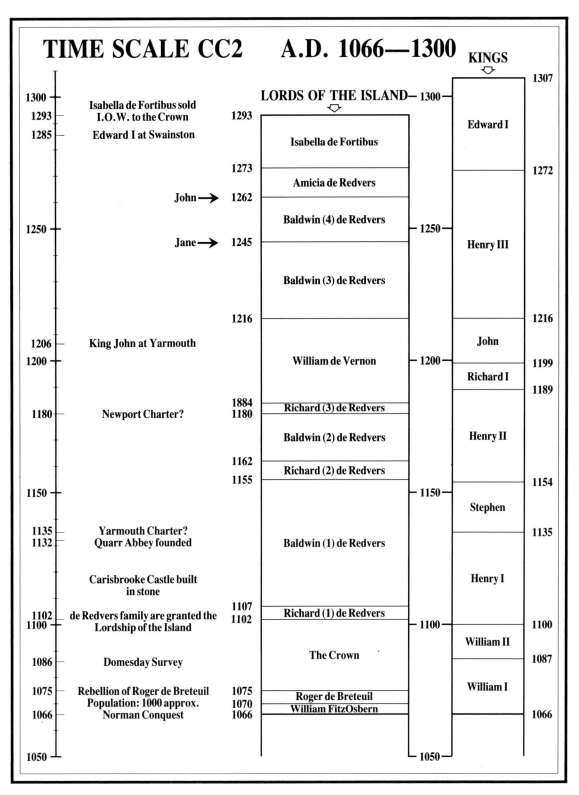

TIME SCALE CC2   A.D. 1066—1300

KINGS

LORDS OF THE ISLAND

Year (left)	Events	Year	Lords of the Island	Year	Kings	Year (right)
1300				1300		1307
1293	Isabella de Fortibus sold I.O.W. to the Crown	1293			Edward I	
1285	Edward I at Swainston		Isabella de Fortibus			
		1273	Amicia de Redvers			1272
	John →	1262	Baldwin (4) de Redvers			
1250				1250	Henry III	
	Jane →	1245	Baldwin (3) de Redvers			
		1216				1216
1206	King John at Yarmouth		William de Vernon		John	
1200				1200		1199
					Richard I	
						1189
1180	Newport Charter?	1884 / 1180	Richard (3) de Redvers		Henry II	
			Baldwin (2) de Redvers			
		1162	Richard (2) de Redvers			
1150		1155		1150		1154
1135	Yarmouth Charter?				Stephen	1135
1132	Quarr Abbey founded		Baldwin (1) de Redvers			
	Carisbrooke Castle built in stone				Henry I	
1102	de Redvers family are granted the Lordship of the Island	1107 / 1102	Richard (1) de Redvers			1100
1100				1100	William II	
1086	Domesday Survey		The Crown			1087
1075	Rebellion of Roger de Breteuil Population: 1000 approx.	1075	Roger de Breteuil		William I	
1066	Norman Conquest	1070 / 1066	William FitzOsbern			1066
1050				1050		

VI —
Priests and People, Lords and Kings

St. Helens old church tower, all that remains of the old Cluniac Priory that became the parish church until the sea swallowed it up.

Within two years of coming to the throne in 1100 Henry I gave away the Isle of Wight to another Norman baron, Richard de Redvers, and for the next 200 years the de Redvers family held sway in the Island. The name Richard was popular in this family, and during this period of 200 years there were three de Redvers of this name who owned the Isle of Wight. The first Richard's son Baldwin succeeded his father in 1107, and Baldwin was an even more popular family name, there being four of them in the next 150 years.

The first Baldwin de Redvers was perhaps the most energetic and successful, and left behind him several reminders of his life in the Island. He it was who first built Carisbrooke Castle in stone, superseding the old earth and timber fort, and producing a very much stronger fortress that was seldom seriously threatened with capture. As a stronghold Carisbrooke Castle dominated the Isle of Wight, and the village that grew up under its protection became the centre of Island life, pre-dating the town of Newport by almost a hundred years.

Possibly the most important achievement of Baldwin de Redvers was his founding of the Abbey of Quarr in 1132. Situated on the shore of the Solent near the stone quarries of Binstead from which it took its name, this great Abbey was the most important ecclesiastical development ever in the Isle of Wight, and for 400 years until the Dissolution of the Monasteries in 1536 it exercised a powerful influence on the Island. The monks of Quarr came originally from the Abbey of Savigny, a Benedictine house set up by a group of monks who wished to follow a stricter rule. They adopted a white habit, and later on in 1147 when the Abbey of Citeaux and other Abbeys had joined Savigny, they became known as Cistercians.

Before the foundation of Quarr the Isle of Wight already had three Priories belonging to other French Abbeys. The first of these, set up sometime around 1090 by the Abbey of Cluny, was at St. Helens, but was never a large foundation. The Priory was suppressed in 1414 together with the other Alien Priories, but the church remained as the parish church of St. Helens until the 18th century, when encroachment of the sea partially destroyed it. Now all that is left is the old church tower, a romantic ruin which has been preserved as a seamark.

Right. *Holyrood Street, Newport, the road that led to the Priory of St. Cross.*

Far Right. *Map of Carisbrooke and St. Cross. A.D. 1120.*

Appuldurcombe Priory bell, now at St. Lawrence.

The second Alien Priory was at Appuldurcombe, this having been set up by the Norman Abbey of Monteburg, c.1100. This also was small, only a Prior and two monks, and after 1414 it was given by the Crown to an Order of Nuns in London, the Minoresses of St. Clare-without-Aldgate, who leased it and its land to an Island family named Fry. Later, in the 16th century it became the site for Appuldurcombe House, the principal Isle of Wight seat of the Worsley family.

The third Alien Priory to be established in the Isle of Wight is in many ways the most interesting historically, for it pre-dated by 60 years the building of the town of Newport. This was the Priory of St. Cross which was founded before 1120 by yet another French Abbey, the Abbey of Tiron, and it was situated in what is now a part of Newport in an idyllic little valley on the banks of the Lukely brook. It is remembered today only by its name, for man has ruthlessly destroyed every vestige of it, but the road that led to it, a road that for centuries was called "the Road that led to St. Cross" is now known as Holyrood Street.

Its history is a sad one, it was damaged in the great French raid of 1377 and never fully recovered. The St. Cross Mill was rebuilt, as was the Priory House, which was later converted into a private dwelling, but in 1888 all was swept away by the Freshwater, Yarmouth and Newport Railway Company, who built their railway station on the site. Alongside the station was a Brewery and the whole area has steadily been engulfed by the expansion of Newport. Railway and Brewery have now in their turn gone, though Whitbreads still have a large yard for their empty barrels, and the station approach is a coal depot, both of them ugly in the extreme. But by some flash of inspiration Medina Borough Council have built on the opposite bank of the Lukely brook (no longer a sylvan stream but now running dirtily between concrete walls) a block of sheltered housing which they have called St. Cross Court, so that once again the name of St. Cross lives on this site. Long may it continue.

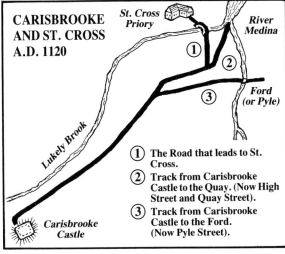

CARISBROOKE AND ST. CROSS A.D. 1120

St. Cross Priory

River Medina

Ford (or Pyle)

Lukely Brook

Carisbrooke Castle

① The Road that leads to St. Cross.
② Track from Carisbrooke Castle to the Quay. (Now High Street and Quay Street).
③ Track from Carisbrooke Castle to the Ford. (Now Pyle Street).

In 1156 a fourth, and the largest, French Priory was built in the Isle of Wight. The Abbot of Lyre had been sending monks over from time to time to organise payment of the tithes and rents to which he was entitled, but as this was obviously not a very happy state of affairs he ultimately requested permission to establish a small permanent Priory in the Island to look after the Abbey's interests. It was only natural that this should be built at Carisbrooke, near and under the protection of the great Norman Castle, and though the Priory buildings have long since disappeared, the nave of the church he built has survived and is still the beautiful parish church of Carisbrooke, dedicated to St. Mary the Virgin.

Another major development carried out during Baldwin de Redvers' ownership of the Isle of Wight was the building of the town of Yarmouth which had been growing in importance due to its geographical situation at the mouth of the River Yar immediately opposite the Lymington River on the mainland. Yarmouth was the first town in the Isle of Wight to be built on the grid system, around a track that led from the landing place up to the road to Thorley. This track became the High Street and roads were built to cross it at right angles. The actual date of building is not known, but tradition has it that the town was granted its first Charter (the first of seven!) by Baldwin de Redvers in 1135. The actual document has been lost however, and we only know of its existence through the record of four witnesses between 1166 and 1179, and the confirmation of its terms in the Second Charter granted by Edward III in 1334. *(For more about Yarmouth see Chapter 16, page 106).*

Grave stone of Hugh, the first Prior of Carisbrooke, who died in 1190.

Baldwin de Redvers "reigned" over the Island for nearly 50 years, but for much of this time was at odds with King Stephen who was King of England from 1135 to 1154. Baldwin regarded Stephen as a usurper and at one time was under siege by the King's forces in his castle at Exeter. He managed to escape however and reached the Isle of Wight and his castle of Carisbrooke, where he felt safer. They patched up their quarrel in due course and it appears that the King created Baldwin earl of Devon, which some historians say was what he had been after all along.

When Stephen died in 1154 he was succeeded by Henry II, and this King's subsequent quarrel with his Archbishop of Canterbury, Thomas a'Becket, had its repercussions in the Isle of Wight. Following the King's querulous remark —

"Will no one rid me of this turbulent priest?"

four of his knights set out for Canterbury to do just that, and one of the murderers was Hugh de Morville, Lord of the Manor of Knighton.

After the murder in Canterbury Cathedral in December 1170 Hugh de Morville fled to the safety of Carisbrooke Castle, where he was protected by Baldwin de Redvers the second, grandson of Baldwin the first, and where he stayed until the public outcry over the murder had died down. When he felt it was safe to leave Carisbrooke he retired to his beautiful house at Knighton and lived there for another 30 years, never being brought to justice.

The next Island town to be built on the grid system was Newport, this being constructed round the track that led from Carisbrooke down to the River Medina. Half way down the track forked, the left hand fork (now the High Street) heading for the river at the highest point reachable by a sea-going ship, and the right hand fork (now Pyle Street) leading to the first ford across the river. Other streets were built at right angles to these tracks — one of these being already there, namely, the road that led to St. Cross. In 1180 Richard de Redvers the third granted a Charter to his "New Port", and this is the name by which the town has always been known.

Another town in the West Wight, not far from Yarmouth, was Newtown, and this enjoyed a brief priod of prosperity which however virtually came to an end in the 14th century when it was burned down by the French. Newtown is situated in the Manor of Swainston and was the property of the Bishops of Winchester for 500 years. The present Swainston House is built on the foundations of the Bishops' summer palace, and this can still be seen in the basement. Without doubt, this site is one of the most historically interesting in the whole of the Isle of Wight. *(See Chapter 18 page 117).*

By the end of the 12th century the Isle of Wight was getting used to being at peace, there having been no fighting for nearly 140 years. The Norman invasion must have seemed a long time ago, and the fourth or fifth generation of the original invaders' children were now in control of the Island. They still spoke French, which was the official language of the country, and indeed there were three languages in current use in England at this time, for the native population spoke English, and the Church used Latin.

Once the private chapel at the Bishops of Winchester's summer palace at Swainston. The 3-light window is an excellent example of early 13th century work, with plate tracery.

But changes were in the air and becoming rapidly more imminent. After over a hundred years of settled life in England the Normans were inevitably becoming anglicised. At first the invaders who also had land in Normandy would split their time between that country and England, but very gradually their English possessions would begin to take precedence, and after several generations England would be their home and Normandy the foreign country. At the same time those Normans who had not come to England would begin to regard their English colleagues as foreigners, resenting their owning of land in Normandy. As they drifted further and further apart, so relationships worsened, and gradually the English Normans began to lose their possessions across the Channel.

In 1199 John inherited the throne of England, and it was not long before he was actually planning an expedition to France to recover some of the territory that had been lost. On 28th May 1206 the King arrived in Yarmouth to supervise the assembly of an invasion fleet, and on 1st June he set sail for La Rochelle. The venture was a fairly dismal failure, and after months of ineffective fighting the King tired of it, and leaving his army behind, returned to England.

King John was back again in Yarmouth in February 1214, this time assembling a fleet for the invasion of Poitou, a venture in which he was joined by the Counts of Flanders and Boulogne and the Emperor of Germany. When he came back he found his barons waiting for him at Runnymead, and he was forced to sign their Magna Carta. There is a legend that following this humiliation the King came secretly to King's Quay, near Wootton, and sulked there for some time, consorting only with the local fishermen, but this is now thought to be apocryphal.

The year 1243 saw a truce between England and France, and this was to last for 50 years. During this period the Isle of Wight came under the control of the last of the de Redvers family, and indeed the last private individual ever to own the Island. This was a woman, Isabella de Fortibus, one of the most remarkable women the Island has ever produced. She took it over in 1262 and for 30 years she dominated the scene and ruled her domain with a rod of iron. It was said of her —

> "A widow when she inherited, she was the equal of any man in a man's world. Beautiful, formidable, intelligent, energetic, patroness of religious houses, another builder who added outstandingly to Carisbrooke Castle, where she kept up a semi-regal state."

She is reputed to have had a passion for litigation, and from the number of law suits she was involved in, it would seem that she found it easy to fall out with people. She indulged in a running battle with the Abbot of Quarr, and with the Abbeys of Breamore and Christchurch in Hampshire, with the city of Exeter and with the town of Newport. In Carisbrooke she harrassed the monks of the Priory, and even went to law with her own mother.

But in her defence it must be said that in her private and domestic life she had much to contend with. Isabella de Redvers was married at the age of 12 to William de Fortibus, Count of Albemarle, and Lord of Holderness, Skipton and Cockermouth. They had five children, only two of

Possibly the only likeness of Isabella de Fortibus, on a corbel in Christchurch Priory. A determined lady if ever there was one.

Typical 12th century 2-light window in the church of St. Boniface, Bonchurch.

whom survived infancy, and both of these died in their teens. Her husband died when she was 23 and a few years later her son Thomas died aged 16. Her daughter Aveline married Henry III's son Edmund Earl of Lancaster at the age of 11, and died four years later when she was 15. So that Isabella was left young, rich, lonely, and bitter. Her brother Baldwin, Lord of the Isle of Wight, died when she was 25, and for the next 30 years, as the Countess of Devon and "Lady of the Isle" she was alone. It is impossible not to compare the sadness of her life with that of Queen Victoria, who several centuries later found the loss of her husband almost too much to bear. Isabella de Fortibus deserves our pity as well as criticism.

In the year 1285 a much respected and feared man paid a visit to the Isle of Wight. This was King Edward I of England who was universally respected for the civilising influence he was having on the country, for the many good laws he had brought in, and for his development of Parliamentary Government. He was respected too, and admired, for his personal bravery, and for his many exploits on the Crusades, in France, and in Wales. But he was also feared for his cruelty and ferocity against anyone who disputed his will.

He arrived in the Island on 5th November, but strangely enough did not stay at Carisbrooke Castle as the guest of Isabella de Fortibus. Instead he stayed at Swainston with the Bishop of Winchester, John di Pontiserra, and there was one purpose for his visit, to dispossess the Bishop and take away from him his Manor of Swainston. The King was not particularly interested in the manor house and its immediate surroundings, delightful though these were, he was interested only in the northern part of the manor which contained Newtown and its natural harbour, a harbour that was capable of accepting the largest warships afloat.

The King well knew that relations between England and France were deteriorating rapidly once more, and that it was only a question of time before an invasion attempt would be made. He was worried about the vulnerability of the Isle of Wight, and its possibly inadequate defences, and he wished to deny the use of Newtown Harbour to the enemy, and indeed might even want to use it himself. The excuse he gave for acquiring the Manor in this way was that John di Pontiserra had been appointed to the See of Winchester by the Pope, and it was an appointment of which he did not approve.

So Swainston became a Royal Manor, and the Bishop not only lost it but was also fined £2000 for good measure. The King however was not satisfied, and when a few years later the French seized his Province of Aquitaine he sought for, and found, a further way of ensuring the safety of the Isle of Wight from invasion. Isabella de Fortibus was taken ill, and when the King heard that she was dying, and that her only heir was a distant cousin of whom he knew little, he sent his officers to her to negotiate a sale of the whole Island. This she was in no position to refuse, and for 6000 Marks (£4000) King Edward put an end once and for all to the private ownership of the Isle of Wight. From that day onwards the Island has remained Crown property.

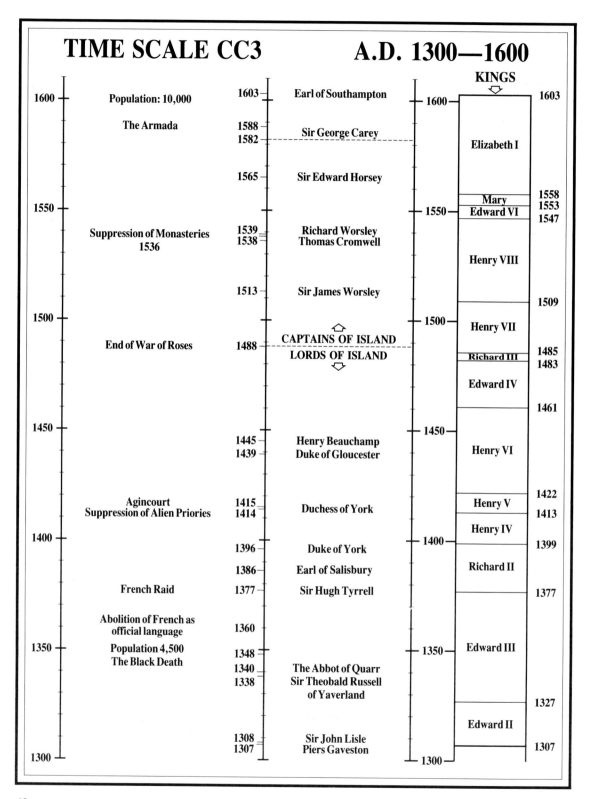

TIME SCALE CC3   A.D. 1300—1600

		KINGS
	1603 — Earl of Southampton	1603 Elizabeth I
1600 — Population: 10,000	1588 — Sir George Carey	1600
The Armada	1582 —	
	1565 — Sir Edward Horsey	1558 Mary
1550 —		1550 Edward VI 1553
Suppression of Monasteries 1536	1539 Richard Worsley 1538 Thomas Cromwell	1547 Henry VIII
	1513 — Sir James Worsley	1509
1500 —		1500 Henry VII
End of War of Roses	CAPTAINS OF ISLAND 1488 — LORDS OF ISLAND	1485 Richard III 1483 Edward IV
1450 —	1445 Henry Beauchamp 1439 Duke of Gloucester	1461 1450 Henry VI
Agincourt Suppression of Alien Priories	1415 Duchess of York 1414	1422 Henry V 1413 Henry IV
1400 —	1396 — Duke of York	1399 1400 Richard II
French Raid	1386 — Earl of Salisbury 1377 — Sir Hugh Tyrrell	1377
Abolition of French as official language	1360	
1350 — Population 4,500 The Black Death	1348 1340 The Abbot of Quarr 1338 Sir Theobald Russell of Yaverland	1350 Edward III
		1327 Edward II
1300 —	1308 Sir John Lisle 1307 Piers Gaveston	1307 1300

42

VII — Wars, and Rumours of Wars

The 14th century was the most calamitous in Isle of Wight history. What with natural disasters and unwelcome attentions from the French and Spanish life was hard for the Islanders. Hence the title of this Chapter. At the beginning of the century the newly established Royal Manor of Swainston was soon in the news again, for within a few years of acquiring it from the Bishop of Winchester King Edward I was at war with Scotland, and orders were sent by him to William Russell, who farmed the manor, to supply quantities of wheat and barley by ship to Berwick-on-Tweed for the use of his army. Shipments began in 1300 and continued on and off for some years, though they were noticeably unsuccessful, the ships taking three months to reach Berwick, and the corn being invariably spoilt *en route*. However, what is of particular interest to anyone studying the history of the Isle of Wight is that the Russell family is still farming in the Island!

Moulding of a Bishop's Mitre on a door jamb in Swainston Manor House. Probably once the front door of the Bishops' Summer Palace.

With the outbreak of war with Scotland a French invasion became a probability, for Scotland and France have always been friends, and for centuries seized any opportunity of combining against the mutual enemy, England. In the Isle of Wight, which was the most likely bridgehead for an invasion, it was felt that the French monks in the Alien Priories constituted a security threat, and they were accordingly moved to the mainland, to Hyde Abbey in Winchester, where a closer eye could be kept on them. This fear was probably very ill founded, for these few poor monks were essentially peace loving men who lived only for their life of industry and prayer, but uprooting them in this way was a typical consequence of the state of war.

The Bishop of Winchester, — who incidentally was also the Abbot of Hyde — decreed that the stock at each Priory should be valued, and the figures for the little Priory at Appuldurcombe make interesting reading —

Cart Horses	20/-	(£1)
Bull	5/-	(25p)
Cow	6/-	(30p)
Young Draft Oxen	4/-	(20p)
Pigs	2/-	(10p)
Sheep	8d — 1/-	(4p — 5p)
Wool	1/6 per stone of 13 lbs.	(7½p)
Chickens	1d	—

The above prices were those ruling almost exactly 700 years ago. In the interim something strange has happened to the value of money!

In 1307 Edward I died, and his proposed conquest of Scotland slowly ground to a halt, partly due to the ineffective leadership of his son Edward II, but also as a result of the splendid rallying of the Scots by Robert Bruce, who once his old tough adversary was out of the way found his task very much easier.

As a king and a leader of the nation Edward II was a disaster. Soon after his accession he married Princess Isabella of France, reputed to be the most beautiful woman of her time, and as high spirited and intriguing as she was handsome. But Edward was already in love with a gay young courtier, Piers Gaveston, and to the disgust of the leading men in the country, and indeed his whole court, he heaped honours and titles on this young man, including incidentally the Captaincy of Carisbrooke Castle, until he drove many of his nobles to the point of rebellion. Some left the country for France, as did the Queen who returned to the French court.

Plotting abroad and disaffection at home combined to weaken the King's authority, and in 1327 he was at last deposed and cruelly murdered, his 14 year old son, Edward, being elected King in his stead. During the last few years of Edward II's reign invasion scares were frequent in the Isle of Wight, and the defences of the Island were continually being improved. In 1324 a system of warning beacons was established, these being the first beacons ever recorded in England. 18 of them were in the West Medine and 13 in the East Medine, at the following sites —

High on Mottistone Down this old track surrounded by gorse is a reminder that beacons once flared up here.

West Medine   (i.e. West of the Medina River)
                  Sconce Point (near Fort Victoria)
                  Headon Hill
                  Chale Down (St. Catherine's Down)
                  Atherfield
                  Lorden Copse (near Gallibury Fields)
                  Hamstead
                  Mottistone Down (Castle Hill)
                  Thorness
                  Northwood
                  Alvington Down
                  8 unidentified sites

East Medine   (i.e. East of the River Medina)
                  Bembridge Down
                  St. Helens Point
                  Sandown
                  Shanklin Chine
                  St. Martin's Down (Wroxall)
                  Appuldurcombe
                  Niton (Cripple path)
                  Arreton
                  St. George's Down (Standen)
                  Wootton Point
                  Whippingham
                  Ryde
                  Wackland (near Newchurch)

The eight unidentified beacon sites in the West Wight could possibly have been at the following — Freshwater (Tennyson Down), Totland, Compton, Brook, Brighstone, Chillerton, Newtown, and Gurnard.

A replica of the Nodes Beacon on Tennyson Down. The Tennyson Monument, which occupies the original site, can be seen on the hill top.

For a few years the boy King Edward III had peace in his realm, but quarrels with France were never very far away, and the new King was soon anxious to retrieve some of the possessions in Scotland and France that his father had foolishly lost. Once again the Isle of Wight seemed destined to be in the firing line. In 1335 a state of emergency was declared, and all Island men from 15 to 60 were called up. The population of the Isle of Wight at this time was about 4500, and the number called up would probably have been around 3000. In 1336 war officially broke out and a French force raided the Island. From this date the war persisted in fits and starts for the next hundred years, and became known as the Hundred Years War. King Edward III, who was now 24 and proving to be a fearless fighter and leader like his grandfather Edward I, decided that attack was the best form of defence and carried the war into Scotland, and in the next year invaded France. He claimed that through his mother he was the rightful king of that country, and in fact styled himself "King of France".

In the Island Theobald Russell (yet another Russell!) Lord of the Manor of Yaverland was put in charge of defences, and immediately set about re-organising the Militia. He was given the title of "Captain of the Men of the Isle of Wight", and was also given the power to compel service. Further invasion attempts were expected and it was not long before both Portsmouth and Southampton were attacked and burned, and the Isle of Wight was also raided.

Because of the uncertainty and danger of living in the Isle of Wight many wealthy landowners decided to leave and take their families to the mainland, where it was safer. This seemed to them to be a sensible thing

45

to do, but of course it did deplete the Island of several able-bodied men and consequently reduced the strength of its defences. The practice was therefore frowned upon and landowners were told that it must cease. In 1339 Bartholomew de Insula, a member of the Norman family who had adopted the name "of the Island" as their own, and who was responsible for the beacon system, was severely rebuked for leaving, and was told that he particularly should be setting an example by staying put. Henry Trenchard of Shalfleet Manor, and several others, were peremptorily ordered to return. These orders were soon found to be justified as in August this year there was another raid on the Island by a combined French and Spanish force.

Men who were called up to become soldiers in these troubled times were of course paid, and a list of typical wages has survived —

Men-at-Arms	12d per day	(5p)
Hobelars (mounted spearsmen)	6d per day	(2½p)
Archers	3d per day	(1¼p)
Sergeant-at-Arms	12d per day	(5p)
Archers on horseback	6d per day	(2½p)
Knights	2/- per day	(10p)
Esquires	12d per day	(5p)
Keeper (of the Isle of Wight)	4/- per day	(20p)

Another interesting figure is given — the cost of crossing the Solent. Passage from Southampton cost 6d, but to return was only 4d, and though this may seem the wrong way round it must be made clear that this was by no means a public ferry service.

1340 was a bad year. The state of emergency still existed in the Island and even the Clergy were called up. They ignored the summons to a man, and complained bitterly to the Bishop of Winchester, who wrote a long letter to John de Kingston who had issued the order. The Bishop told him he had no right to do such a thing and said that surely there were more profitable ways in which he could employ himself other than harrassing the Clergy. If anyone called the latter up it would be he, the Bishop. Having issued this rebuke he then went ahead and ordered the Clergy to muster. The Abbot of Quarr was also involved in the defence of the Island. He was already supplying ten Men-at-Arms, and in 1340 he served for a year as Warden of the Island.

There was another French raid in the summer, and a number of men were killed, including the Commander-in-Chief, Theobald Russell. He had only recently married Eleanor de Gorges and so become Lord of Knighton Gorges as well as Yaverland, and it was to Knighton that he was taken when he was badly injured in the field at St. Helens, and it was there that he died.

The following year (1341) there was a further invasion scare in April, and orders were issued that no one was to leave the Island, nor was any corn to be exported. To make sure this rule was obeyed a control was put on to all boats in the Island, and it was decreed that there should only be

The 'Eremue' Ship, still the crest of Yarmouth Town.

three recognised ports where boats could be kept — La Riche (now Ryde), Shamblord (now Cowes), and Eremue (now Yarmouth). Each port had a Warden whose job it was to implement the law, but no doubt if you knew him well enough, and had the wherewithal, it was possible to circumvent the regulations.

In 1346 Edward III decided to invade Normandy. He was now 33 years old and at the height of his considerable powers. He had been married when only a boy to Philippa of Hainault and now had a son of his own aged 16. While preparing for the invasion the King set up his headquarters in Yarmouth and Freshwater, and set sail from St. Helens on 11th July. The number of ships he took with him is given first as 750, then as excitement grew and exaggeration set in, 1000, and ultimately 1500. Whatever the truth, his efforts were crowned with great success, and on 26th August against enormous numerical odds he defeated the French at the battle of Crecy, his young son, known as the Black Prince, particularly distinguishing himself.

This victory must have brought some comfort to the men and women of the Isle of Wight who had suffered French punitive raids for many years, and who were probably aware that their ordeal was not yet over. They little knew the extent to which they were still to be tried in the years to come, but enthusiasm for the war was high at the time, and in 1347 the Island contributed 13 ships and 222 seamen to Edward's campaign that led to the reduction and capture of Calais.

Calais was the climax of this phase of the war. King Edward besieged the town for a month before it surrendered, and was then preparing to wreak terrible vengeance on its inhabitants for having resisted for so long. But his Queen, Philippa, travelled over from England and interceded with him for the burghers of Calais and persuaded him to spare them, and avoid any more bloodshed. Incidentally, on her way to France Queen Philippa stayed in Sandwich in Kent for a few days waiting for a fair wind. The house where she lodged, the Old Customs House in Upper Strand Street is still there, and was for some years the home of the present writer. The bedroom in which she slept is to this day known as Queen Philippa's Room.

The capture of Calais was followed by a truce, and just as England appeared to be entering a new period of peace and prosperity, the most terrible disaster occurred — the Black Death. This great calamity, not only in its immediate impact but also in its long term effects, was the most significant event in the whole of English history, and hence in the history of the Isle of Wight.

The plague appears to have started in China in 1333 during an extraordinary period of drought, famine, earthquakes, and floods. It moved steadily westwards, and by the time it reached Europe had killed 37,000,000 people. Continuing its westward course it crossed Europe, killing a further 25,000,000 of the population. In England, to which the disease arrived through the Dorsetshire seaports, and from whence it spread steadily through the whole country, it is estimated that one third of the population succumbed, and this figure applies also to the Isle of Wight.

The disease was terrible not only in its nature but also in the swiftness with which it killed. It attacked principally the young and strong, not the weak and feeble, and men were more susceptible than women. There was no cure nor antidote and it killed within three days, receiving its name from the purplish-black blotches that broke out on the skin. From the first appearance of these to the time of death was only a matter of hours. It was highly contagious, a fact that helped breed panic.

No one knew what had caused it, or thought of connecting it with the appalling unclean habits of the age. Some said it could only be a visitation from God. In Europe for a time a rumour spread that the Jews were responsible for contriving the calamity by poisoning the wells, and many thousands of these unhappy people were destroyed on false evidence produced under torture. England was spared this additional tragedy since in 1290 Edward I had ruthlessly expelled all Jews from his kingdom. Later it was believed that the infection was carried by the fleas that lived on rats, but an alternative theory was developed when it was discovered that the Monastery of Christ Church in Canterbury had practically no trouble from the plague, and this community had recently installed a piped supply of pure water from the hills outside the city.

The immediate effect of the Black Death in the Isle of Wight was a chronic shortage of labour, and as in other agricultural areas this meant difficulties in looking after stock and at harvest time. The Island was possibly less affected than other parts of England, but the problem was severe enough and it brought a new power to agricultural workers, who found they were in a position to bargain for higher wages and better conditions. This had a lasting effect, and though inequalities were by no means ironed out, and there was still a tremendous gap between the poor and the rich, yet it was at least a step in the right direction.

Some of the other long term effects were strange. The plague was at its height in 1348 and then died out, with spasmodic recurrences, but when the immediate onslaught was over and life was returning to something like normal, statistics show that the birth rate was considerably increased, and that twins and triplets became more prevalent. Also, those born afterwards tended to grow fewer teeth than before.

It was many years before the Island economy fully recovered from the effects of the Black Death, and indeed there was no respite from the stresses and strains of living in the Isle of Wight for the truce in the 100 years war with France came to an end in 1355 when King Edward organised another invasion and achieved a further outstanding victory at Poitiers. The Island Home Guard, or Militia, was kept permanently on the alert for fear of retaliation from across the Channel.

In 1359 a levy of 6d in the £ was imposed on all merchandise leaving Yarmouth, and this was followed by a complete embargo on the exporting of corn. King Edward invaded France again and continued to be conspicuously successful. In 1360 a temporary peace was established, England by this time being in control of all western France north of the Rhone, and to emphasise still further our national identity and superiority over France, the French language was abolished as the official language of this country, its place being taken by English.

But the French did not forget, and prepared for the day when they could hit back. Though the peace lasted for nine years war broke out again in 1369, and all through that summer the French fleet was assembling, its avowed intention being to destroy England. New regulations were issued for the Island stating that all residents were to remain and give all possible help. All available men were to be equipped and trained, and all inlets and bays were to be protected by walls and dykes. In addition, a more careful watch was to be kept at the ports, since in spite of all the precautions it was believed that horses, gold and money were still being exported.

In the summer of 1370 invasion was expected almost daily, and the Island was divided into nine defensive areas, five in the East Medine, and four in the West, as follows, the names of the Commanding Officers being:

East Medine

> William Russell, Lord of Yaverland, Bembridge and Brading.
> (Lord of Woolverton in Bembridge, Lieutenant)
> Peter de Heyno, Lord of Stenbury. For Stenbury, Whitwell, Wroxall, Bonchurch, Apse, Cliff, Crab Nyweton, Sandham.
> (Lord of Wathe, Lieutenant)
> Theobald de Gorges, Lord of Knighton. For Knighton, St. Helens, Kern, Ride, Quarr, Binstead, Newchurch.
> (Reynold Oglander, Lieutenant)
> John Urry, Lord of East Standen. For East Standen, Arreton, Whippingham, St. Catherines, Rookley, Nettlecombe, Wootton.
> (Lord of Wootton, Lieutenant)
> Bailiffs of Newport to undertake defence of the town.

West Medine

> John de Kingston, Lord of Kingston. For Kingston, Shorwell, Carisbrooke, Park, Northwood, Watchingewell.
> (Sir John Lisle of West Court, Lieutenant)
> Lord of Brook. For Shalfleet, Thorley, Yarmouth.
> (Prior of Christchurch, for his Manor of Ningwood, Lieutenant)
> Adam de Compton, Lord of Compton. For Compton, Afton, Freshwater.
> (Robert de Afton, Lord of Afton, Lieutenant)
> Thomas Cheke, Lord of Mottistone. For Mottistone, Newtown, Calbourne, Brixton.
> (Thomas Langford, Lord of Chale, Lieutenant)

The next seven years were uneasy ones for the Isle of Wight, a patchwork of fears and hopes. In '72 official prayers were said for peace, but England, lost a sea fight off La Rochelle, and both Portsmouth and the Isle of Wight were attacked. In '74 Spanish chronicles were recording attacks that they had made in the Island, but all these pinpricks were merely rehearsals and preparation for the big attack which the French and the Spanish were jointly planning. And this came in 1377. This year was indeed a black one in the history of the Isle of Wight, and coming so soon after the Black Death the humiliation it brought by our enemies was a crippling blow, and it took a full 150 years for the Island to recover.

An attack had of course been expected, and all landowners were ordered to be back in the Island by 1st April. Sir Hugh Tyrell, Keeper of Carisbrooke Castle and the Island, was ordered to prevent anyone leaving, the Bishop of Winchester called up all the Clergy. The Island was as ready as it could be, but was not prepared for the onslaught that followed.

There were two waves of attack along the south coast, the first starting on 24th June and continuing through the whole month of July. Rottingdean and Lewes were taken, and Folkestone, Portsmouth, Dartmouth and Plymouth were sacked. Incredible though it may seem, during these invasion attempts London was celebrating the coronation of the 11 years old King Richard II, Edward III having died in June.

The second wave involved the Isle of Wight, a combined French and Spanish fleet arriving in the Solent off Yarmouth on 15th August. There seems to have been little opposition, many people were killed, and Yarmouth was set on fire. The invaders then travelled eastwards and completely destroyed Newtown, and from thence they went to Newport and burned it to the ground.

Elated with their success they then tackled Carisbrooke Castle, but this proved a much harder nut to crack, and they sat down outside it to starve the garrison into submission. During this siege, which lasted until 10th September, the invaders were not without their problems, tradition having it that one day a party of Frenchmen were ambushed and killed not far from the Castle in a narrow lane, which was later given the name Deadman's Lane, but is now known as Trafalgar Road.

The end of the siege is also a tradition in Island history. Apparently the French Commanding Officer was in the habit each evening of approaching the Castle walls to reconnoitre, and he was spotted by Peter de Heyno, one of the Militia leaders who was inside the Castle. De Heyno, who was renowned as a marksman with his bow, requested permission from Sir Hugh Tyrell to take a shot at the Frenchman, and this having been granted he lay in wait for him. Sure enough, the Frenchman came close to the Castle for his usual reconnaissance, and Peter de Heyno was able to shoot him. This disheartened the French, who decided to call off the siege, but before doing so they demanded, and were paid, a ransom of 1000 Marks, thus completing the humiliation.

As a result of the French Occupation, Newport is said to have been so badly damaged that no one lived in the town for two years, Yarmouth was left to lick its wounds, and took a long time to rebuild, Newtown of course never recovered. During the rest of the 14th century other attacks took place, as for example in 1381 when the French returned to Newport and burned down the watermill at St. Cross Priory, which they themselves had founded 260 years previously, but after the events of those dreadful August days in 1377 these forays were something of an anti-climax.

But the 14th century was indeed a sad and sorry time for the Isle of Wight.

Carisbrooke Castle entrance today. It must have looked very forbidding to a 14th century invader!

50

VIII — *The Mixture as Before*

The White Horse Inn, Whitwell, built in 1454.

In 1396 King Richard II of England was 30 years old, and he married the Princess Isabella of France, who was 10. Child brides were by no means uncommon at this time, but this was a political move, designed to bring to an end the long drawn out war with France, one of the terms of the marriage settlement being a truce between the two countries for 25 years. Unfortunately, only three years later in 1399, Richard was pushed off the throne by Henry Bolingbroke, Duke of Lancaster, and it was not long before war broke out again, and indeed the old pattern of "tip and run" raids on the Isle of Wight went drearily on for the next 50 years or so.

Because of the deposing of Richard by Henry of Lancaster the French now had an additional grievance against England. In their eyes the rightful Queen of England was Isabella, who was now 13 years old, and demands were made that she should be returned to France together with the dowry that had been paid on her behalf, and all her jewels. These demands were supported by armed raids on the Island, some of them quite large. In 1402 the Curate-in-Charge of Northwood Church recorded in his register —

> "The French landed in the Isle of Wight 1700 men, burnt two villages and a few cottages, but hearing the people of the Island were assembled, they made haste to their ships and returned home."

It would seem that the Militia had established a reputation that was causing the French to be cautious!

One of the loudest voices coming from France was that of the Count de St. Pol, who was believed to be in league with Lord Henry Percy, son of the Earl of Northumberland. Percy was known to be a supporter of ex-King Richard, and in fact organised two separate rebellions against King Henry, and it was St. Pol who led several raids on the Isle of Wight. These were probably not serious attempts to invade, but rather to try out the defences preparatory to an invasion.

In 1403 St. Pol arrived with 1000 men in December, and announced his intention of spending Christmas in the Island. They rounded up a large number of cattle and were proposing to take these back to France, but the Militia set about them, chased them back to their ships, and they left several dead behind. French records do not comment on this end to the raid, they merely say that the French King knighted several men for burning down villages in the Isle of Wight.

The next year they were back again, this time demanding that the Island should be given up, and the traditional story told in the Isle of Wight is that the Militia sportingly invited them ashore and offered them six hours in which to prepare for battle, an offer which the French declined, and decided to return home. Another story that has been handed down is that the French demanded tributes to be paid in the name of King Richard and Queen Isabella, but the Islanders expressed surprise at this request and pointed out that King Richard had been dead some time, and that the Queen had returned home to France, so that any tribute was inappropriate.

King Henry IV died in 1413, having had anything but a peaceful reign, and was succeeded by his young son Henry who was a dashing and popular hero. Henry V very quickly decided to invade France, but before doing so solved once and for all the problem of the Isle of Wight's Alien Priories — he closed them all down — so that never again was there any need to worry about French monks being spies in time of war.

Henry V's exploits in France are well known, thanks largely to Shakespeare — his capture of Harfleur, and his extraordinary victory in the battle of Agincourt over a huge French army, leaving him virtually master of much of France. At least two Island men fought at Agincourt, though the first of these possibly never lived here. This was the Duke of York, Lord of the Island, who was related to the King. He fell off his horse during the battle and had the misfortune to be suffocated inside his armour which was so heavy that he could not get up. The other was Harry Hawles who lived in Arreton. He came back safe and sound and lived for another 15 years in the village, and was buried in the chancel of Arreton Church. His grave can still be seen, surmounted by a brass (alas now headless) of a knight in armour.

King Henry's success in France considerably relieved the pressure on the Isle of Wight. He married a French princess and in 1419 signed a treaty of "perpetual peace", but alas he died in 1422 and all the goodwill he had built up crumbled away. He was succeeded by his nine month old son (Henry VI) and it is a sad fact of English history that no king who came to the throne in his infancy was ever successful — which does not say much for the quality and integrity of those who have acted as Regents. In France Joan of Arc came on the scene in 1429 and was largely instrumental in reviving in the French a desire to drive the English out of the country. After some success her own countrymen burnt her at the stake in 1431 as a heretic, a crime which to our shame we did nothing to prevent.

Henry VI continued on his ineffectual way, and in 1445 crowned a young favourite of his, Henry Beauchamp, son of the Earl of Warwick (the kingmaker) as King of the Isle of Wight. This proved to be too much for the Island gentry who protested loudly, but Beauchamp himself solved the problem in the following year by dying. He did leave hs mark behind him though, and we are still reminded of him to this day. His coat of arms con-

Sign of the old Bugle Hotel, Newport, one of the town's most historic inns, now alas no more. It has been 'developed'.

tained a "supporter" in the form of a young bull, called in Latin "bucullus", from which has sprung the word "bugle", and there are still two inns — now hotels — in the Island known as The Bugle — one in Brading and one in Yarmouth. Until recently there was a third, in Neport.

The middle of the 15th century saw the end officially of the Hundred Years War with France, though sporadic outbursts still occurred, but its place was taken by civil war in England — the Wars of the Roses — between two powerful families, the Houses of Lancaster and York. The Isle of Wight has always suffered through being geographically sited between England and France, with the attendant danger of becoming a battleground, but in the Wars of the Roses the few miles of water between the Island and the mainland of England acted as a buffer, and spared the inhabitants the tragedy of seeing Englishmen slaughtering other Englishmen.

The middle of the century saw a return to peace, and in the Island even a mini-building boom, in which several old houses were rebuilt, some of which survive to this day. Notable amongst these, and at the head of the list, stands Mottistone Manor, the east wing of which was built by Thomas Cheke at this time, and built so well that 500 years later it is still one of the finest Island houses. Another building of a very different type, but of equal age, is the White Horse Inn in Whitwell, which claims to be the oldest surviving Island inn, having been built in 1454, and known then as "Chiddles".

The second half of the 15th century was not a period of English history of which we may feel proud. It was a period not only of war and bloodshed, but of cruelty and atrocity, treachery, and broken promises, and a pathetic display of greed and lust for power on the part of our would-be rulers. At one time, believe it or not, there were two Kings of England — Henry VI and Edward IV — neither of whom was in a position to govern the country, for they were both held in captivity by the opposing side. Edward IV lasted the longer, for Henry VI was mysteriously murdered, but when Edward died in 1483 — still in his forties, but apparently worn out by the profligate life he had been leading — worse was to follow, and in the dramatic events that ensued it was not long before the Isle of Wight was once again involved.

Edward IV left six children, two boys and four girls. His eldest son Edward, aged 13, was his rightful heir, and theoretically became Edward V, but his father also left an ambitious and unscrupulous brother, Richard, Duke of Gloucester, who was determined to get the throne for himself. The first thing Richard did was to seize the boy King Edward and his younger brother and put them in the Tower of London — for security reasons he said — he felt they would be safer there, but in fact they were never seen alive again, and history has named them "The Princes in the Tower".

Edward IV's widow, Queen Elizabeth, realising that her own life and the lives of her daughters were in jeopardy, fled with her children to the Sanctuary of Westminster Abbey, where even Richard dare not follow them, and where they lived for several months under conditions of extreme hardship and suffering. One of her daughters was Princess Cecily, 14 years old at the time, and the effect of this voluntary imprisonment on her and her sisters can be imagined. Later, after Gloucester had systematically liquidated everyone who stood in his way, and achieved his ambition of becoming King Richard III, the Queen Dowager and her daughters came out of the Sanctuary. In due course Cecily was married off to a Commoner old enough to be her grandfather, and though she had two children neither they nor her husband lived for very long.

And then at last, when she was over 30, Princess Cecily fell in love. The man she fell for was one Richard Keynes, of Keynes Court in Niton, and when they were married they came to live in the Island, at Great East Standen Manor, near Arreton, a most secluded and peaceful spot, and one very far removed from the hurly-burly of Court life. Perhaps here she found the peace and happiness that had so far been denied her, though sadly this did not last for many years. She died in 1507 and the Abbot of Quarr requested the honour and privilege of burying her in his Abbey Church. His monks carried the body from Great East Standen, up Burnt House Lane to Downend, then along the Briddlesford Road to Wootton, and so to Quarr. With tapers alight they chanted prayers for the soul of the dead Princess, and the procession was followed by practically all the gentry of the Island, a sombre and moving spectacle.

Briddlesford Road today. Along this road (minus white lines) the monks of Quarr bore the body of the Royal Princess Cecily, tapers burning and prayers being chanted.

IX — *Creed and Greed*

In 1509 a new king sat on the throne of England — Henry VIII. His father, Henry VII, the first of the Tudor dynasty, had transformed England since seizing the Crown in 1485. As head of the House of Lancaster, with a strongish claim to the throne, he had defeated and killed Richard III at the battle of Bosworth and thus put an end to the line of Plantagenet kings, the kings whose emblem had been a sprig of broom, the French *"plante genet"*, a name that gardeners in this country still use in its Latin form "genista".

Henry VII had then brought a swift end to the Wars of the Roses by marrying Princess Elizabeth of York, elder sister of Princess Cecily, and in his 24 years reign had brought stability and peace to the country. In the Isle of Wight a small but significant change had taken place in administration, the old feudal title of Lord of the Island being abolished. In future the Head of the administration was to be known as Captain of the Island, and his power was no longer absolute.

But under the new King Henry VIII the prosperity and peace that had been built up by his careful father soon came to an end. Within two years we were once again at war with France, and before many more had passed the King had squandered the fortune that his father had so painstakingly put together. The extravagance and wastefulness of the King was incredible. He had fifty palaces, the upkeep of which meant that he was always needing more and more money, and he succeeded in impoverishing not only himself but the whole nation. His foreign policy was blundering, reckless, and based on self-aggrandizement, as was his quarrel with the Church of Rome over his divorce, and he chopped off his subjects' heads at the slightest pretext. It is necessary to remember these unpleasant things to appreciate the climate in which men lived at this time.

But the Isle of Wight benefitted in one way early on in Henry's reign in that a local man was made Captain of the Island. This was Sir James Worsley of Appuldurcombe, and he was the first Islander to be thus honoured. As a boy James Worsley had served as a Page at the Court of King Henry VII, and as he happened to be the same age as the Prince Henry (later Henry VIII) he chanced to be elected the latter's whipping boy. This position arose out of the law that it was a crime to offer physical violence to a Prince of the blood, and to get round this a boy of the same age was appointed so that there was someone to take the punishment if the Prince did anything wrong.

We may think today that this was a rather cock-eyed rule, but nevertheless young James Worsley was whipped every time Prince Henry did anything naughty. Actually this did no harm at all to James Worsley, and when he grew up, and Prince Henry had become King Henry, he was rewarded by being knighted, made Yeoman of the Wardrobe (a responsible position at the Court of King Henry VIII, who loved dressing up) and was appointed Captain of the Isle of Wight. Any possible damage done by this strange custom was only to the Prince, who might have grown up to be a better man had he received a few sound thrashings which he no doubt deserved as a boy.

In 1536 a new blow fell on the Isle of Wight. Short of money and egged on by his Chancellor, Thomas Cromwell, the King decided to close down the smaller monasteries in the country and confiscate their possessions and incomes, and this decision affected Quarr Abbey. To accomplish the dissolution it was necessary to persuade Parliament to pass an Act, and there was considerable opposition to this by the Commons, who were horrified at the thought. When he heard that the Commons had thrown out the Bill the King was furious, as he was with anyone or anybody who thwarted his will, and he summoned the Commons to meet him. Bluntly he told them that he meant to have this Act passed, and that if there was any further opposition he would have to apply to them his favourite remedy for stiff necks. The Commons knew exactly what he meant — he had already chopped off so many heads that a few more would make no difference to him — so they trooped back to Westminster and passed the Bill through.

So Quarr Abbey, that for over 400 years had exercised a benign influence over the Island, suddenly came to an end, and on 22nd July 1536 its property and possessions passed to the King. An inventory was made at this time which stated that Quarr housed 10 priests, 10 waiting servants, 2 servants in the Church, 8 officers in the household, 2 "lavenders", 6 servants in the dairies, and 1 "corridur" servant. The value of its stock, ornaments and plate was £330 and its yearly income was assessed at £156.10.1d.

The Abbey buildings were entrusted to the care of a rich Southampton merchant, John Mill, but alas, within a very few years the Abbey Church and the majority of the monastic buildings had been demolished and the stone sold for building purposes. No one at that time, or indeed until Queen Victoria came to the Island, seemed to be worried by the desecration of the Church, or the abandonment of the graves it contained, amongst which were those of Baldwin de Redvers, founder of the Abbey, and the Princess Cecily, daughter of Edward IV.

Sir James Worsley, Captain of the Isle of Wight, died in 1538 and was succeeded by none other than Thomas Cromwell, Henry VIII's Chancellor. This was no doubt a great honour for the Island but it did not last for long, for, as so often happened with Henry's ministers, Cromwell ran out of royal favour, his crime being that he led Henry to believe that Anne of Cleves was beautiful and nubile when in fact she was neither of these things. So poor Cromwell lost his head, and once again the Island had a local Captain — this time Richard Worsley, son of Sir James.

This Richard Worsley — who may be nick-named "The Fortifier" to distinguish him from two others of the same name in later years — was young, dashing, aggressive, a capable and energetic commander, and full of new ideas. He introduced firearms to the Militia, and added considerably to the fortifications, building castles at Sandham (now Sandown), and at East and West Cowes. He re-organised the Militia into 10 Centons of 150—200 men and insisted that each parish should have a cannon, "a fawconet of brasse or yron", and that men should become proficient in their use. The guns were to be kept in the parish church and were to be taken out regularly on muster days for practice, certain farms being responsible for providing horses to draw the gun carriages. The Militia fired them regularly and became expert gunners, though in the event none of these pieces was ever fired in anger.

At the Dissolution of the Monasteries Richard Worsley had been appointed a "Commissioner for the Sale of Church Plate", so he was obviously known to the King, though he lost some of his popularity when the King came to stay at Appuldurcombe as his guest. He took the King hunting for pheasant and partridge but failed to find any, and Henry was not amused. In his "thank-you" letter, if such it was, the King advised Richard to make sure that on his next visit there were plenty of game birds available, or else . . . Was he perhaps hinting at his favourite cure for stiff necks? (For more about the Worsley family see Chapter 25 page 148).

King Henry paid a visit to Portsmouth in 1545, and had the misfortune to clash with an armed French raid on the Island. The King was reviewing

Richard (The Fortifier) Worsley decreed that each parish cannon should be housed in the church. The Shorwell gun chamber was later blocked up and is now the Vestry.

the fleet, which contained his latest new ship, the *"Mary Rose"*, when the French arrived in Spithead, sailing up the east coast of the Island from Bembridge, and Henry was hurriedly whisked ashore to the safety of Southsea Castle, from which he was able to watch proceedings. There was very little wind so that action between the two fleets was minimal, and when a breeze finally did get up the King was a helpless, and no doubt infuriated witness of the accident to the *"Mary Rose"* which in turning across the wind heeled over. Her lower gun ports were open, and for some reason her guns were not secured, so that they crashed from one side of the ship to the other, whereupon water rushed in and she sank, drowning practically all of her crew.

The following day the French landed 2000 men on the Island between Seaview and Bonchurch, but found the Militia ready for them. They managed to do some damage in the Manor of Wolverton in Brading, an area now covered by Centurion's Copse, but were ultimately driven back to their ships, losing several of their company, including one of their chief Captains, the *Chevalier d'Aux*. King Henry, suitably enraged at the impertinence of the French, issued immediate orders to Richard Worsley that these raids must be stopped, and as a result the defences were further strengthened, and a Castle was built at Yarmouth (of Quarr stone), and it is a fact that since this was done the Isle of Wight has had no more raids from France. So at least we have something to thank Henry VIII for.

During his reign the Reformation in Europe was in full swing, and in England it was given additional impetus by Henry's quarrel with the Pope, resulting in his becoming Head of the English Church, his divorce from Catherine of Arragon, and later by the Dissolution of the Monasteries. When he became Head of the Church the King did not wish to change in any way the religion of the country. He was perfectly happy with the Roman Catholic faith, and once he had expunged the word "Roman" from the name and substituted the word "Anglo" he was content.

But willy-nilly he had released reforming forces that were more powerful than he imagined, and which he was unable to control. The full effects of these forces were not felt immediately, but after Henry's death in 1547, and his replacement by the young and weak Edward VI, the zeal of the reformers knew no bounds. As with most reforms the pendulum swung wildly and too far, and before long practically every church tradition was being swept away. Of course, some of the changes made at this time, as for example the publishing of the first prayer book in English, were for the better, and brought the people into closer contact with the Church. The effects of the Reformation on the lives of people living in the Isle of Wight are discussed in Chapter 37, page 212.

When Edward VI died in 1553 his sister Mary Tudor became Queen and immediately re-established the Roman faith, and stopped the reforms that were going on. The Captain of the Island, Richard Worsley, who had assisted Henry VIII zealously in suppressing the Monasteries and grabbing their valuables, thought it prudent to resign his Captaincy, and during the five years of Mary's reign he kept a very low profile, and so managed

Top. Yarmouth Castle built in 1545 (of Quarr stone) following the 'Mary Rose' disaster.

Bottom. In 1560 Queen Elizabeth granted Yarmouth its 6th Charter. Within the 'E' of Elizabeth is a portrait of the Queen.

to keep out of trouble.

When Richard himself died in 1565 Queen Elizabeth was on the throne and England's fortunes were beginning to look a little brighter. The next Captain of the Island was Sir Edward Horsey, an old sea-dog who proved to be an energetic and able leader. He enthusiastically continued the same defence policy and even imported saltpetre into the Island so that he could make his own gunpowder. He also enjoyed an energetic and enthusiastic private life in the Island, declining to live in Carisbrooke Castle, his official residence, which he found cold and unfriendly. Sir Edward was married to a French woman, but this lady preferred to live in France, so that he perforce had to make other domestic arrangements. He met an attractive and lively young widow, Dowsabelle Mill of Haseley Manor, and it was not long before he moved in with her.

The gentry were scandalised at first by this irrgular behaviour on the part of their Captain, but Sir Edward and Dowsabelle kept open house, and criticism was soon stilled. Anyone who dispenses free food and drink on a liberal scale is usually assured of popularity, and in an average week they are said to have roasted two beef cattle and eight sheep with all the associated trimmings. The mind boggles at the number of people they must have entertained.

Sir Edward died in 1582, being replaced by another energetic, if somewhat autocratic, Captain, Sir George Carey. Carey was an entirely different type to the jovial, ex-sea captain Edward Horsey, being a martinet, with strong ideas on duty and conduct, together with a healthy regard for his own importance. He was a great nephew of Anne Boleyn, the Queen's mother, and was married to Elizabeth, daughter of Sir John Spencer of Althorp, a lady even more autocratic than himself, who believed there were only three ladies in the whole of the Isle of Wight suitable to be her companions — namely, Sir John Oglander's mother, Lady Meux, wife of Sir John Meux of Kingston, and Mrs. Hobson, an ex-Chelsea lady who had been living for many years in Ningwood. Sir George and Lady Carey lived in high and imperious state in Carisbrooke Castle, entertaining their chosen friends in the grand style, but not endearing themselves to the population.

But there is no doubt that Carey was the right man at the right time for the Isle of Wight. It was common knowledge that Spain was preparing a massive fleet for the invasion of England, with the avowed intention of restoring the Roman Catholic faith in this country, and becoming the head of a Roman Catholic dominated world, and it was firmly believed that their first objective was to capture the Isle of Wight. Carey energetically continued the work of improving the Island's defences that had been carried on by his predecessors, and he stepped up the arming and training of all the able-bodied men in the Island.

His priority was the provision of more muskets for his men, and adequate training with this comparatively new weapon, and he organised competitions and gave prizes for prowess, not only with muskets but with pikes, bows, and halberds. He established a new beacon arrangement, with three beacons on the Downs at each end of the Island, permanently manned. If up to 30 enemy ships were sighted then one beacon had to be fired, if between 30 and 50 ships two beacons, and over 50 ships all three beacons were to be set alight. The watchmen were also charged with the responsibility of running to the nearest church and ringing the bells. A further precaution, and perhaps a very necessary one, was that every 15 minutes all watchmen were to blow a whistle or horn to prove they were awake.

Out of a total Island poplation approaching 10,000 the Militia numbered 1856 officers and men, 1158 armed with muskets, 109 archers, 116 pikemen, and 473 armed with halberds or bills, a force which, together with the parish cannon, must be regarded as highly commendable.

Two other regulations were promulgated by Sir George Carey, one being that all his men should go to church regularly, and receive Communion. This was perhaps a surprising demand, but it was the law, and one that was no doubt resisted by many, but at least the Islanders knew that they had a leader with high principles, and who was not afraid to issue commands. From time immemorial men have always responded to bold and positive leadership, and Carey certainly supplied this.

His last rule was not in the least surprising, but was not well received. It was that no grain should be exported from the Island, nor should anyone leave without his permission, and though this was acceptable in such a time of emergency, he was not popular when he let it be known that he would be happy to sell anyone a permit. This upset many Islanders who discovered very soon that a "Captain's Licence" was necessary before almost any business could be transacted, and it was felt that in exploiting the inhabitants for his own personal gain Sir George was going a bit too far — particularly as he was soon styling himself "Governor" of the Island.

The work that Sir George Carey carried out on improving the defences included an elaborate addition to the fortification of Carisbrooke Castle, and an interesting item in his accounts concerns payment for work performed between 25th March and 24th November 1587. This had been approved by the King, and a sum of 1000 Marks allowed for it, but this had to be collected from London. Sir George sent his deputy, John Leigh, to fetch it, and the cost of his journey is detailed as follows —

> "John Leigh, Gent, for the Expenses and Charges of himself,
> 5 men and 6 horses for 12 days travelling from the Isle of Wight
> to London, staying there and bringing down the thousand
> marks approved for the Fortifications . . . . £4.0.0d."

In these days of transferring large sums of money simply by means of a piece of paper it is interesting to realise the problems involved when money was real and heavy!

The anticipated invasion attempt finally came in 1588. On 5th July a small 80 ton Island ship called *"Rat of Wight"* sailed into Portsmouth under its Captain Gilbert Leigh, with the news that an Armada of over 120 ships had sailed from Spain and was already on its way, its target being the Isle of Wight. On the 25th July the Armada was sighted from the Island, almost becalmed, but being followed and harrassed by the English fleet who were already making life difficult for the Spaniards.

The Spanish galleons and galliasses were huge, unwieldly ships carrying thousands of soldiers, their tactics being to grapple with an enemy and board him, so that their soldiers could then deal with the enemy crew. Unfortunately for them the English had abandoned this race to build bigger and bigger ships carrying more and more men. Under Sir William Winter, Chief Ordnancer to the Navy, the English tactics had been changed to building smaller, faster, and more handy ships armed with cannon, the simple theory being that it was only necessary to sink a Spanish ship and the sea would effectively deal with the men who were aboard.

In the event the Armada did not succeed in sailing into the Solent and capturing the Isle of Wight, and it may be that they never intended to do this. On the other hand it could be that the absence of wind, or too much attention from Sir Francis Drake and his ships deterred them. But they continued on their stately way up Channel towards their projected meeting with the Duke of Parma's army off "the Cape of Margate". This meeting, of course, never took place and the Armada suffered a series of mishaps. They anchored off Calais and in the night the English drifted a number of fire-ships down on them, which caused some damage but more panic. There was then a battle off Gravelines in which the English ships were by far the more manoeuvrable, and the Spanish ships found themselves in difficulty in shallow water.

After Gravelines the Armada was in disarray and was driven to the north east in rapidly worsening weather, with the English fleet in pursuit. The chase was called off at the Firth of Forth and the Spanish Commander, the Duke of Medina Sidonia, sent a signal to his fleet to follow him to the north of Shetland and round Ireland to home. Those ships that obeyed him made it, but many cut the corner and were wrecked off Ireland. Out of the 130 Spanish ships that set out from Spain only 60 returned.

The jubilation in England was naturally tremendous, and nowhere was there more thankfulness than in the Isle of Wight. After years of tension and preparation the sudden removal of the threat produced an enormous feeling of relief and relaxation, and men sincerely believed that there was now going to be no more war. Prosperity followed, and during the next 35 years while peace lasted there was a great wave of building, many fine houses that are still with us today being built, or rebuilt, at this time, including Arreton, Barton, Merston, Sheat, Great Budbridge, Kingston, North Court, West Court, Wolverton, Shalfleet, and Yaverland.

The heartfelt feeling of thankfulness that pervaded the Island was ideally expressed by the Rev. John Baker, Vicar of Carisbrooke, who on 26th July 1588 wrote in his diary —

> "The very year that the great and huge fleet of the Spaniard came by the Isle of Wight was at Maudlintide in the year of our Lord God 1588, in the which God defended us. God preserve our Queen and realm this day and for evermore, and send us truth and quietness within ourselves."

62

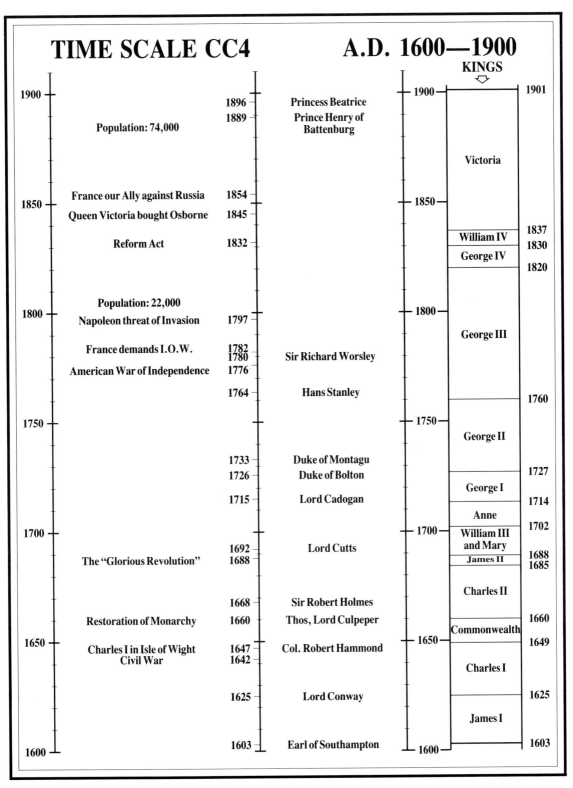

TIME SCALE CC4 A.D. 1600—1900

KINGS

1900		1901
	1896 Princess Beatrice	
Population: 74,000	1889 Prince Henry of Battenburg	Victoria
France our Ally against Russia	1854	
1850 Queen Victoria bought Osborne	1845	1850
		1837 William IV
Reform Act	1832	1830 George IV
		1820
1800 Population: 22,000		1800 George III
Napoleon threat of Invasion	1797	
France demands I.O.W.	1782 1780 Sir Richard Worsley	
American War of Independence	1776	
	1764 Hans Stanley	1760
1750		1750 George II
	1733 Duke of Montagu	
	1726 Duke of Bolton	1727
	1715 Lord Cadogan	George I
		1714
		Anne 1702
1700		1700 William III and Mary
	1692 Lord Cutts	1688 James II
The "Glorious Revolution"	1688	1685 Charles II
	1668 Sir Robert Holmes	
Restoration of Monarchy	1660 Thos, Lord Culpeper	1660 Commonwealth
1650 Charles I in Isle of Wight	1647 Col. Robert Hammond	1649 1650
Civil War	1642	Charles I
	1625 Lord Conway	1625
		James I
1600	1603 Earl of Southampton	1600 1603

63

X — Of Cabbages and Kings

At the beginning of the 17th century changes were in the air. In 1603 Queen Elzabeth, the last of the Tudors, died and was succeeded by a Scotsman, James VI — who became James I of England. So England had a new king, and at the same time the Isle of Wight had a new Captain and Governor, for Sir George Carey's father had died, and Sir George found himself the second Baron Hunsdon.

The new Governor of the Island was a young man, Henry Wriothesley, 3rd Earl of Southampton, who had already had a fairly adventurous career. As a courtier a rather disgraceful *affaire* with one of Queen Elizabeth's waiting women had caused him to be banished from Court. He then got into very bad company and was involved in the abortive revolt organised by the Earl of Essex, for which he was stripped of his title, his lands and his money, and sentenced to death. The Queen then took pity on him — she had a soft spot for good looking young men — and commuted his sentence to life imprisonment.

Luckily for Henry Wriothesley the Queen herself then conveniently died, and James I, in the euphoria surrounding his accession, pardoned him, gave him back his title, his lands and his money, and appointed him Captain and governor of the Isle of Wight — a change of fortune that can only be described as spectacular, and one that bears out the truth of the saying that it isn't what you know that is important — it is who.

Henry Wriothesley did not relish living in the austerity and draughts of Carisbrooke Castle, and being determined to enjoy himself, bought the Manor of Great East Standen and established himself there in that idyllic spot under the lee of St. George's Down. On the Down itself at the back of the house he built a bowling green, and every Tuesday and Thursday invited all the gentry of the Island to play bowls with him. No doubt they drank the odd glass of wine too, and if it was wet repaired indoors to play cards. Understandably, he was a very popular Governor.

But the most interesting fact about the 3rd Earl of Southampton is his friendship with William Shakespeare, for this was close and intimate. Shakespeare dedicated to Wriothesley his two great love poems, "Venus and Adonis" and "The Rape of Lucrece", and also the Sonnets, many of which are erotic, and it has been suggested that there was some sort of homosexual relationship between the two men. Shakespeare was the elder by eight years, and it is intriguing to speculate as to whether the poet ever visited his friend in the Isle of Wight.

Henry Wriothesley, 3rd Earl of Southampton, and friend of Shakespeare, as a young man.

The whole of this period is in fact full of intriguing possibilities. Sir George Carey, when he was Captain of the Island, had entertained on a lavish scale in Carisbrooke Castle, and one of the friends who was a guest there was Henry Wriothesley. Both Carey and Wriothesley were enthusiastic patrons of the arts, and Carey, when his father died, not only succeeded to the title of Baron Hunsdon but also followed his father as Lord Chamberlain and patron of the leading company of actors, the "Chamberlain's Men". William Shakespeare was the most prominent member of this company, so that it is at least possible that Shakespeare knew the Island even before his friend the Earl of Southampton became Captain and Governor in 1603.

The 3rd Earl of Southampton, older (and wiser?) than in the previous picture. Governor of the Isle of Wight.

But in these early years of the 17th century another star was rising in the Island firmament, another personality was developing, one that was destined to play a leading part in Island affairs and to whom we owe a priceless debt for the information he has left behind. This was Sir John Oglander of Nunwell, who has turned out to be our principal source of information about life in the Isle of Wight at this time. The Oglanders of Nunwell are dealt with more fully in Section II of this book; suffice it to say here that they arrived in the Island from Normandy soon after the Conquest and lived at Nunwell for an incredible 800 years. (See Chapter 27 page 164).

Sir John was born in 1585, three years before the Armada, and in his early twenties was already a Justice of the Peace and beginning to take part in the administration of the Island. He was for many years a Deputy Governor of the Island and served both as High Sheriff of Hampshire, and Deputy Governor of Portsmouth. For a time he was also Member of Parliament for Yarmouth. But his great value to posterity was that he was a compulsive scribbler of notes and never threw any of them away, the net result being that a veritable treasure trove of information about his daily life was inherited by his descendants, and has survived. A small portion of these notes has been transcribed and published, and has proved of inestimable value to future historians.

Typical of the information he has left us is the following list of the "gentry" of the Island in 1610 who were the guests of the Governor, the Earl of Southampton, at his manor of Great East Standen. Sir John writes

> "I have seen with my Lord of Southampton on St. George's Down at bowls, from 30 to 40 knights and gentlemen, where our meetings was then twice every week, Tuesdays and Thursdays, and we had an ordinary there (i.e. a meal) and cards and tables."

He then gives the list of those usually at these meetings. The names of their houses has been added for identification, and those marked with an asterisk are the subject of further information in Section II of this book. It is not until we learn about the people who actually lived in the Island that its history comes to life.

Sir Robert Dillington*   (Knighton Gorges)
Sir Richard Worsley*   (Appuldurcombe) Aged 21 at the time.

Sir Thomas Fleming	(Haseley) Son of a Newport Merchant who became Lord Chief Justice of England. One of the Judges at the Gunpowder Plot Trial in 1605.
Sir John Meux	(Kingston)
Sir John Leigh*	(Shorwell)
Sir William Lisle*	(Wootton)
Sir Bowyer Worsley	(Ashey)
Sir John Dingley	(Wolverton)
Sir John Oglander*	(Nunwell)
Sir Edward Dennis	(West Court)
Mr. Bowreman	(Brook)
Mr. Barnaby Leigh	(Wellow)
Mr. Thomas Cheke*	(Mottistone)
Mr. Edward Cheke	(Merston)
Mr. Lisle*	(Briddlesford)
Mr. Barnaby Colnet	(Pan)
Mr. Jermyn Richards	(Yaverland)
Mr. Erlesman	(Westover)
Mr. Wayte	(Waytes Court, Brighstone)
Mr. Richard Baskett	(Apse)
Mr. Rice	(Bathingbourne)
Mr. Leigh	(Brading)
Mr. Thomas Hobson	(Ningwood)
Mr. Hobson, Junior	(Ningwood)
Mr. Thomas Urry*	(Thorley)
Mr. Philip Fleming	(Combley)
Mr. John Worsley*	(Gatcombe)
Mr. John Harvey	(Alvington)
Mr. Emmanuel Badd	(St. Helens) A Brewer
Mr. Urry	(Afton)
Mr. Knight	(Landguard)
Mr. Streapor	(Hale)
Mr. Legge	(Stenbury)
Mr. Shambler	(Arreton)
Mr. Loving	(Langbridge)
Mr. Champion	(Carisbrooke)

and others

In the Oglander Memoirs Sir John lists four separate attempts made to put a dam across Brading Haven, and writes in detail about the last disastrous effort made in 1620. Originally Bembridge was a tidal island, and a successful attempt to connect it to the main part of the Isle of Wight was made in the 14th century at what is now Yarbridge. This prevented the tide from running right round Bembridge, and the silting up that inevitably followed encouraged further attempts to reclaim large areas of the Haven. These were made in 1562, and again in 1594, and then in 1620 Dutch engineers were employed to build an embankment from St. Helens. At first this was highly successful, and indeed the embankment held for nearly ten years, but in 1630 the tide finally made a breach at a time when a period of heavy and continuous rain was followed by several very high spring tides, and before action could be taken to plug the gap too much damage was done and the embankment was gradually washed away. No further attempt at reclaiming the Haven was then made for another 200 years until the coming of the railway when a satisfactory embankment was built, and this has proved to be permanent.

During the first twenty years of the 17th century an unaccustomed peace had reigned in the Isle of Wight, but in 1622 the threat of war with Spain was again raised. Rumours reached the Island that the Spaniards, still smarting from the defeat of their Armada in 1588 were preparing an even bigger and more formidable fleet with the object of sailing against England. The details of this new Armada were rather strange, and perhaps were intended to frighten us out of our wits, for the armament included the following —

120	ships built after the English fashion
300	Spanish ships
20	Castles
200	Galleys and Galliasses
8,000	Voluntary noblemen and gentlemen
23,000	Sailors
6,000	Soldiers
300	Galley slaves
20	Armed elephants sent from Persia
420,000	Poisoned bullets
200,000	Hollow bullets filled with wild-fire
12,000	sets of musket-proof armour

Elizabethan ships, built 'after the English fashion'.

From the proposed use of poisoned bullets and wild-fire it would seem that the old fashioned, rather gentlemanly rules of warfare were now a thing of the past, and from henceforth no holds were to be barred. Wild-fire, a highly inflammable liquid difficult to put out when once ignited, and possibly based on phosphorus, had been used in warfare previously by the Byzantines, and had been known as Greek fire. It was flattering that they intended to build a number of ships after the English fashion, and with the inclusion of armed Persian elephants the force was obviously going to have an international flavour.

This Armada never materialised, but rumours and invasion scares continued, and there were occasional false alarms indicative of the general state of tension that existed in the Island. One such alarm in 1623 resulted in a full scale mobilisation and even the King was roused from his bed in the middle of the night to be told of it. This was caused by the arrival in St. Helens roads of a fleet of 30 Hamburg merchantmen, presumably calling for water — St. Helens water being famous for its purity and longevity — and being mistaken for Spaniards. Many St. Helens residents left their homes and fled inland, including one old man of 89 who had been bedridden for five years, but who nevertheless managed to walk three miles. There were reports of up to 1000 men having landed, and a beacon was fired, but in fact no one came ashore, and the face of the Deputy Governor of the Island, Sir John Oglander, was very red. He received a stinging rebuke from the Governor, the Earl of Southampton, with a curt request that no more accidents of this sort should happen, but four years later an almost identical false alarm occurred which roused the whole of the south of England. The Isle of Wight could be said to be a rather nervous place in which to live at this time.

Lord Southampton died in 1625 and was succeeded by Lord Conway, a strange Governor who for two years never even visited the Island. He had been appointed Secretary of State in 1623, a post for which he was ill equipped, for he knew no Latin and his handwriting was so bad that no one could read it. One of the favourite jokes of King James I was that he had been given a Secretary who could neither read nor write.

At the time of Lord Conway's appointment Sir John Oglander was required to make a return of all the able-bodied men, and their Commanders, available for the defence of the Island, and the figures which he gave, and which are quoted below, were later publshed by Sir Richard Worsley in his *"History of the Isle of Wight"*.

Sir John Oglander (Nunwell)	97	
Sir Edward Dennis (West Court)	210	
Appuldurcombe	261	
Mr. Dillington (Knighton Gorges)	122	
Sir John Richards (Yaverland)	109	
Mr. Cheeke (Mottistone)	154	
Sir William Meux (Kingston)	261	
Mr. Leigh	95	
Mr. Bowreman	115	
Mr. Hobson (Ningwood)	170	
Mr. Urry (Afton)	122	
Newport	304	Total: 2020

They were armed as follows —

Muskettes	1088
Collivers	33
Corslettes	263
Bare Pickes	196
Halberdes	10
Men Unarmed	297
Officers	133

In 1627 a minor calamity befell the Isle of Wight — a regiment of Scottish Highlanders descended on the Island. They were on their way to France on an expedition to the Isle of Rhé, and were expected to stay here only for a few days. Unfortunately the expedition failed before they managed to join it, and in the event they were billeted in the Island for just over a year. Their habits and customs were foreign to the Isle of Wight and they scandalised and terrorised the inhabitants. Strong representations were made against their long stay, particularly as no money was forthcoming for their keep, and ultimately the King himself (Charles I) visited the Island to inspect the regiment. Soft words were spoken and promises made, though it was confessed that the advantage of keeping the Scots in the Island was that they found it very difficult to desert. However, within a week of the King's visit the Scotsmen (or the "red shanks" as Sir John Oglander called these kilted warriors) departed.

One of the gentlemen in the list above, Mr. Robert Dillington of Knighton Gorges, was related to the Oglander by marriage, but Sir John had an extremely poor opinion of him, and described him as —

> "Base, proud and miserable, not caring for any but those by whom he may gain; in all his actions he hath relation to his own ends; doing a courtesy no further than may stand with his own profit; one that would seem wise, yet a fool in all things, gain excepted."

But Mr. Dillington, through excessive thriftiness and his own business acumen, became one of the wealthiest men in the Island, and in 1628 purchased for himself a baronetcy, thus elevating himself in the social scale and becoming second in precedence only to Sir Henry Worsley of Appuldurcombe. As can be imagined this was not a move designed to endear himself to the other gentry of the Island, and it was only made possible by the fact that the great Duke of Buckingham, favourite of both James I and Charles I, had given away 40 baronetcies to his friends and supporters with permission to sell them for what they would fetch. The going price was £150 to £200 each.

A Dillington funerary hatchment in All Saints Church, Newchurch.

Among the gentry of the Island social position was a very important and rather touchy business, particularly in matters concerning the Militia, and Lord Conway was moved to publish a list under the heading —

"Captains of the Isle of Wight as they are to take place and be ranked when they shall appear in the field with their companies, and in all meetings on martial business.

Sir Edward Dennis	Knights, my Lieutenants in the Island
Sir John Oglander	

The West Medham

Sir William Meux, Knight	(Kingston)
Sir John Leigh, Knight	(North Court)
Mr. Bowerman, Esquire	(Brook)
Mr. Hobson, Esquire	(Ningwood)
Mr. Harvey, Esquire	(Avington)
Mr. James	(Cosham Manor, Newport?)
Mr. John Urry	
The Town of Newport	

The East Medham

Baronet Worsley	(Appuldurcombe)
Baronet Dillington	(Knighton Gorges)

Sir William Lisle, Knight	(Wootton)
Mr. Edward Cheke, Esquire	(Merston)
Mr. Baskett, Esquire	(Apse)
Mr. Thomas Rice	(Bathingbourne)

Inevitably these various lists of the Island's leaders give a very one sided picture of life in the Isle of Wight, and suggest a society that is all Chiefs and no Indians. Unfortunately this cannot be helped, since all the information we have comes from the "Chiefs", but it must be borne in mind that the figures given on page 69 for the Militia probably give a fair indication of the balance throughout the Island population between the number of "haves" and "have nots". The figures quoted gave 133 officers out of a total of 2020 able-bodied men, so that there would have been 1857 other ranks, a ratio of approximately 1 to 14. In Section II of this book some information can be found about wages, prices, and the condition of life for the "have nots" in the Island at various times. (See Chapter 34 page 194).

In January 1628 Sir John Oglander headed a deputation of the "gentlemen of the Island" to London to petition the King for money —

> ". . . to have our castles and forts, some amended, others new erected where most required, and also to have a place of retreat, if so we should be beaten, *videlicet;* Freshwater for our cattle and the main body of our companies, and Yarmouth for the better sort of people . . . "

The plan was, firstly, to let the sea in at Freshwater Gate so that it would flow into the River Yar and turn Freswater into an island, and secondly, to cut the neck of land on the road leading out of Yarmouth to the east so that Yarmouth too became an island. To us today this seems a crazy sort of plan, apart from it being socially indefensible, but it was received kindly by King Charles and his advisers. They thought the Island gentlemen were worrying themselves unduly, but made vague promises to do something about it before long, but nothing was done at that time. 40 years later the Yarmouth part of the plan was carried out, but after two years of the inconvenience of having to use a drawbridge at the entrance to the town, it was abandoned. Some of the stones were later taken to Freshwater and used for building, but traces of the work can still be seen in the thicket of brambles nearby.

An interesting sidelight on Sir John Oglander's journey to London is given in his description of the crossing of the Solent to Portsmouth —

> "I went in so great a wind at south from Ryde to Portsmouth that I went over in half an hour by my watch, with only half the foresail, and the wind was so great that, when we came ashore at Portsmouth, we could not stand nor knew well how to land."

Nowadays we are used to crossing the Solent in much larger ships and are able to keep dry, warm and safe, but it does no harm to remember that until the coming of the Ferries the crossing could be hazardous and uncomfortable. Those of us who are used to sailing these waters in small boats know just how rough and wet it can be. There were six in Sir John's party

— Sir Edward Dennis, Sir William Meux, Mr. Barnaby Leigh, Captain Cheke, Captain Hobson, and himself. Plus of course the boatman, who incidentally would have to get back to Ryde in this head wind blowing a gale from the south — a very wet trip.

Concern about the Island's defences continued to be felt, until in 1642 a new excitement and danger, the Civil War in England, seems to have swept other problems aside for a while. The Civil War had little impact on the Island to begin with, for there was no fighting, but loyalties became very sharply divided. The gentry were generally Royalist in their sympathies to begin with, led by Sir John Oglander, who was outspoken to the point of indiscretion in his support for the King, but the bulk of the population were for the Parliament, many seeing this as a great opportunity to better their conditions.

It was not until 1647 that the Island became fully involved in the struggle, when suddenly, with the arrival of the fugitive King seeking asylum, the Isle of Wight found itself the focus of attention.

Many questions were posed as a result of the precipitous flight of King Charles I to the Isle of Wight in November 1647. Did he really believe he would be safe here, and that his friend Sir John Oglander would be able to protect him? Was he really ignorant of the pro-Parliament feeling in the Island? Did the Parliament connive at his flight from Hampton Court, and guide his steps towards the Island? Was the appointment of Colonel Robert Hammond as Captain and Governor of the Isle of Wight only a few weeks before the King's arrival deliberate? Did Colonel Hammond really have a battle of conscience over his treatment of the King?

There is no doubt that the Parliament were seriously embarrassed to find they had a beaten and disgraced King on their hands as a prisoner. This was a situation without precedent, and for a time they had not the faintest idea what to do with him. To let him go was far too dangerous, but to kill him was (at first) unthinkable. There must have been many who regretted sincerely that Charles had not been killed during the war; life would have been so much easier for them.

For the first few weeks of his stay the King was allowed almost complete freedom, and no one wished to take responsibility for restricting the movements of one who so vehemently believed that he held his position as monarch by Divine right. He visited Nunwell and stayed the night as the guest of Sir John, he went sightseeing at the Needles, and was entertained to a banquet at Thorley. Indeed it was not until an attempt to rescue him was being planned that his freedom was curtailed, the story being that the King was visiting Edward Worsley at Billingham Manor when information reached Colonel Hammond about the plot, and he was so worried that he despatched a troop of horse to Billingham to escort the King back to Carisbrooke.

During the year he was imprisoned in the Castle several attempts to help the King escape were made, but all came to nought. Towards the end of his stay a Treaty was proposed between the King and Parliament, and for this purpose the King was allowed to leave the Castle, on strict parole, and live

Right, Top. The building inside Carisbrooke Castle in which Charles I was imprisoned.

Bottom. The King's lodging in Newport during the Treaty of Newport negotiations.

The silver-gilt hand mace presented to the town of Yarmouth in 1660 by King Charles II in recognition of kindnesses shown to his father.

in Newport where the Treaty was to be negotiated. After much speculation it is now believed that he stayed in a house at the corner of Lugley Street and Holyrood Street. This building later became the Sun Inn, and is now a Wine Store. The Treaty itself is believed to have been negotiated in the Old Grammar School in Lower St. James Street, with the Royalist supporters and lawyers housed in the George Inn, which has long since disappeared but was situated on the south side of the High Street almost opposite Boots the Chemists. The Parliamentary delegation were housed in other inns nearby, the principal one probably being the Bugle in the High Street.

The so called Treaty of Newport never came to fruition as neither side was prepared to give way, and after some weeks of frustration and growing irritation the Army took the law into its own hands and removed King Charles, not only from Newport but also from the Island, imprisoning him in Hurst Castle on the mainland. This happened on the last day of November 1648, and exactly two months later the King was executed in Whitehall.

So the Isle of Wight's brief moment of full national publicity ended rather quickly and sadly. And there was a sad sequel too, for two of King Charles's children — the Princess Elizabeth and Henry, Duke of Gloucester — were sent to Carisbrooke Castle. The Princess was 15 years old, but within a month of arriving in the Island she was dead, (in September 1650), having been caught in a rainstorm from which she took a chill. She was buried unostentatiously in Newport parish church with no stone marking her grave, and it was not until Queen Victoria and the Prince Consort rebuilt the church 200 years later that she was provided with a suitable monument. This monument was commissioned by Queen Victoria and executed by the Italian sculptor, Baron Marochetti, and is a thing of beauty that everyone should see.

The Island also lost its greatest character in 1655 with the death of Sir John Oglander at the age of 70. His Royalist sympathies and his outspokenness had made him very unpopular and had brought him two spells of imprisonment, during the second of which his wife had died. The death of his eldest son George also upset him greatly, as did the execution of the King, and the fact that his own godson, John Lisle, was a fanatical Parliamentarian and one of the judges who sentenced the King to death. Sir John's last years were full of bitterness and depression and he spent them quietly at Nunwell, looking after his estate, and, as he himself wrote:

> ". . . riding in black or some sad-coloured clothes over the Downs to take the air, morning and evening . . ."

But he left the Island an inestimable legacy of information about life here in the 17th century, a legacy that has never been equalled.

There is an old saying that when one door shuts another one opens, and the death of Sir John Oglander was followed within a few years by the arrival of another great character, a man out of a very different mould, flamboyant and extrovert — Sir Robert Holmes — who became Governor of

Sir Robert Holmes, one of the Island's most extraordinary Governors.

74

the Isle of Wight in 1668. Sir Robert's career reads like the script of an Errol Flynn film. As a young man he distinguished himself as a soldier, as a sailor, and as a ladies man, and during the Commonwealth had roamed the high seas with his friend Prince Rupert, romantically supporting the cause of the exiled Charles II. On the Restoration he became the dashing leader of two expeditions to West Africa, where his piratical activities on the Dutch held Gold Coast were instrumental in provoking a war with Holland. It was the gold that Sir Robert brought back from the coast of Guinea that was minted into coinage and brought the word "guinea" into our language.

Holmes was a born leader, the type of man that inspired intense loyalty in those under him, and if he had a fault it was that he could not always get on with those above him. He had a love-hate relationship with Charles II, and with the Duke of York who later became James II, and was often in all sorts of trouble. In 1668 he was involved in a duel as a second to the Duke of Buckingham, and not only was Buckingham's adversary, the Earl of Shrewsbury, killed, but Holmes also despatched the Earl's second, and was lucky not to be charged with murder.

Perhaps he felt that the time had come to retire from the London scene, for later that year he purchased the Governorship of the Isle of Wight from Lord Culpeper, and established himself in Yarmouth in the house next to the Castle which is now the George Hotel. From this centre he organised a piratical empire, extending far into the English Channel, which added to his already considerable wealth and must have been something of an embarrassment to Whitehall.

He survived the Rebellion of 1688 with its change in kingship, and transferred his loyalty to William and Mary, but by then he was ill and had lost much of his sparkle. When he died in 1692 an era came to an end, and the Island was poorer for his passing.

The beautiful staircase at the George Hotel, Yarmouth, once the home of Sir Robert Holmes.

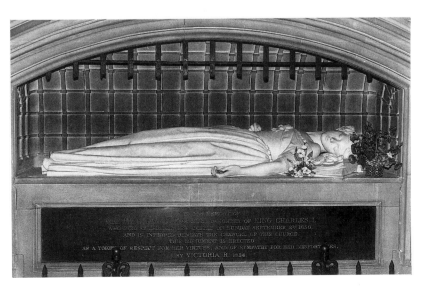

Monument to Princess Elizabeth in Newport Parish Church.

XI — *A Country Rotten with Wealth*

John, Lord Cutts, Governor of the Isle of Wight 1692—1707, once described as being "as brave and brainless as his sword".

The history of England during the 18th century is a story of booming agriculture and trade, a boom such as had never been seen before, typified by the making of huge fortunes by a small number of *entrepreneurs*, accompanied by fierce political in-fighting. In Parliament the two-party system of government developed, with Whigs opposing Tories, and there was a large increase in bribery and corruption. The poorer classes imitated the behaviour of the wealthy, moral values continued to decline, and there was a startling boost to violence and excesses of all kinds.

Charles II had set an all-time low in moral standards, and his subjects followed suit. In the next reigns money became god, wealth being the yardstick by which men were judged, and the poor old Church of England, which should have been there to lead and guide the nation, was silent and ineffective. The so-called "Glorious Revolution" of 1688 split the country neatly in two, and within a year we were once again at war with France, where Louis XIV had sworn to re-instate the Roman Catholic James II on the throne of England.

One saving grace of the 1688 Revolution however was the hammering out of the British Constitution, the unique balance of power between the Crown, the House of Lords, and the House of Commons, which contributed largely to Britain's subsequent greatness, and which ever since has been the envy of the rest of the world, and has been copied by many nations.

Not that Parliament was democratic by any means. The House of Lords was of course hereditary, and of the 558 members of the Commons 294 were returned by constituencies with less than 250 electors, and most of the remainder were "nominated" by local landowners, many new and large centres of population had no representation at all. In short, the system was rotten from top to bottom.

In the Isle of Wight the situation was an exact replica, on a smaller scale, of the above. The Island returned six members to Parliament, two each from Yarmouth, Newtown and Newport, and ever since the time of Sir George Carey there had been a battle between the Governor and the "Gentlemen of the Island" as to who should nominate these six M.P's. There was of course no question of holding an election, or anything like that; the Governor regarded it as one of his perks, and the Gentlemen strongly resented this. Many men were prepared to pay up to £2000 to become a Member of Parliament, so that six seats constituted quite a valuable commodity to have for sale.

The row over who should sell these seats erupted into the open in 1696, soon after the appointment of a new Governor, Lord Cutts. Cutts was a soldier who had distinguished himself by his bravery in the field, but he was an autocrat and he soon fell out with the Gentlemen of the Island. The quarrel was bitter and long drawn out, but in the end it was agreed on both sides to call a truce, and a "Friendship Agreement" was drawn up. This was signed by the Governor and by four of the Island's leading gentlemen, Sir Robert Worsley, Bart, James Worsley Esquire, Anthony Morgan Esquire, and Henry Holmes Esquire, signing on behalf of themselves and all other Gentlemen of the Island. The clauses in this Agreement are quoted in full below, since it is such an extraordinary document, and is an example of how intelligent, educated, and wealthy men can behave like schoolboys.

The Agreement contains the following clauses —

> "THAT there shall be a real, sincere, mutual and lasting friendship between the Governor and Gentlemen, as also between their dependants, friends and servants, to all intents and purposes.

"THAT all quarrels, lawsuits, animosities and the like, relating to corporations and elections, that have at any time happened between them . . . shall *ipso facto* cease and be absolutely forgotten, as if they had never been.

"THAT Sir Robert Worsley, his friends and the partys who have signed these articles will assist any persons recommended by the Governor to be chosen members to serve for the Corporation of Newport for the ensuing Parliament.

"THAT the Governor shall . . . call at Hall at Newtown, examine Witnesses concerning the ancient method of choosing members to serve in Parliament, and effectually restore the Corporation, and all who have a just pretence to be members of it to their ancient rights of Burgage-Tenure; providing that the Governor be put in possession of a qualifying Burgage-Tenure to enable him to be an elector of the Corporation. He paying for the same.

"THAT election of M.P's for the several corporations in the Island shall be managed by all who shall at any time hereafter stand for the same, and by such as recommend or appear for them, with all Calmness and Good Nature, and no Animosity or harsh proceedings to be encouraged or practised on either side.

Newtown Town Hall.

"THAT when any persons stand for M.P. who are not Island men, the Governor's recommendation shall be preferred to them.

"THAT all due respect be paid to the Governor.

The identity of the four men who signed for the Gentlemen is of interest. Sir Robert Worsley, though only a young man, was head of the most influential family in the Island, and was at this time building himself a palatial new house at Appuldurcombe, a house that even today in its ruined state is an architectural treasure. Anthony Morgan and Henry Holmes are the most interesting ones, for they were the leaders of two factions who were involved in a bitter struggle for power and the right to control the Borough of Yarmouth and its two members of Parliament. This struggle went on intermittently for over 50 years, and there is no doubt that it contributed substantially to the downfall of Yarmouth which ultimately lost its municipal status. Henry Holmes was the nephew of the great Sir Robert Holmes and married Sir Robert's illegitimate daughter Mary when she was 15, and inherited a large fortune.

The Friendship Agreement did not prove to be permanent, and when Lord Cutts died in 1707 the Gentlemen were in fact squabbling among themselves. Albin's *"History of the Isle of Wight"*, published in 1795 has the following to say about the corrupt state of affairs in Yarmouth —

> "Yarmouth contains about 50 houses, cottages included. The right of election (to Parliament) is in the capital and free burgesses. The capital burgesses are chosen from the free burgesses which are unlimited by the constitution of the borough, but at present there are only nine.
>
> Mr. Holmes and Mr. Jervoise Clarke Jervoise have each their friends and dependants as burgesses, and by mutual compact have agreed that each shall nominate one of the two members. The capital burgesses are equally divided between the two parties."

Yarmouth Town Hall.

Henry Holmes died in 1738 and was succeeded as head of the Holmes family by his son Thomas, who continued the struggle and was able to gain control of the Newport nominations. Albin has the following comment to make —

> "It is plain that the four members of Newport and Yarmouth are returned by only two persons; three by Mr. Holmes, with the Minister's assistance, and one by Mr. Jervoise. The members for Newtown are chosen at present by four persons; in all six members by six electors only; and this small body may be further diminished by an union of interests in the borough of Newtown, between the Worsley family and Mr. Holmes; in which case four men would return six persons to represent them in Parliament. If this unadorned recital does not impress on the mind the fullest conviction of the absolute necessity of some reform in the representation, it is surely fair to conclude that the utmost power of reason and eloquence would be exerted in vain."

In 1760 plain "Mr" Holmes became Thomas, Lord Holmes. To them that hath shall it be given!

Outside, in the great world beyond these Island shores, the struggle for power, and the changes that this conflict brought about, went on with increasing momentum. England's economy and her overseas possessions were expanding more rapidly than at any previous time, an example of the prodigious growth of commerce being that imports rose from £6 million in 1720 to £10 million in 1760, and to a fantastic £37 million in 1789. Much of this increase was due to the trade in Indian tea and West Indian sugar, and of course in the process of this expansion England was acquiring an empire.

In parallel with this commercial explosion there was a boom in the arts. In 1741 Handel produced his "Water Music" for King George II, and "Rule Britannia" was also published. In the next year Handel came out with "The Messiah". In 1749 Daniel Defoe wrote "Robinson Crusoe", and in 1750 Gray wrote his "Elegy in a Country Churchyard". And so it went on, there seemed to be no limits to British achievements.

Not quite such a pleasant feature of the boom was that the gap between rich and poor was ever widening. The rich were getting richer and the poor poorer, and by the end of the century the labouring classes had never had it so bad. In the north of England the Industrial Revolution added more misery and privation to the bulk of the population, but all this was overlooked and ignored in the general atmosphere of prosperity in the country, and the frantic grab for greater profits.

In the intervals of peace between the ever recurring wars with France and Spain wealthy young men travelled the Continent, doing the "Grand Tour", and coming back loaded with works of arts and new ideas. There was a revival of classical architecture and huge houses were built all over the country. In the Isle of Wight the Worsleys built Appuldurcombe at the beginning of the century, and Gatcombe House in the middle, and it became fashionable to include in one's house a Venetian window. Many of these can still be seen in Island houses, as for example in Nunwell, Haseley, Gatcombe, Wolverton, and North Court.

Gatcombe House, built by Sir Edward Worsley in 1751 was originally intended to be twice this size.

Most large Isle of Wight houses were built of Island stone, though this was getting rarer as the quarries were gradually worked out, and brick was beginning to be used, notably at Merston Manor and in Billingham. In the latter, which was rebuilt in 1722, very effective decorative use was made of blue or plum coloured "headers", and towards the end of the century many small terraced town houses were built, particularly in Newport, where alternate red and blue bricks added considerably to their attraction.

England's aspirations and achievements suffered a hiccough in 1776 when her American colonies revolted and became independent, and for a few years it looked as though England had at last over-reached herself. Her enemies, and there were many, including almost all the European nations, were delighted, for they all saw the startling rise in England's power as a threat. France was smarting under the loss of Canada, which we had taken from them, Spain felt the same about Gibraltar, and Russia, Denmark and Sweden were all anxious to limit England's maritime power. Nearer home the Irish were in revolt.

The culmination of this period came in 1782 when Horace Walpole, the Prime Minister, announced that the French, elated at our loss of the American colonies, and delighted in the down-turn in our fortunes, had been insolent enough to demand that the Government should cede the Isle of Wight to them forthwith. Previous attempts by the French to win back the Channel Islands, our possession of which must have rankled, had failed, but fortunately their request for possession of the Isle of Wight was turned down out of hand, otherwise the history of the Island might have taken a very different course.

The Isle of Wight at this time was having its own problems, and was still suffering from the shock of the loss of the *"Royal George"* off Ryde. This ship, a first rater, and the flagship of Rear Admiral Richard Kempenfelt, was anchored in Spithead undergoing a minor repair to her timbers.

There was not thought to be any danger, and a number of wives and families were aboard, but her bottom suddenly gave way and she sank, drowning about 1000 people. Subsequently it was claimed that she was rotten and ought never to have been at sea, but by then it was too late. Many of the bodies were washed up on Ryde beach and given mass burial under what is now the boating lake.

In 1793 we were once more at war with France, but by this time that country was no longer a monarchy, the Revolution of 1789 having seen to that. This war marked the beginning of a long period of anxiety for the Isle of Wight, with many invasion scares, for France was in the ascendant under the inspired leadership of a young military genius, Napoleon Buonaparte, who was intent on the subjugation of England. Until his final defeat at the battles of Trafalgar (at sea) and Waterloo (on land) the Island was under continual threat.

No gentleman's residence in the 18th and 19th century was complete without a Venetian window.
This one is actually in Osborne House, where there are dozens.

XII — *Victoria and Alfred*

Norris Castle, in which Queen Victoria spent her first Island holiday at the age of 12.

One of the most romantic sights in this part of the world is the view of Norris Castle from the sea. This rugged and battlemented pile is everyone's idea of what a Norman Castle should look like, but Norris was in fact built at the end of the 18th century for Lord Henry Seymour, who wanted a holiday home in the Island. The architect, James Wyatt, gave his client exactly what he asked for — a genuine, authentic medieval stronghold, destined to be the envy of all who saw it.

Lord Henry was just one of the hundreds of wealthy and titled men who had discovered the Isle of Wight and were rapidly turning it into the most fashionable holiday resort in England. The boom had started with the little fishing village of Ryde in 1705 when one Henry Player bought part of the manor of Ashey, built himself a large house near the seashore, and seeing the possibilities of the place, divided his land up into building plots and became the first developer. The development was highly successful and before long several other large villas were built and the popularity of Ryde was assured. By 1795 the population had reached 600, and then in the next 25 years it exploded. In 1821 it had rocketed to 3000.

Other parts of the Island too got caught up in the boom, and for example Ventnor was not far behind Ryde in attracting important and

Right. Osborne House, Queen Victoria's "place of one's own, quiet and retiring", designed for her by Prince Albert.

Statue on the terrace at Osborne.

influential visitors, but of the many members of the nobility who began to frequent the Isle of Wight, by far the most significant was the Duchess of Kent, who took a lease of Norris Castle in 1831 and spent the summer there with her 12 year old daughter, Victoria.

The young princess never forgot her first holiday in the Isle of Wight, and years later when she had become Queen of England and had married, it was to the Island that her thoughts turned when she and Albert decided they must have a retreat somewhere so that they could "get away from it all". Their attempts to buy Norris Castle failed, the Seymour family obviously miscalculating and asking too high a price from their Royal buyer, and it was the nearby Osborne estate that Victoria and Albert ultimately bought, an estate which during the next 60 years was destined to become the centre of the expanding British Empire, and which brought people flocking to the Isle of Wight. For where Queen Victoria went, so the elite of the country, and indeed the world, followed. Today, nearly 90 years after the death of the Island's most famous resident, the Queen of England, Empress of India, and Head of the greatest Empire the world has ever known, the glamour may have worn off slightly but the magic of Victoria still attracts the tourists in their thousands.

But other things were happening in the Isle of Wight in the early years of the 19th century. In 1815 a number of gentlemen interested in the sport of salt-water yachting met in a tavern in London and formed an organisation which they called The Yacht Club. With an initial membership of 42,

and led by the enthusiastic Hon. C. A. Pelham, (who later became the first Lord Yarborough, and incidentally married the niece and heiress of Sir Richard Worsley of Appuldurcombe), the Club was so successful that within two years the Prince Regent himself had expressed an interest in joining. When the Prince came to the throne as George IV in 1821 the Club became the Royal Yacht Club, and in 1825 the Headquarters were moved from London to Cowes. In 1833 the new King William IV agreed to the name being changed to The Royal Yacht Squadron, expressed his approval of the organisation as being of national utility, and was "graciously pleased to consider himself its head". At this time it was antici-pated that in the event of a war the many large yachts owned by members of the Squadron would play a significant role. Since these early days con-tact with the Royal family has been continuous and close, and for over 150 years the Squadron has been acknowledged as the premier yacht club in the world, and its Headquarters, and consequently Cowes itself, as the chief international yachting centre.

The Royal Yacht Squadron.

In 1851 the Royal Yacht Squadron invited the New York Yacht Club to send a yacht over to compete in English waters, and they were pleased to comply. The yacht they sent was the 170 ton *"America"*, and the whole world knows what happened. Not only did she win the Challenge Cup put up, but subsequent attempts to win it back were such failures that it became known as *"the America's Cup"*, and over the years competition for this trophy has given birth to a multi-million pound industry.

The first race was conducted in the presence of thousands of enthusi-astic spectators, the Solent beaches being crowded, and there were said to be over 100 yachts anchored in Cowes Roads. These spectators did of course see the *"America"* win the race and the cup, but few people seem to have been aware of the fact that without British help she might never have done it.

To begin with, the *"America's"* crew were mainly English seamen, lent to her for the occasion by the English yacht *"Surprise"*. Secondly, the *"America"* was skippered by a Cowes pilot named Underwood, and thirdly, in a 10½ hour race the margin between the *"America's"* time and the English yacht, the 47 ton *"Aurora"*, was only 8 minutes, and the *"Aurora"* had in fact mis-read the instructions and had sailed a longer course round the Nab, without which detour she would certainly have won. This information, after 140 years, must now be catalogued as "in-teresting, but useless", and had the *"America"* not won, the subsequent design of fast sailing boats would not have progressed so rapidly, and the public would have been denied many hours of sporting entertainment.

Cowes Roads, with 'Britannia', during Cowes Week.

Boat deign was progressing in another direction too with the invention of the steam engine and its adaption to the propulsion of boats, for this revolutionised water-borne transport and gave man some release from the tyranny of wind and tide. To those who lived in the Isle of Wight it brought a whole new way of life, for with the coming of mechanical propulsion came the possibility of a regular and reliable ferry service, running to a time-table.

The first such service, between Portsmouth and Ryde, began in 1817, and though it was not all that reliable in its early stages, yet it was a beginning. Southampton to Cowes started in 1820, and 10 years later the Lymington to Yarmouth ferry was inaugurated. This spelled the end of the Island's immemorial isolation, and opened the way for the mass tourist trade, which began at this time.

The next boost to this trade came with the opening of the railways, both on the mainland and in the Island. The London to Portsmouth and London to Southampton lines brought the Island within reach of the Capital, the new steam ferries carried people across the Solent, and once on the Island a network of railways transported them to all parts. The first passenger trains ran in the early 1860s from Cowes to Newport and from Ryde to Ventnor. The Freshwater, Yarmouth and Newport Railway opened in 1888 and provided one of the most scenic routes in the whole Island, and by the time the web of railways was complete no part of the Isle of Wight was secret any longer.

The advent of the railways and steam ferries has been described as resulting in a completely new way of life for Islanders. This is no exaggeration, for not only were visitors now able to reach the Island with ease, but for the first time the mainland was opened up to Islanders, trade was increased, and exciting new markets were capable of being developed. The economy of the Island underwent as revolutionary a change as it had seen in hundreds of years. *(For more information about the Island's economy see Section II, Chapter 33, page 190).*

On the political front too revolutionary changes were taking place. The Reform Bill of 1832 shook the whole country with the far reaching nature of the proposed changes, 60 boroughs with a population of less than 2000 losing their franchise. This meant that Newport, Newtown, and Yarmouth all lost the right to send two representatives to Parliament, and in their place the Island was allowed two members only.

The Reform Bill did not have an easy path through Parliament, and on its second reading in the Commons was passed by only one vote. The Government felt that on such a major and controversial issue this was insufficient to enable them to proceed, and so they decided to go to the country.

The new Parliament met in June 1831, and this time the second reading of the Bill was passed with a majority of 136. The third reading had a majority of 109, but it was then thrown out by the Lords. By this time the country was in a ferment of excitement, and the failure of the Bill resulted in civil disturbances and rioting in various places.

The Government persevered however, and ultimately sent the Bill to the Lords for the second time. The debates here were long and acrimonious, and it was only passed after a threat had been made that if necessary a sufficient number of new peers would be created to swamp the opposition. This evokes memories of the past, and though this threat is not as drastic as the one Henry VIII used to persuade the Commons to pass his Dissolution of the Monasteries Bill, yet it had the desired effect and the

Farringford, for many years the home of Alfred, Lord Tennyson.

Act became law. The King himself (William IV) became involved in the struggle, which aroused such high passions in the country that for a time there was a distinct threat of Civil War, and though he gave his Royal Assent to the Bill, he is said to have been so hurt by the coercion to which he had been subjected, and by the insults heaped upon himself, the Queen, and all belonging to him, that nothing could persuade him to go to the House and give his Assent in person.

While all this political activity was causing bewildering changes at home, strange things were happening abroad. Way back in 1797 Napoleon had said "The time is at hand when to destroy England we shall have to seize upon Egypt", his theory being that before reducing the British Isles themselves it was necessary to break up the English power in India, and to do this meant capturing Egypt and disrupting our lines of communication. This young man certainly figured things out on a global scale, and though his subsequent Egyptian campaign was a failure, his continued successes in Europe kept the Isle of Wight permanently on its toes until he switched his attention to Russia, with disastrous results that contributed to his final downfall.

And then a strange thing happened, for only 40 years later we ourselves were at war with Russia, and believe it or not, France was our ally, and indeed the senior partner. Peace broke out in 1856, but it was an uneasy truce, and two years later our relationship with France had once more deteriorated to the point when the possibility of invasion was again causing concern, this time interest being focussed on the Isle of Wight and the possible sacking of the naval base in Portsmouth. In 1859 the Government set up an enquiry into the defence of Portsmouth and Spithead, which naturally involved the Isle of Wight, and this ultimately led to the building of the Spithead and other forts.

At this point the sad comment must be made that international politics, which cause wars to break out, and allies and enemies to be swapped, appear to be distressingly futile. There are many reasons why men cannot get on with each other, but unfortunately when they fall out at international level thousands of innocent people are liable to be killed.

Queen Victoria's residence in the Isle of Wight and the interest this created in the Island, resulting in crowds of visitors from the mainland, was very nearly matched by the effect that one other person had when he came to live here in 1853. This was Alfred Tennyson, the poet, who took a three year lease on Farringford House in Freshwater, with an option to buy. He liked what he found in the Island, and at Farringford, and what is equally important, so did his wife. When the lease expired they had no hesitation in making the purchase.

Tennyson had then been Poet Laureate for six years, and the great success of his poetry had already turned to fame. He was a shy and complex character, with a passion for seclusion and a morbid fear of celebrity hunters. He could, and did, mix with local people but could not stand being watched or pried upon. And unfortunately this is exactly what happened to him. His fame brought thousands of people flocking to Farringford, mainly with the object of catching sight of him, though there were so many notabilities who came to visit him — poets, writers, painters, and artists, etc. — that there was often a rich harvest for the sight-seer, besides the great man himself. Farringford at this time had been described as one of the intellectual centres of England, and it is no exaggeration to say that Tennyson was one of the most eminent of many eminent Victorians.

Ultimately the blatant invasion of his privacy by the crowds of tourists became too much for him, and he bought a house on the mainland to which he retreated in the summer, returning to the Island only when the visitors had gone. But for 40 years Farringford was a Mecca that attracted pilgrims in their thousands from every level of society, and together with Osborne helped to establish the Isle of Wight at the top of the Holiday Island League.

It is strange that two people — Queen Victoria and Alfred Lord Tennyson — both shunning the limelight, both desperately wanting peace and quiet, could have done so much to publicise the Isle of Wight. They were both respected, venerated, and indeed idolised, but they both attracted the crowds, and between them they revolutionised the character of this small Island. Tennyson died in 1892, the Queen survived for another 10 years. In the great celebrations that had attended the old Queen's Diamond Jubilee in 1897 the people of Cowes erected a banner across the street. The message it contained was of course addressed to the Queen, but it was typical of the affectionate and humorous regard in which she, and Tennyson too, had been held. It read —

"A Good Sovereign — No Change Required!"

XIII — *Landmarks and Milestones*

The 20th century opened quietly enough, though experiments were being carried out in the Isle of Wight that were destined to shake the world, and were a prelude to a century of technological devlopments such as had never been seen before, nor even dreamed of. These experiments had started in the last years of the old century in Alum Bay, conducted by an Italian scientist, Signor Marconi, who had managed to establish wireless communication with Bournemouth, and who was now racing ahead extending the range of his transmissions, firstly from England to France, and then — miracle of miracles — from England to America.

On the other side of the Island the old Queen passed away, and though her influence lingered on, it was the end of an era. It is said that when one door shuts another one opens, but at this time no one could possibly foresee the future and forecast the fantastic changes that this new century was going to bring into our lives. In America Orville and Wilbur Wright were stumbling into the sky in a heavier than air machine, and Henry Ford was founding his famous motor company. In England Sir John Fleming invented the thermionic valve, the road speed limit was *raised* to 20 m.p.h., and Mr. Rolls met Mr. Royce.

In the Isle of Wight the new King of England, Edward VII, lost no time in getting rid of Osborne House where he had spent much of his childhood, and of which he had very unhappy memories, but he retained the neighbouring estate of Barton Manor as a *'pied à terre'* in the Island, and somewhere he could entertain his friends. On one such occasion in 1909 his guests were the entire Russian Royal Family, Czar Nicholas II, his Empress Alexandra Feodorevna, and their five children. The photographs taken at the time of their visit are a pathetic reminder that this was the last State visit the Russian Royals made to this country, for only a few years later the whole family — with the possible exception of the Grand Duchess Anastasia — were murdered during the Bolshevik rising of 1917.

The Russian Royal House Party at Barton Manor, 1909, hosted by King Edward VII. From L. to R, Standing: Prince Edward of Wales, Queen Alexandra, Princess Mary, Princess Victoria, Grand Duchess Olga of Russia, Grand Duchess Tatiana of Russia. Seated: Princess of Wales, Czar Nicholas II, King Edward VII, Empress Alexandra of Russia, Prince of Wales, Grand Duchess Marie of Russia. On ground: Czarevitch Alexis and Grand Duchess Anastasia of Russia.

In 1908 Quarr Abbey came to life again. A group of French Benedictine monks who had left their own country in 1901 due to political persecution and had settled in Appuldurcombe House, moved to Quarr and built a new and magnificent monastery in brick, so that after a silence of nearly 400 years the Abbey bells could once more be heard calling the brethren to prayer.

These were spacious and gracious days in the first decade of the century and Edwardian society patronised the Isle of Wight and brought it renewed prosperity. Holidays at the seaside were firmly established as a national pattern, and the Island resorts with their wide sandy beaches and unpolluted sea attracted the more well-to-do. The Royal Yacht Squadron went on from strength to strength. King Edward VII was an enthusiastic member, and as the Squadron's Admiral he headed an aristocratic organisation which refined the art of snobbery to the nth degree. Membership was jealously controlled and only those with the bluest of blood were permitted to join. Even Sir Thomas Lipton, who spent a fortune in trying to win back the *America's Cup* was excluded from membership of the Squadron until he was 80 years of age. And of course, for many years no woman was allowed inside the hallowed premises on Cowes Esplanade.

One member who was jealous of King Edward's popularity was his nephew, Kaiser Wilhelm II of Germany, who was also an enthusiastic yachtsman and visited Cowes regularly with a succession of large yachts, all called *"Meteor"*. Indeed, Cowes became increasingly international in character, and in 1909 three visiting monarchs — the Emperor of Germany, the Czar of Russia, and the King of Spain — were all present in their yachts to add something to the glittering scene.

When Edward VII died in 1910 his son, George V, took his place as Admiral of the Squadron, and so it went on. But these halcyon days were coming to an end. In 1914 a Review of the Fleet was held in Spithead, this providing an incredible and frightening display of British maritime power, there being no fewer than 68 battleships, 218 destroyers and 76 submarines among the many ships drawn up for the King to review. But any triumph he may have experienced was short lived, for on 4th August war broke out between England and France on one side, and Germany and Austria on the other. Life in the Island was immediately disrupted, all yachting ceased, the ferry service with the mainland was discontinued, and for the

*Westland Aerospace
works in East Cowes,
previously the British Hovercraft Corporation, and for
many years before that —
Saunders Roe.*

Right. *The corner of Church
Litten and South Street,
Newport, once the site of
Cosham Manor, which
Charles I visited when he
was Prince.
Now a supermarket!*

Below. *But the Island is still
a beautiful place. View from
Bowcombe Down.*

next four years the Isle of Wight was isolated.

When it was over it was a long time before life returned to normal, and indeed things were never quite the same again, though Cowes recovered much of its popularity and position, and yachting experienced a boom which, with the exception of the seven years of the second world war, has lasted right through the century. Besides being a yachting centre Cowes was of course important in shipbuilding. One of the leading firms — J. Samuel White — built a variety of craft for the navy, though concentrating on destroyers, which they had helped to develop, not only with regard to speed but also in armament. White's also built submarines and lifeboats and were involved in the development of the seaplane.

Another prominent firm in the building of boats also graduated from them to aircraft. This was Saunders-Roe, set up in 1912 by S. E. Saunders who built a record breaking hydroplane, as well as lifeboats, and later built *"Bluebird"*, Sir Malcolm Campbell's boat that established a world water speed record of 126.3 m.p.h. in 1936, and topped it two years later. In conjunction with Sopwith, Saunders had developed the flying boat in the early years, but it was their partnership with the aircraft manufacturer A. V. Roe in 1928 that really produced results, a number of commercially attractive large flying boats being built. The last and largest of these, the *Princess*, looked like being a winner but unfortunately the Government lost interest in flying boats and decided to concentrate on land craft. Seaplanes too never fulfilled their true potential, though for many years the *Schneider Trophy Race* was held over the Solent, the starting and finishing line being Ryde Pier, and the seaplanes designed by R. J. Mitchell for Supermarine were the ancestors of the *Spitfire* which in the second world war played such a large part in saving Britain from defeat.

During this war the Militia, now known as the Home Guard, came back into its own, and once more the Island, as in so many times in the past, became an armed fortress. Many hundreds of men joined the Home Guard, training was taken very seriously, and once uniforms, weapons and ammunition had been supplied, this civilian force developed into an efficient fighting unit. Had they ever had to face a full scale German invasion the day would have ultimately and inevitably gone badly with them, but they would have sold their lives dearly.

Perhaps the most remarkable fact about the Home Guard was the astonishing feeling of comradeship that developed, especially at the time of the Dunkirk withdrawal when our fortunes were at a very low ebb and it seemed certain that the next move of the German Army would be an onslaught on the south coast. At this time within the Home Guard all class barriers, prejudices, and local animosities evaporated as if by magic, and it became a privilege to serve in and with such a body of men. Anyone who experienced this period of the war in the Home Guard will remember the feeling almost of exaltation, that came from the knowledge that here, in the face of imminent danger, was complete unity and singleness of purpose.

Though this feeling did not survive once the immediate danger was over, yet the war ended on a note of hope, with many men believing that it would be possible to build a new order of things based on justice and social equality. There was much talk of a shorter working week with everyone enjoying more leisure time, but alas it did not work out that way. Our worn out and old fashioned economic system was not capable of ensuring a fair distribution of wealth, and before long we were back to a state of every man for himself, with greed being the motivating force.

During the second half of the century the national economy showed every sign of instability, and it soon became apparent that no political party knew the secret of how to make it work fairly for the whole community, or even how to keep it on an even keel. There was an even greater swing towards the worship of material things, and the rich grew richer and the poor poorer. The motor car became a god, and even in the Isle of Wight the number of vehicles on the road was allowed to grow to the point where traffic reached ludicrous proportions, and parking became a complicated exercise.

In a pathetic attempt to control matters every road was painted with yellow lines or white lines, or both, and we became so accustomed to this desecration of our highways that we could no longer see what an indictment it was of our mis-management of the transport system. To add to the confusion and danger we continued to straighten roads out, to make them wider, and to give them smoother surfaces, with the result that more motor cars were encouraged to use them, and speeds were increased to even greater levels of danger. If and when we felt that a limit had been reached, then the only antidote we could devise was to build across the road at intervals "sleeping policemen" to slow the traffic down!

Nationally too, our television programmes were allowed to glamorise violence and sex, as well as the motor car, and inevitably many young people copied the heroes and heroines they watched on the screen. To many a young man an exciting car chase on the box acted directly as an incitement to go out and do likewise, and it was regarded as manly and grown-up to drink and drive.

The Government of the day paid lip-service to the problem of inflation, and regularly produced complacent figures to show that the situation was really not very serious, but regardless of these statistics the wages and prices spiral continued its escalation to almost ridiculous heights. One of the worst price explosions was in property, house prices increasing to such fantastic heights that very few buyers could pay cash for their house, and more and more people risked financial ruin by borrowing beyond their means. We became a nation living on tick.

Island prices and wages traditionally have lagged behind those on the mainland, and in the 1980s this encouraged a flood of developers with beautifully prepared schemes, all anxious to invest in the Island and provide us with amenities we were not sure we wanted. Sometimes it was not easy to see that a developer's motives were not altogether altruistic, and that his activities were slowly eroding away the unique beauty and charm of the Isle of Wight, and the peace and quiet which has always been a

92

feature of the Island, and for which so many of our visitors desperately seek.

Many people still find the Isle of Wight a place of retreat and refuge, and a safe haven where they can live at a slightly slower pace and recover from the nervous strain of life on the mainland. Attempts to connect us to England by means of a bridge or a tunnel crop up from time to time, but fortunately good sense has so far prevailed, for though there would be many advantages to be gained by a fixed link, yet we should lose for ever our character as an island.

Our three local Councils continue to put their party political allegiance before the well-being of the Island, and so far no one has had the courage or the strength to cut this Gordian knot and relieve the Island from what can only be described as excessive over-government. Nevertheless, in spite of its many problems, and the bewildering speed with which changes are taking place, the Isle of Wight and its people are in reasonably good heart. The wife of one landowner who farms a few hundred acres in the centre of the Island, and who perhaps is wiser than most of us, said —

> "We do not regard ourselves as owners of the land, but rather as custodians, just one link in a long chain of people who have lived here from way back in the remote past to far ahead in the future. The land belongs to God; we only look after it."

As we move towards the 21st century perhaps we should all re-examine our attitude towards this beautiful little Island in which we are privileged to live. If we do, then perhaps we may realise that in the short time we are here we have a duty to care for the Isle of Wight and pass it on to others in as good a shape as possible.

Thrift on the cliff tops near Freshwater Bay, Tennyson Down beyond.

Section II

Section I was a chronological account of events from the earliest times up until the present day. Section II looks at the Isle of Wight from a different point of view; it deals with various aspects of life in the Island, with people and places, and tries to show some of the reasons why it is such an *"Enchanted Isle"*.

From Bowcombe Down looking north-east towards Newtown, with the Solent in the background. An enchanting view that over the centuries many travellers must have enjoyed.

XIV — *Isle of Wight Place Names*

There have been many theories put forward to explain the meaning of the word WIGHT, one of the most likely being that it springs from the Celtic word "Guith", which means a separation. This is a logical explanation, going back to the times of the known Celtic invasions of the Island some hundreds of years B.C., and the name may have referred to the separation of the Island from the mainland, an event which had happened earlier still.

When the Romans came they changed the name to *"Insula Vectis"* (the Island of Vecta) and this name was used all through their occupation of 400 years, but when they left in the 5th century the old name seems to have come back. In A.D. 530 the Anglo-Saxon Chronicle was referring to *"Wihte ealand"*, and with minor variations this spelling has survived. In passing it should be noted that in Saxon times the word *"wight"* also meant a human being or person, either male or female, and it is a strange coincidence that of the two principal British off-shore islands, one is called the Isle of Wight, and the other the Isle of Man.

The acknowledged authority on Isle of Wight place names is not an Englishman but a Swede, Helge Kokeritz, who spent some considerable time in the Island in the years before the 1939—1945 war. He chose the Island deliberately for his research, which was sponsored by Harvard University, since he felt —

> ". . . that the Isle of Wight, geographically well-defined and historically significant, would undoubtedly offer an interesting and profitable field of research, furthermore that the limited size of the Island would make it possible to acquire intimate acquaintance with the whole area, so essential for correct identifications and plausible interpretations."

His work, which was published in Uppsala in 1940, is scholarly and not easy to read, and though he is infuriatingly vague about some names, and has nothing at all to say about others, yet the mass of information he gives is of the utmost value to historians and all those anxious to learn about the Isle of Wight.

Apart from the name of the Island itself, place name evidence of those early Celtic settlers is almost non-existent, one of the few Celtic names to have survived being Carisbrooke. Roman names are equally scarce and it is not until the Jutish and Saxon invasions of the 5th, 6th and 7th centuries that new names were given to the places they inhabited, many of which have survived in recognisable form to this day.

Possibly the oldest of these names are those ending in *"—ham"* or *"-hamm"*. These are Saxon words, a *"-ham"* meaning a homestead, and a *"-hamm"* a river meadow, and it is logical that words with these endings should be of very early date. Typical examples in the Island are Newnham, Ninham, Sainham, and of course Hamstead. There was also at one time a Faselham, in Gatcombe parish, but this name has been lost.

Another group of names of equal age, and even more interest, are the *"-ing"* names (*"-ing"* meaning very roughly 'the land of'), and particularly the compound words where *"-ing"* is one of the syllables. Brading is the best example of a plain *"-ing"* name, but there are many interesting ones compounded with *"-ham"* or *"-hamm"*, such as Billingham, Whippingham, Wilmingham, and Tidelingham (a lost name). The *"ingham"* names are thought to be Jutish.

"-ton" is another ending (Saxon), this one meaning a township or settlement. Examples of this Saxon name are Wolverton, Mottistone, Niton, Alverstone, Wootton, Arreton, Merston, Chillerton, Afton, Brighstone, etc., etc. *"-ton"* can also be compounded with *"-ing"*, as in Eddington and Lushington.

The *"-ing"* syllable can also be compounded with other words, and it is curious that many of these refer to, and are near, water. For example, Farringford, Bathingbourne, Huffingford (Blackwater), Horringford, and Watchingwell, all of which are early names.

Another early Saxon name ending is *"-bury"* or *"burh"*, this being the name they gave to an old Celtic fortified place, examples being Stenbury (a fortified place in stone), Bigbury and Dunsbury (fortification on the Downs). One of the earliest of all names is "Wihtgaraburh" where a battle took place in A.D. 530 and many of the old Celtic inhabitants were slain, (see Chapter 3, page 18).

"-combe" is a Saxon ending meaning a valley, and is the same word as the Celtic *"cwm"*. Examples, Luccombe, Appuldurcombe, Nettlecombe, Gatcombe, Whitcombe, and Shalcombe. *"-or"* is a Danish ending, meaning a strand or beach, as in Ventnor or Bouldnor, *"-den"* means a boundary, as in Standen, *"-bourne"* means a stream, and *"-fleet"* a creek.

Finally, another name ending that has perhaps not been given enough attention is the Saxon *"-field"* or *"-feld"*. Professor W. G. Hoskins maintains that a Saxon place name ending in *"-field"* often betokens a site they found already in cultivation and complete with boundaries, and hence one of Romano-British origin, or even earlier.

In the Island there are at least 35 place names ending in *"-field"*, and research into these could release some very interesting information about the period of the Roman occupation. Two names in particular appear to be significant. It is known that the Romans imported and farmed oysters in the River Medina, and that their oyster beds were probably either in the bight of the River below Whippingham (where very much later on the Folly Inn became a notorious *rendez-vous* for the young bloods of the Island), or at Claybrook, above Whippingham, the *"luck"* or fishponds of which were still being farmed a thousand years later by Quarr Abbey.

Here at Claybrook, on either side of the "Luck" are two farms, Heathfield and Binfield, and it is possible that these were the centre of Roman oyster farming in this part of the Island. Both farms are connected with ancient tracks that would lead naturally to the Roman Villas at Newport, Combley, and Brading. Binfield is particularly interesting in that it is situated half way between Claybrook Luck and what is now the North

97

Fairlee Road, and the track that passes through the farm does a double right angle bend, often a sign that the settlement was at one time much larger.

If Professor Hoskins is right about the meaning of "*-field*", then with up to 35 of them in the Island there are exciting possibilities of further research into possible Roman sites, and the existence of Roman roads.

The place name endings listed above cover the majority, though not all, of the pre-Conquest Island names, and armed with this information it is possible to look at the Island in a new light, and detect many examples of early colonisation by the Romans, Germans and Scandinavians. A list in date order of some of these early place names makes interesting reading, and throws up one or two other varieties.

A.D. 530   **Wihtgaraburh** is mentioned. Believed to be the Saxon name for Carisbrooke.

683   **Brading.** The people living on the edge of the Down.
Yaverland. Originally probably *Overland*, i.e. the land over the other side of Brading Haven, in what is now Bembridge.

725   **Whippingham.** The homestead (or river meadow) belonging to Wippa's people.

826   **Calbourne** probably takes its name from the stream on which the village is situated (the Caul Bourne), though Kokeritz suggests it means "the valley where cabbages grew".

Winkle Street. This attractive row of tourist-haunted cottages could possibly get its name from a freshwater snail at one time found in the 'Caul Bourne' here. (There are other theories).

828	**Shalfleet**, the shallow stream or creek.
880	**Arreton**, originally Eaderingtune, "the township of Eadhere's people."
	Wellow takes its name from the willow trees that grow there.
959	**Atherfield**, in Domesday Survey given as Avrefel. One of the 35 Island *"-field"* names meaning open or previously cleared land.
960	**Bathingbourne.** The stream of Beadda's people.
968	**Sticelett** has several suggested meanings, all of which refer to the second element of the name, which means a muddy creek or estuary.
	Watchingwell is not far from Sticelett and is a compounded *"-ing"* name for which Kokeritz gives several possible derivations. The favourite would seem to be a derivation from the Saxon name of the locality *"Whatine"*, but it could also mean "the place where wheat was grown". In Domesday it is given as *"Watingwell"*, where *'wat'* could mean *'wet'*, i.e. "the wet place". Finally, a map of 1775 named the ancient track past Lower Watchingwell as "Holy Lane", and this arouses all sorts of exciting possibilities.

The following are a few more Island place names, arranged alphabetically for easy reference, and with the date (in brackets) of the first known reference. In reading this list it must be borne in mind that —

1. The derivation given is not necessarily the only one available. Experts do not always agree, and indeed like lesser mortals they are frequently groping in the dark for a suitable explanation.
2. The majority of the names quoted are Anglo-Saxon, (c.440—c.1000) but were not recorded until the date shown, which in many cases is much later. Over the centuries the spelling and pronunciation of names changes, sometimes quite dramatically. This is particularly true of the early centuries when few people could write, and names were passed on by word of mouth. The more uneducated the person the more likely he was to get the pronunciation wrong. One only has to look at old Church Registers to see the truth of this.
3. To help get the quoted dates in perspective see the Charts C.C.1 (page 6), C.C.2 (page 35), C.C.3 (page 42), and C.C.4 (page 63).
4. The list given below is far from complete and must be regarded as a selection only. There are many, many more place names, the whole subject being one of infinite scope and interest.

Afton	*"Aeffa's farm"* or alternatively "the wet and muddy farm", the Saxon word *"aeffa"* meaning a wet and muddy place. It is interesting that Afton is close to the marshy source of the River Yar. *(1086)*
Appleford	"The ford near the apple tree" *(1086)*

Appuldurcombe	"The valley of the apple trees" or *"Apelder's valley"*. Alternatively it has been suggested that in the ancient Armoric language *"pul"* is a bottom, or ditch, or pool, and *"dur"* is water. *(1255)*
Apse	Derived from "aspen tree". *(1100)*
Barton	Generically "a farm", Barton, in Whippingham, was once an Oratory, later a manor belonging to Queen Victoria. *(1274)*.
Bembridge	"The land lying inside the bridge", a name that must have been given to it after the building of Yarbridge. *(1316)*
Bierley	"A farm meadow" *(1341)*
Binstead	Kokeritz says "The place where beans were grown". This seems a very prosaic name for a place as old and romantic as Binstead with its quarries. *(1086)*
Bonchurch	*"Bana's church"*, or "the church built by a murderer as an act of atonement". *(1086)*
Botany Bay Mill	Nickname given to the East Medine Mill built at the mouth of Claybrook Luck on the River Medina.
Bouldnor	A cliff facing the Solent near Yarmouth and having a shape resembling a bull. *(1181)*
Bowcombe	"The place above the valley". Once the meeting place of the Bowcombe Hundred, one of the three Hundreds into which the Island was divided at the time of Domesday, (the others being Calbourne and Hemreswell) *(1086)*
Briddlesford	"A ford suitable only for horseback" *(1086)*
Brighstone	*"Beortwig's farm"*. Once known as Brixton. *(1212)*.
Brook	Takes its name from the stream that flows through it. *(1086)*
Budbridge	"A bridge of tree trunks or logs" (over the eastern River Yar). *(1248)*
Carisbrooke	"The deep valley through which the brook flows", or "The rock past which the brook flows". The brook is of course the Lukely Brook. *(1071)*
Chale	A "throat" or gorge, i.e. Blackgang Chine. *(1086)*
Chessell	"A burial place under the hill". Anglo-Saxon. *(1250)*
Chillerton	"The farm in the valley with an enclosure or yard" ("Chill" having the same root as "Chale"). *(1086)*
Clatterford	"The ford where small stones make a clattering noise". Kokeritz is non-commital about this one. *(1255)*
Colwell	"The cool spring". *(1417)*
Compton	"The farm in the valley". *(1086)*

The Causeway at Freshwater spanning the River Yar — which was originally called the Freshwater.

100

Cowes	A comparatively modern name (15th century), and originally called Shamlord. The new name sprang from two sandbanks off-shore — the East and West Cows. *(1666)*
Cranmore	Kokeritz is vague, the first element meaning "crane" and the second one "moor". *(1235?)*
Debourne	"The deep brook". *(13th century)*
Dolcoppice	A farm originally owned by one William Dolecope. *(13th century)*
Duver	A south country word meaning a sandy piece of waste land near the sea. *(1771?)*
Easton	"The eastern farm", in Freshwater. (Similarly Weston, Norton, Middleton, and at one time Sutton). *(1244)*
Farringford	"The ford of the people living in the ferny place". The ford was either at Sheepwash cottage or near Blackbridge. *(1287)*
Fishbourne	Probably the original name of Wootton Creek. The Abbey of Quarr had fishponds here. *(1267)*
Franchville	The original name of Newtown, and meaning "A free town". *(1254)*
Frenchman's Hole	A cave near Totland, possibly so called because a Frenchman once concealed himself in it and starved to death.
Freshwater	Originally the name of the (western) River Yar. *(1086)*

Gatcombe	"The goat valley." *(1086)*
Gladices	Walter Gladhouse, the first of a long line, owned this farm near Chale. *(1391)*
Godshill	Self explanatory. *(1342)*
Golden Hill	"Downland subject to some form of tax". The site of a Napoleonic Fort. *(1299)*
Gurnard	"The marshy shore". *(1279)*
Hamstead	"A homestead". Once a Grange of Quarr Abbey. *(1086)*
Haseley	"The hazel wood". *(1086)*
Havenstreet	Name of doubtful origin. "The street built, or used by heathens (Celts?)", or "The street through heather covered land". The site of a possible Roman road? *(1248)*
Headon Warren	"The rabbit warren on the heather-clad Down." Rabbits were a very important 'crop' at one time. *(1324)*
Heathfield	"Open land covered in heather?" There are several instances in the Island. *(1246, 1341, etc)*
Hulverstone	"Hunthrip's farm." *(1287)*
Hunny Hill	"The hill where wild honey could be gathered". *(1274)*
Merstone	"The farm by the marsh." *(1086)*
Middleton	"The middle farm", (from its situation between Easton and Weston). *(1246)*
Monk's Farm	"Mowne's land." According to Kokeritz, nothing to do with Monks. *(1417)*
Mottistone	Named after the Neolithic menhir, the Longstone, which in Saxon times was used as a Meeting Stone. *(1086)*
Needles	The three famous rocks at the extreme western point of the Island. A fourth one, 100 feet high, crashed into the sea in 1764. *(1333)*
Newbridge	Self-explanatory and indicating that there was a bridge here previously (over the Caul Bourne). *(1378)*
Newchurch	Self-explanatoy. *(1228)*
Newtown	Modern name for Franchville. *(1254)*
Ningwood	"The wood which had been enclosed" *(1086)*
Niton	"The new farm" *(1086)*
Norris Castle	Castle built in 1799 on land once held by the Norris (le Noreys) family. *(1259)*
Northwood	"The north wood" (of Parkhurst Forest) *(1248)*

Osborne	Once spelt 'Austebourne' — "The brook at the sheep-fold. *(1316)*
Parkhurst Forest	"The King's Forest." "Park" = an enclosure, "hurst" = a wooded hillock. *(1200)*
Porchfield	At one time spelt Portsfield, i.e. land owned by the Port family. *(1559)*
Puckaster	Thought by some to have been a Roman Camp connected with the Tin Trade. Kokeritz traces the name to "Puck" (a goblin) and "Tor" (a rock or high hill). *(1608)*
Queen's Bower	Queen Anne (1702—1714) is said to have had a 'Bower' here where she came for the excellent hawking. *(1781)*
Rew Street	"Rew" = a hedgerow, so the name could possibly indicate a boundary. *(14th century)*
Ryde	The local word "ride" or "rithe" means a small stream. *(1257)*
St. Helens	The place takes its name from the church. At one time called Eddington. *(1248)*
Sandown	"The sandy river meadow" *(1086)*
Sconce Point	Literally "the sharp point", originally "Sharpenode". Sir George Carey built a small fort here — Carey's Sconce. *(1324)*
Shalcombe	"The shallow valley" *(1086)*
Shalfleet	"The shallow stream or Creek" *(828)*
Shamlord	Previous name for Cowes. Also spelt Shamblord. *(13th century)*
Shanklin	Takes its name from the famous Chine, which was called by the Anglo-Saxons *"Scene"* (the Cup). In the Anglo-Saxon language *"Sc-"* had the same pronunciation as our modern *"Sh-"*. *(1086)*
Shide	Possibly the name of an early bridge over the Medina River. *(1086)*
Shishford	"The ford near the corner of land" *(1255)*
Shorwell	Below the steep hill (Anglo-Saxon *"scora"*) is a spring of beautiful clear water, hence "Shorwell". The stream once powered a fulling mill in the village, and another mill at Yafford. *(1086)*
Stenbury	"The stone fort" *(1086)*
Swainston	"Sweyn's Farm" *(1213)*
Thorley	A Celtic name? "The pasture near the *'tor'* or hill" *(1086)*
Totland	"The protruding, or prominent, land". Alternatively "The look-out land" *(1608)*

Ventnor	Derivation obscure, the ending *"-or"* possibly meaning a strand. But Kokeritz suggests it might come from either a "vintner" who lived there, or from a "vintener" who was a second-in-command of a Milita leader. *(1617)*
Walkers Lane	In Shorwell. So called because the men who trampled the cloth in a fulling mill were known as "walkers".
Warden Point	Warden = watch hill. *(1591)*
Watcombe Bay	*"Combe"* means valley or low ground. *"Wat"* means wet, or *"what"* means wheat. Take your choice. *(14th century)*
Werrar	"The river bank where there is a weir". Actually, Werrar is believed to be the "safe haven" used by Danish invaders as their winter quarters c.1006. *(1199)*
Westover	"The western bank of the Caul Bourne" *(1331)*
Whitcombe	"The white valley" *(1086)*
Whitwell	"The white spring" *(1212)*
Wilmingham	"The homestead of Wilhelm's people" *(1086)*
Wootton	"The farm in the wood" *(1086)*
Wroxall	Derived from *"Wroc"* meaning an escarpment, or hillside, and also meaning a bird of prey, such as a buzzard. Above Wroxall is the very steep St. Martin's Down, on which incidentally buzzards could well have nested. *(1038)*
Wydcombe	"The wide valley" *(1255)*
Yafford	"The ford by the dam" *(1086)*
Yarmouth	"The muddy estuary" *(1086)*

XV — Island Towns: Introduction

The Guildhall in the Island's county town, Newport. Designed by John Nash in 1813, though the clock tower was added in 1887, in celebration of Queen Victoria's Jubilee.

Oscar Wilde once said that age is no guarantee of respectability of character. He was of course referring to a lady of advanced years, but the remark applies equally well to towns, some of which in their old age are not very attractive to look upon. In the Island we are lucky. All our towns are old, some older than others, and they exhibit between them a wide range of characteristics, but it can truthfully be said that respectability is one shared by them all.

Experts tell us that the most common form of town is the planned town, and that very few just grew because they were at suitable locations. As a generalisation this may be so, but it would not seem to be true of our Isle of Wight towns, for of nine settlements that can claim to be called towns, only three — Yarmouth, Newport and Newtown — were completely planned from scratch. The remainder, and particularly the seaside holiday towns of Ryde, Sandown, Shanklin, and Ventnor grew, even mushroomed, in a very short space of time. Naturally, each of these had some planning content, but their ultimate shape was influenced as much by the haphazard ownership of land as by a deliberate and conscious planning effort. The other two towns, Brading and Cowes, developed because of their geographical position alongside navigable waters.

The following notes are not intended by any means to be a comprehensive guide to these nine towns, but merely to sketch in the history of their growth, and to emphasise that they are all worthy of further acquaintance and study.

XVI — *Island Towns: Yarmouth*

Not the first town to be mentioned in the Isle of Wight — that honour goes to Brading — but certainly the first to be planned and built as a town, at a date in the middle of the 12th century. The mouth of the western River Yar is directly opposite the mouth of the Lymington River on the mainland, and in the days when boats were very small and propelled by either sail or oar, calm water for a landing place was very desirable, and these two river estuaries provided just that — at Lymington on the mainland, and at Thorley in the Island — Thorley pre-dating Yarmouth by many, many centuries as a port.

Roman coins have been found at Thorley, and the very name Thorley Street suggests a Roman road, and it is at least possible that there was a Celtic settlement here before Vespasian and his 2nd Legion arrived in A.D. 43. Incidentally, one other advantage of a landing place well inland was the protection it gave you from pirates.

All through the centuries that followed the Roman arrival the estuary of the River Yar — the name men gave it was Ermud, the muddy estuary — gradually silted up, and it became more and more difficult to reach Thorley except when the tide was in. Ultimately another landing place, nearer the sea, had to be found, the requirements being not only some protection from the sea and the weather, but also a dry and shingly beach so that landing could be achieved without getting too muddy.

The spot that was decided on was near the river mouth and on the east bank, and it is now well buried under Yarmouth Quay, though at that time there was nothing there but a sandy or shingle beach and the wild saltings. At this spot men could draw their boats up beyond high water mark, and could walk the mile or so to Thorley.

The route they took can still be followed today, over a thousand years later. From the beach they made a track eastwards along the peninsula, and this track is now Yarmouth High Street. Once clear of the peninsula the track turns sharp right into what is now Thorley Road, and descends from the high ground (the 'Tor') into the estuary and marshes of the Thorley Brook. When the tide was out it was possible to cross the brook fairly easily, and a glance at today's Ordnance Survey map will show how the track crossed the estuary, meandering from shingle bank to shingle bank to maintain as dry a crossing as possible.

As time went on, more and more activity was transferred from Thorley to the new landing place near the mouth of the river, and sooner or later sheds would be erected for boats, gear and merchandise. Gradually, the settlement at the Yar mouth grew, but it was not until the early years of the 12th century that Baldwin de Redvers, the Norman Lord of the Island, decided to build a proper town. This he did by using the existing track as the spine of his town — the High Street — and across it at right angles he built a number of streets — now called Market Square, St. James Square and St. James Street; Refuge Lane and South Street; Love Shore Lane and Baskett's Lane; and higher up still the High Street was ultimately crossed by Snakes Lane and St. John's Lane.

Yarmouth Square from the Castle overlooking the gardens of the George Hotel. Another hotel, the Bugle, opposite, and cars, cars, cars.

From its inception Yarmouth prospered and grew. Tradition has it that in 1135 Baldwin de Redvers granted his new town a Charter, which raised the status of its inhabitants and made them free men, and also established the town and gave it dignity. This Charter has unfortunately been lost, and there is consequently some doubt as to its date, but what is important is not the actual date but the fact that a Charter was granted in these early days of the town, and that it was the first of no less than seven similar Charters which in the succeeding centuries were given to Yarmouth. The other six were all Royal Charters, and they constitute a splendid record of honours bestowed on this small town and port.

By the beginning of the 13th century Yarmouth had two churches, one at the east end of the town dedicated to St. John the Baptist, and the other in the market place dedicated to St. James. A Hospital, known as The Refuge, was established in the High Street, its site being now occupied by one of Yarmouth's larger houses, The Towers. In 1295 the town was invited to send a representative to Parliament for the first time.

The 14th century proved to be disastrous for the town. There were many invasion scares, and armed raids from the French, and in 1334 Edward III granted the town its second Charter as a morale booster, confirming the provisions of the first one. But Yarmouth was in for a bad time.

In 1348 the Black Death swept across Europe and arrived in England, killing approximately one third of the population. The disease attacked mainly young and strong men, and Yarmouth lost the cream of its population of about 300.

Before the town had recovered from this blow a combined French and Castillian fleet sailed into the Solent in August 1377, and an invasion force landed at Yarmouth bringing death and destruction to the inhabitants. Another morale boosting Charter was granted by Richard II in 1385 and a fourth in 1439, but Yarmouth was still reeling from the double blow it had received, and it was almost 150 years before it fully recovered.

The Charter of 1439, granted by Henry VI, gave the town enhanced status as a Borough, and in the next year a Mayor was elected for the first time. It is a proud boast in Yarmouth that in spite of many subsequent changes in municipal government the town has had a Mayor ever since. In the first half of the 15th century there were many unwelcome visits from the French, and Yarmouth must have frequently regretted that it was the principal Port of Entry to the Island. The middle of the century however saw the establishment of peace with France, and the town slowly continued the process of getting back on to its feet.

In the 16th century under Henry VIII however Yarmouth was once again in the firing line, and is reputed to have been attacked and burned by the French in 1543. Two years later another raid, this time on Spithead, was witnessed by the King himself, who had the mortification of seeing the accident that sank his ship the *"Mary Rose"*, but as a result of which the King ordered a Castle to be built at Yarmouth, and it is a sober fact that since this was done there have been no more hostile visits from our neighbours across the Channel.

A survey carried out in 1559 shows that Yarmouth had only 26 houses, so that its total population could not have been much more than 100—150. The following year Queen Elizabeth, who had come to the throne in 1558, granted the town its sixth Charter, and in 1584 increased its representation in Parliament from one member to two.

The final Royal Charter, and by far the longest, was given in 1609 by King James I. During the whole of his reign England was at peace with France, but soon after he died and was succeeded by his son Charles I, concern about the defences of the Island began to be felt, and in 1628 the plan to make Yarmouth into an island and fortress (described in Chapter 10 page 64) was put forward. It was over 30 years before this plan was put into effect, by which time Charles II was on the throne. Incidentally, soon after the Restoration in 1660 the King presented the town with a silver-gilt hand mace as a token of his gratitude for Yarmouth's loyalty to his father, and this mace is still one of the town's most prized possessions.

In 1668 the Isle of Wight's new Governor, Sir Robert Holmes, decided to live in Yarmouth, and he brought to the town a sense of excitement and importance that had previously been lacking. For nearly 30 years he was the dominating character in Yarmouth, and even after he died in 1692 his influence was still felt, and his white marble statue in the Church remained

The old swing bridge across the harbour, never built for heavy motor traffic, and now replaced.

The Pier, erected 1876, and recently magnificently restored.

as a perpetual reminder of a quite extraordinary man.

The 18th century saw yet another down-turn in Yarmouth's fortunes, with corruption and squabbling amongst those responsible for the management of the town. The struggle for power went on intermittently throughout the century, and gradually spread until quarrelling engulfed the whole Island. With hindsight it is obvious that there could only be one outcome, and it is no great surprise to find that under the Reform Act of 1832 Yarmouth was deprived of its representation in Parliament. (See Chapter 12 page 82). Later, in 1880, the Municipal Corporations Commission decided that Yarmouth was a "Rotten Borough", and in 1891 the town was stripped of its Borough status.

Life went on of course, and there were many technological developments in the 19th century that helped inhabitants to forget the shame of their muniucipal punishments. The regular steam ferry service with Lymington brought more trade to the town, in 1847 the breakwater round the harbour was constructed, in 1860 a bridge across the River Yar was opened, in 1876 the Pier was built, and in 1889 the Freshwater, Yarmouth, and Newport Railway proudly began to operate.

With all these changes taking place the population of the town gradually increased, though due to its geographical limitations — the sea to the north, the river to the west, and the Thorley marsh to the south — it was unable to sprawl and be spoilt like so many other towns at this time. A population of 240 in 1750 had grown to 570 a hundred years later, and to 850 in 1950. In the next 30 years it topped 1000, but the growth rate was slowing down and the total is not likely to get very much higher.

As a result Yarmouth has kept its compact, almost medieval character, and this in spite of the fact that in summer it is thronged with tourists, its ferries disgorging thousands of cars each day, and its little harbour often so full of visiting yachts that the "Harbour Full" sign has to go up. In the winter it is a very different story. Of a winter's evening when the last ferry has gone, the streets are deserted, and silence descends on the town. Silence — and the wind, for there are few days when no wind from the sea blows round the street corners in Yarmouth. In the High Street then it is easy to imagine those early days when the town was first built, and life was less complex than it is today.

Yarmouth Town Hall, dated 1763, but the site of a market for centuries before then. A market is still held downstairs on Wednesdays and Thursdays, and the town Council meet in an upper chamber.

XVII — *Island Towns: Newport*

The junction of High Street (on the left) and Pyle Street (on the right). This was where the track from the Castle to the river, forked, long before Newport was built. Later, the cattle pound was sited here, and one of the town pumps.

Newport, the County Town of the Isle of Wight and its administrative centre is ideally situated for the role it has to play. Geographically almost at the centre of the Island, and at the extent of navigation of the Medina River, a glance at the map will show that major roads radiate from the town to all parts. But Newport has not always been the centre of Island affairs.

In the days of the Norman Conquest of England, and even before, power and control of the Isle of Wight was vested in the owner of Carisbrooke Castle, and in those days Newport did not even exist. The Castle, a commanding and virtually impregnable fortress, is believed to have been built originally as an earth and timber fort by the Saxons. It was rebuilt in stone in the 12th century by the first Baldwin de Redvers, but at this time, apart from the village of Carisbrooke which nestled underneath its protective walls, Carisbrooke Castle was an isolated strongpoint, surrounded by open country.

There were no roads in the Island, and the only access to Carisbrooke was via the Medina River. From the Castle to the river ran a track, a track that forked before it reached the river, the left hand arm leading to the highest point on the river that could be reached by the ships of the day, and the right hand arm leading to the first ford across the stream. These two tracks have survived the passage of time, the left hand arm having developed into Newport High Street and Quay Street, and the other into Pyle Street, Pyle being an earlier name for a ford. (See the map in Chapter 6 facing page 33).

As time went on development inevitably occurred along these tracks, and ultimately Richard de Redvers, a descendant of Baldwin, planned and built a town on the grid system and around these two tracks. As in the building of Yarmouth, streets were constructed at right angles to the High

Street and Pyle Street, and these are still with us today, namely Mill Street, St. James' Street, Holyrood Street and Town Lane. Two other streets were provided parallel to High Street, these being Lugley Street and Crocker Street, and from this basic pattern Newport continued to develop as a typical country market town. Richard de Redvers christened his town "the new port for his Castle of Carisbrooke", and so it has always been known. Its first charter was granted c.1180, and there are records of no fewer than 15 further Charters.

And so, for 750 years, everyone believed that that was the beginning of Newport, until one day in March 1926 workmen digging the foundations for a garage at Cypress Road stumbled across some very much older foundations — those of a Roman Villa. The remains of this Villa had lain undetected under the soil for nearly 1900 years, and it is now believed that it was built in the very early days of the Roman occupation c.A.D.50, and was occupied for about 250 years. The Villa would in effect have been a farmhouse, the centre of a cultivated area sloping down to the river, and specialising probably in corn and sheep. It is believed to have come to a violent end c.A.D.300, destroyed in a piratical raid, and sadly in the corner of one room were found the remains of a woman who was killed at this time.

So Newport's history goes back very much further than was thought, though strangely there appears to have been no development other than this one Roman Villa until the Normans took over the Island and settled in Carisbrooke. In 1120 a group of monks from the Abbey of Tiron in Normandy established the small Priory of St. Cross on the banks of the Lukely Brook, and only a few years later the town of Newport was built. Richard de Redvers divided his town up into building plots of ¼ — ½ acre each, but retained 13½ acres of these "places" for himself. This area, which was triangular, had its apex at the fork where Pyle Street split off

The triangular piece of ground between Castlehold Lane and the junction of High Street with Pyle Street was once under the separate jurisdiction of the Castle, hence its name.

Newport Quay. The old warehouses have now been converted and are in use again.

from the High Street, and its base was a lane joining the two streets which to this day is called "Castlehold", indicating that the area was the personal property of the owner of the Castle.

The town thrived, and has always been a busy, bustling place, full of life. For many years there were three market places — the *Beastmarket* (now St. James' Square), the *Cornmarket* (now St. Thomas' Square) and the *Buttermarket* (at the junction of High Street, Quay Street and Watch-bell Lane). At the north-east corner of St. Thomas' Square stood the *Cheese Cross*, where on market days the farmers' daughters would display their wares, and on the north side of this Square were the butchers' stalls, known as the *Shambles*.

The Church of St. Thomas a'Becket was built at the same time as the town, but was a dependant chapel of Carisbrooke and not a full parish church. This explains why the Church has no graveyard surrounding it, as all burials had to be carried out in Carisbrooke. During a particularly vicious attack of plague in 1584 an appeal was made for permission to bury the dead in Newport due to the difficulty of carrying so many bodies, over very poor roads, and to an already overcrowded graveyard. This was granted, and the *Archery Butts*, on the perimeter of the town, were turned into a graveyard, since known as Church Litten, and now a pleasant green open space.

Incidentally, tradition has it that the house at the top end of Holyrood Street, where God's Providence House now stands, escaped the plague, and that this gave rise to the name "God's Providence", though of course the present house was not built until nearly 200 years later.

The old Church survived until 1854 but became very dilapidated and had to be demolished. The Prince Consort himself laid the foundation stone of the new building, and the 17th century pulpit from the original church was retained, together with the elaborate tomb of Sir Edward Horsey, Governor of the Island from 1565 to 1582. It was during the rebuilding of the Church that the grave of Princess Elizabeth, daughter of Charles I, was found under the chancel floor, where it had been forgotten, and this prompted Queen Victoria to erect the beautiful memorial that is now such an attractive feature.

In its time Newport has had four water mills powered by the Medina River, plus two tide mills further down-stream, and an astonishing five mills operated by the little Lukely Brook, plus another two in Carisbrooke. The four Medina Mills were Ford Mill (at the bottom of Pyle Street), Pan Mill, and Lower and Upper Shide Mills, and the two tide mills were the East Medine, (nicknamed Botany Bay Mill and situated at the entrance to Claybrook Luck), and the West Medine (on the opposite bank of the river and nicknamed Port Jackson Mill). These last two Mills were both built by William Porter, an 18th century Newport character.

The five Lukely Mills were West Mill (off Carisbrooke Road), Westminster Mill (in Westminster Lane, and now turned into flats), Home Mill (at the foot of Mill Street, now completely disappeared and superseded by Unigate Dairies factory), Towngate Mill (at the bottom of Lower St. James' Street), and St. Cross Mill (a forlorn remnant of which survives at the back of St. Cross Court). Of the two Carisbrooke Mills one is in Castle Street and was latterly known as Kent's Mill, and the other was at the foot of Carisbrooke High Street, and originally belonged to Carisbrooke Priory. The site of Priory Mill is now occupied by the Southern Water Authority, and the mill pond is an attractive feature to the rear of the Eight Bells Inn.

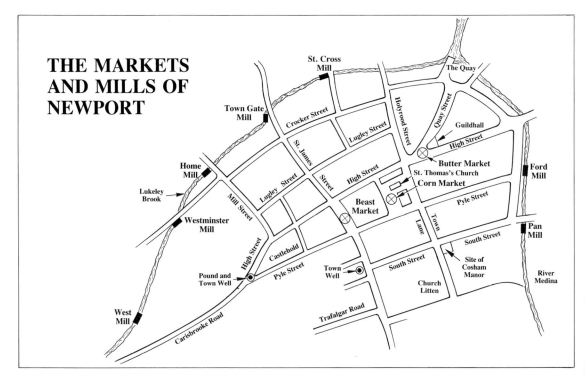

THE MARKETS AND MILLS OF NEWPORT

One other Mill should perhaps be mentioned, though this was at Clatterford, the other side of Carisbrooke. This was a paper mill, powered by a tiny tributary of the Lukely Brook and bringing the total of mills on this diminutive stream to eight, all within a distance of about a mile and a half.

Newport was of course completely destroyed by the French in August 1377, and it is said that it was a full two years before it became inhabited again. No buildings of this age, or anything like it, have survived, the oldest being of late 16th century date. An interesting small house in Crocker Street was built in 1580 and is still in good shape today. It has been well looked after, and contains some fine linenfold panelling. Another old building, one with considerable historical interest, is the Old Grammar School in Lower St. James' Street which was founded in 1612. This building was in the national limelight in 1647 when the negotiations for the so called Treaty of Newport between Charles I and his Parliament were held here. Latterly it has been used as a Youth Club, but plans have been put forward to turn it into a museum.

Charles I visited the Island several times before his ill-fated final sojurn in Carisbrooke Castle, and there is a record that on 27th August 1618 he dined at Cosham Manor as the guest of Andrew James. Cosham Manor was an old and rambling Elizabethan manor house on the corner of Church Litten and South Street, which in the 17th century was called Cosham Street.

The 18th and 19th centuries saw significant changes in the life of Newport. As in other parts of the Island there was a great increase in the interest taken by the gentry in local politics, and the power struggle that developed amongst them inevitably concentrated itself in Newport. It became fashionable for the well-to-do in all parts of the Island to acquire a town house in Newport, so that they could be at the centre of things, particularly in the winter when the appalling state of the roads made travelling difficult and sometimes almost impossible. Power ultimately became concentrated in comparatively few hands, and the big families such as the Worsleys and the Holmes dominated Island life.

At the same time as this increase in opulence and power among the gentry developed, there was a similar rise in the number of poor people, and a calamitous fall in the conditions under which they lived and worked. For example, at this time, and right up to the end of the 1914—18 war, South Street was a notorious slum area in Newport where hundreds of people were living in one-up-and-one-down houses with no sanitation and no gardens. Overcrowding was the order of the day, dirt and degradation were commonplace, and for the people in the slums the only relief obtainable was in the local pubs, of which there were many.

Fortunately those days are now well behind us, and though Newport still has its housing problems — and indeed problems of overcrowding in its prisons at Parkhurst, Albany, and Camp Hill where society has not yet learned how to deal with our weaker brethren who find it difficult to conform and keep within the law — yet for the majority of the poor, living conditions are at least bearable. Hopefully the future will bring further changes for the better. There are of course plenty of changes going on in Newport's townscape, and particularly in South Street, where developers have succeeded in transforming the old cattle market (and the site of Cosham Manor) into a stereotyped red-tiled complex of buildings for all the world like a gigantic stable block, complete with bell-cote or clock tower.

The following few Newport street and place names are probably worth listing, together with their derivations —

Broadlands	Late the home of the D.H.S.S. but once a lace factory, set up in 1826 by a Mr. H.W. Nunn who had developed a machine that could make lace as fine as a spider's web.
Castlehold	Land between the west part of the High Street and Pyle Street, once the demesne of the Castle.
Cockram's Yard	An alleyway connecting St. Thomas' Square to South Street. Possibly named after a Boyce Cockram who lived in Newport c. 1850.
Coppins Bridge	Well known to all who travel in Newport, its name commemorating a William Copping who lived in 1577.
Cosham Street	One time name for South Street, and for many years the southern boundary of the town.
Crocker Street	Named after a John Crocker, A.D. 1341.
House of Industry	Established in 1770, the second Incorporated Workhouse in England.
Lugley Street	A 13th century name, possibly from the same root as *"Luck"*, meaning a pool or dam. Alternatively, there was a William Lugely who was Provost or Reeve in Newport at the end of the 13th century.
Nodehill	Or "Noddies Hill", *Noddies* being dead men, and specifically the Frenchmen ambushed in 1377 who were buried hereabouts.
Pyle	From *"Pil"*, a pile or stake, but also believed to mean a ford.
Scarrot's Lane	Named after Christopher Scarrot who had a house and orchard in the street in 1720.
Snook's Hill	Prior to 1828 a Mr. Snook was a well-known blacksmith with a forge at the top of the hill, left hand side going up.
Trafalgar Road	Name given in 1861 to Deadman's Lane, formerly (in 1461) "Dedmanstret", either from the ambushing of a party of Frenchmen in the 1377 raid, or (more likely) from a dead body having been found there.

116

XVIII — *Island Towns: Newtown*

Junction of High Street and Broad Street, with the Town Hall in the background.

Anyone in search of true peace and quiet cannot do better than to go to Newtown. Here, as in very few other parts of southern England, it is possible, not just to get away from it all, but to be so immersed in nature, to be so surrounded by creeks and inlets, by marshes and saltings, as to be able to forget the artificial world of today, with its noise and pollution, its telephones and motor cars, and refresh one's tired spirit, in exactly the same way that in a hot bath one can refresh the tired body. Here in Newtown is a silence that can almost be felt, a silence broken only by the lapping of water, the cries of the marsh birds, and the rustling of the breeze in the sedge. Many people these days come to the Nature Reserve which is Newtown in desperate need of refreshment, and few go away disappointed.

The fact that Newtown is so peaceful and relaxing may have something to do with its great age, and also that the whole of this part of the Island belonged, for many hundreds of years, to the Bishops of Winchester. This may sound fanciful, but there certainly are spots on this earth where the influence of early Christian occupation has lingered on, and the ancient manor of Swainston-in-Calbourne, of which Newtown is a part, may be one of them.

This great ecclesiastical manor in Calbourne was granted to the monastery of St. Swithun at Winchester in A.D.827 by King Egbert, and there is an even earlier record of a grant of land to St. Swithun's in A.D.735, these dates giving an indication of the great age of the manor, which was huge in size, stretching right across the Island from north to south, from sea to sea. The Domesday Survey of 1086 lists the manor as follows —

> "Walchelin, bishop of Winchester, holds Swainston-in-Calbourne. It was always the minister's . . ."

this entry showing not only its age, but the fact that the Bishops of Winchester were also Abbots of St. Swithun's monastery. It must be remembered too that at this time Winchester was the Capital of England, which meant that the Bishop of Winchester was one of the most powerful prelates in the land.

The Bishops built themselves a palace — their summer palace, it was called — at Swainston, and in the basement of the present Swainston manor house can still be seen part of the walls of this venerable building, together with one of the most astonishing sights in the Isle of Wight, the original front door, which has a moulding of a bishop's Mitre on each jamb of the doorway.

In the year 1236 is the first mention of Newtown, in the form of a Charter granted by Aymer de Valence, Bishop-Elect of Winchester.

The Bishops' Hall and Chapel, Swainston. It was possibly in this very building that Aymer de Valence signed the Charter incorporating his 'New' Town.

118

The deserted Haven, once one of the best harbours in the south of England.

"... to his burgesses of Franchville or Newtown of all liberties and free customs which the burgesses of Taunton, Witney, Alresford and Farnham enjoyed ... "

It is not clear whether this "New Town" or "Free Town" was built under this Charter, or whether it had been there for some time, but what is obvious is that the Bishops of Winchester, in building a town on the banks of the safest deep water harbour in the Island, were becoming increasingly powerful, and were sailing in waters normally reserved for the monarch alone. It may be that this contributed to their downfall.

On 5th November 1285 King Edward I arrived at Swainston and stayed until the 11th as the guest of the then Bishop, John di Pontiserra, and while he was there he did two things. Firstly, he confirmed the terms of the Charter granted to Newtown by Aymer de Valence, and secondly he picked a quarrel with Bishop Pontiserra.

In spite of his Italian sounding name the Bishop was an Englishman — John Sawbridge — indeed "Pontiserra" is a fairly straightforward translation of the name into Italian — and one wonders whether he actually came from Sawbridgeworth in Hertfordshire. The King's quarrel with the Bishop was, at first sight, perhaps a little petulant, but retribution was swift and severe, and it altered the course of Island history. Albin, writing in 1795, described it thus —

High Street.

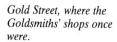

Gold Street, where the Goldsmiths' shops once were.

> ". . . the King deprived John di Pontiserra of this manor because the Pope had forcibly intruded him into that See, contrary to the King's inclination and pleasure, and the King harrassed him frequently by divers acts of displeasure openly manifested and declared. At length the bishop, to purchase the King's peace, agreed not only to surrender the manor of Swainston into his hands, and for himself and his successors for ever to quit claim to the said manor, but to pay a fine of two thousand pounds for the quiet and peaceable enjoyment of the other temporalities belonging to the bishopric."

But there must have been more to it than that, and there is little doubt that what the King really wanted was Newtown with its large natural harbour. He was worried about the vulnerability of the Island to French attacks, and probably also had his eye on Newtown as a base for possible invasion plans of his own. A few years later he went one stage further and purchased the whole Island from Isabella de Fortibus, and this transaction marked the end of private ownership of the Isle of Wight. (See Chapter 6 page 36).

In 1318 Edward II confirmed to the Earl of Chester, who was presumably the Lord of Swainston at the time, a weekly market on Wednesdays, and an annual fair on the vigil, the feast, and the morrow of St. Mary Magdalene (July 22nd) at "La Neuton" (a spelling of the name that had not previously been used). This was a straight confirmation of the Charter granted by Aymer de Valence, and at this time it must have seemed that Newtown was firmly established and could look forward to a calm and prosperous future. No one could have guessed at the terrible events that were shortly to happen, events that were to destroy the town for ever.

In 1348 the Island was visited by the Black Death, and just as in Yarmouth and in Newport, a third of the population, including practically all the young men, were wiped out. And before the town had time to recover from this devastating blow, the French arrived. In August 1377, flushed with their success in burning down Yarmouth, they landed in Newtown and repeated the exercise, killing, looting, raping and burning, with very little opposition from the inhabitants.

Attempts were made to re-build, and indeed only 16 years later Richard II confirmed the terms of the Charter. There was a further confirmation by Henry V in 1413, but it was no use, the town did not recover. Spasmodic revival attempts continued from time to time, in 1584 the borough was invited to send two representatives to Parliament, and in 1598 Queen Elizabeth granted a further Charter, but by this time the town had completely lost all its importance as a port and a borough, and its economy, based to a large extent on the manufacture of salt, was in shreds.

The road into Newtown from the south, crossing the bridge at the head of the Haven.

In 1677 the town hall was built, a building that now stands forlorn and alone, overlooking the haven. In 1696 the town found itself in the centre of the quarrel between the Governor and the Gentlemen of the Island (see Chapter 11 page 76), and during the long period of corruption that followed how could the borough possibly revive when the few men in power were interested only in their own ends? The Reform Bill of 1832 classed Newtown with Yarmouth and Newport, and marked the end of the town as a borough with its own representation in Parliament.

The Town Hall, sometimes confused with the Bishops' Hall and Chapel, Swainston, but built at a much later date.

Today all is a memory. The old burgage plots and streets can still be traced, and names are remembered — High Street, Gold Street, Broad Street, Horsefair — but gradually nature has triumphed over man, and it is difficult now to imagine the once bustling medieval town. Only the annual fair, the Newtown Randy, has survived. After a period when it too was dropped it has been revived, and once again attracts the crowds.

The harbour does not contain a lot of water these days, but there is enough for small boats, and from the entrance several branches reach out inland like the fingers of a hand. These constitute a veritable paradise for small sailing boats, and it is possible to land at one spot and walk to a farm shop where water and other necessities of life may be obtained, and at another spot to land and walk to the pub in Shalfleet. Apart from these facilities there is thankfully nothing else to spoil the natural beauty of Newtown, the "Free Town" that is still free and available to all who yearn for peace and quiet.

XIX — *Island Towns: Ryde*

Hovercraft leaving for Portsmouth, with the Pier in the background.

In the beginning was Ashey — a large agricultural tract of land in the north-east corner of the Island, a tract that was first mentioned in the reign of King Ethelred the Unready. There were few people living in Ashey before the Norman Conquest, just a handful of men cultivating various parts of the manor, and perhaps one or two fishermen living on the coast near the mouth of a little stream that emptied itself into the Solent. This stream, or *"Rithe"*, gave its name to the small village that grew up at its mouth.

Later, sometime during the 12th century, the monks of Quarr Abbey were given about six acres of meadowland beside this stream and it became known as the *"Monkenmeade Brook"*. The name is preserved to this day in Monkton Street, though regrettably the brook itself has disappeared, buried underground as being a thing of no importance and a hindrance to building development. By the 13th century the cluster of fishermen's huts was being referred to as *"La Ride"* or *"La Riche"*, and in 1341, when strict controls on the movements of boats were introduced because of the frequency of French raids, *La Riche* was one of the three recognised ports where boats could be kept. (See Chapter 7 page 43).

The manor of Ashey itself passed into the hands of the Benedictine Abbey of Wherwell near Andover, and from then until the beginning of the 16th century it remained in the possession of these absentee landlords. (Perhaps we ought to say *landladies* since the Abbey of Wherwell was a Nunnery). At the Dissolution in 1536 it had become the property of Giles Worsley, one of the first of that illustrious family to settle in the Island, and at this time Ryde was still a small fishing village, though there were the beginnings of another hamlet on the high ground just a little way inland.

But the development that really started Ryde on its meteoric transformation from a humble fishing village into one of the country's leading seaside resorts was the advent of Henry Player in 1705. As described in Chapter 12, page 82) he bought part of the manor of Ashey, built himself a large house and became in fact the Island's first *overner* developer. Henry Player only lasted for another six years but his plans were carried on by his son Thomas, and for the next 250 years the Player family, and their descendants the Brigstockes, dominated Ryde and fostered its growth.

In 1719 Thomas Player built Ryde's first church, dedicated to St. Thomas the Apostle, and though this was officially only a chapel of ease to Newchurch, in which parish Ryde then was, it fulfilled a great need in the village, which for the next 60 years was to remain as two separate communities, Upper and Lower Ryde, divided by a 12 acre area of woods and fields known as *Node Close*. Lower Ryde at this time contained only fishermen's cottages, but Upper Ryde, the district now marked by the High Street, was beginning to acquire a few larger houses. John Albin, writing in 1795, has left us a charming description of Ryde at this time —

> "Upper Ryde, which is the principal part of the place, is situate on the top of an eminence, in a clean and pleasant air, which induces many gentlemen to have a summer residence there, and has occasioned several good houses to be built in it; so that it has become a neat and respectable village.

> Of Lower Ride, indeed, we cannot say much in its favour, being a straggling place, and mostly inhabited by fishermen and coasting seamen; it also has some slips for building small vessels, and, as the nearest point to Portsmouth and Gosport, being only about 5 miles distant, has a constant communication with the opposite shore."

Albin also refers to the fields that separated Upper and Lower Ryde and mentions an inn on the edge of the area, 100 yards in front of which was a seat —

> "From this commanding seat, a full, extended and complete prospect of the whole length of Spithead, and of every anchored ship therein, and of the towns of Gosport and Portsmouth, burst suddenly and distinctly upon our enraptured sight."

Could this inn have been the Anglesea Tavern, which must have had a spectacular view before the hillside in front of it was built up? Or was it possibly the Crown?

One of the oldest pubs in Ryde, the Anglesea, stood on the edge of the upper village and had magnificent sea views.

124

Union Street, the road that joined the two villages of Upper and Lower Ryde.

In 1780 the two villages were joined together by the well named Union Street, and from then on the town of Ryde never looked back. George Player, who was head of the Player family and Lord of the Manor of Ashey and Ryde at the time, and hence in a position of power, stipulated that there should be no shops in the new street, and therefore to begin with Union Street contained only rows of elegant houses, which must have provided a fine sight. It is possible now, with the benefit of hindsight, to appreciate what a major development this joining together of the two villages was, for it marked the birth of the town as we know it today. From this point on the population steadily grew.

A number of large houses were built, the largest being Appley House, erected by a wealthy man named Boyce who had made a fortune, reputedly by smuggling. The story is told that Mr. Boyce, who was illiterate, decided to have a library in his new house, and ordered £500 worth of "best books" from a London bookseller. The bookseller, who was something less than honest, realising that his client could not read, supplied him with a set of excellent and attractive bindings, but the contents were books that he had been unable to sell, and many of them were duplicates.

In 1805 the first regular ferry service with Portsmouth was inaugurated, though the timetable was necessarily flexible. As a sailing boat the ferry was dependent on weather conditions, the standard crossing time being one hour, but it could sometimes take as long as four hours. In 1817 the first steam ferry appeared, but this was soon withdrawn owing to the

125

Ryde Pier.

difficulties experienced with rough seas, high winds, and strong tides, and it was a further eight years before a regular service was established, by a steamer appropriately called the *"Union"*, the average crossing time by which was 34 minutes.

As a matter of interest the *Union's* vital statistics were 76 feet overall length, 12.2 feet beam, and 8 feet draught, and she was powered by an engine that developed all of 16 horsepower! Fares were ridiculously cheap in these early days, and were kept down by rising competition. In 1836 they were 1/6d aft (7½p), or 1/- forward (5p). Return fare was 2/- (10p). Presumably it was cheaper to travel up forward since one got a little wetter there. In the ensuing 150 years and up to the introduction of the fast catamarans in the 1980s the crossing time did not alter very much. Only the astronomical increase in fares indicates the frightening change that has overtaken the value of money. Instead of 10p the return fare is now £7.00!

The establishment of the ferry service was aided and encouraged by the building of the Pier, which is still the second longest in the country. This solved the problems of getting ashore at low tide across a wide expanse of beach, and development of the town as a fashionable resort was again speeded up. More and more well-to-do members of the aristocracy decided to build houses in Ryde, attracted by the healthy climate and the miles of golden sands. Sheridan, writing in 1834, quotes the Duke of Buckingham, Lord Vernon, Sir Richard Simeon, and perhaps most importantly Earl Spencer, who had been First Lord of the Admiralty, all of whom built large houses. The final accolade was given, not only to Ryde, but to the whole Island, when the Queen herself decided to make it her home.

The population of Ryde in 1700 was about 250, and in 1800 it had increased to 1000. By 1850 it was 10,000, and by 1950 it had doubled again to 20,000. Inevitably, with this tremendous growth in population, some of the exclusivity of the town was lost, and as travel became easier, so the well-to-do gradually drifted further and further south in a search for new playgrounds — first the south of France and the Italian Reviera, then Greece and Spain. But Ryde still prospered as a family resort, there were military band concerts in the Western Gardens, concert parties and Pierrots at the other end of the Esplanade, Punch and Judy on the sands, and hundreds of holiday-makers enjoyed a Sunday evening stroll on the Pier.

Sadly, the days of such simple pleasures as these gradually came to an end, and after recovering from two devastating wars, in which for the first time the civilian population found themselves in the firing line, the nation succumbed to the twin blandishments of television entertainment at home, and cheap package holidays to the Mediterranean, leaving our Island holiday resorts forsaken and bewildered, struggling to keep up appearances on a considerably reduced income. To date a solution has not yet been found to the competition of foreign resorts which though they may not be able to offer much in the way of scenic beauty, can guarantee unlimited sunshine.

Ryde, however, has survived in its own right, for as well as its sands and holiday attractions it has much more to offer. It has of course to give pride of civic place to Newport, which is the administrative centre of the County, but Ryde is a thriving and lively business community, and its supporters will claim that it has the best shops in the Island. And its proximity to Portsmouth, with the fast crossing times now possible, will always ensure its popularity and prosperity as a principal gateway to the Isle of Wight.

A hovercraft, fast but noisy.

127

XX — Island Towns: Sandown and Shanklin

From Dunnose to Culver Cliff is very nearly six miles as the crow flies, and a good bit longer if you go round by the coastal path, but these two headlands enclose Sandown Bay and some of the finest holiday beaches in the Isle of Wight. They also enclose two of the most popular seaside towns — Shanklin and Sandown — which along with Lake, the village that joins them together, have a resident population of about 20,000, a population which is multiplied many times in the summer.

The two resorts are slightly different in character. Shanklin has high ground behind it, indeed Shanklin Down immediately to the south of the town is one of the highest spots in the Island, whereas Sandown is backed by the wide and flat valley of the River Yar as it flows on through Brading to reach the sea between St. Helens and Bembridge. What the two places have in common is glorious sandy beaches, and the best sunshine record in the south of England, making both of them ideal for family holidays.

Sandown and Shanklin are both old, both in fact mentioned in Domesday. But Roman finds have been made all along this coast of the Island from Brading to Freshwater, and in the Hyde area of Shanklin an amphora containing 600 coins was discovered. In this area is Hungerberry Copse, long associated with Roman occupation, and there may be further treasures to find. This copse had a brief moment of glory only a few years ago, for during the liberation of Europe at the end of the Second World War it hid an enormous header tank which was part of the PLUTO project for pumping fuel across the English Channel to France.

In earlier times Sandown also played a military role, for its long flat beach was one of the few places on the south coast of the Island regarded

Right. Sandown Bay from Shanklin, Sandown and its Pier in the distance.

128

The Chine is a fascinating and attractive natural feature.

Some of Sandown's glorious small hotels.

as attractive to a foreign invading army, and Henry VIII had a fort erected here in 1537. This fort, which was built by Richard Worsley, Captain of the Island, fell into the sea c. 1630 due to erosion, and though it was replaced in 1632 this one also was built too near the edge and was ultimately demolished in Victorian times.

It was of course in Victorian times that Sandown and Shanklin blossomed as holiday towns, their rapid rise starting a little later than Ryde and Ventnor but being in full swing by 1875. At the end of the 18th century Shanklin had a population of only 100, Sandown being still "the village by the sandy shore", with only a very few inhabitants. But change was in the air. The notorious John Wilkes was one of the first notabilities to build a house and live in Sandown, bringing a touch of colour and eccentricity to the place, and a reputation that lingered on from his wild and mis-spent youth. Fashionable society in the Isle of Wight during the 1780s was centred in Knighton Gorges and Appuldurcombe, and Wilkes was a member of the set which included the Governor of the Island, Sir Richard Worsley and his young wife, Seymour.

Later regular visitors to Sandown included Lewis Carroll and Charles Darwin, and for good measure such diverse characters as Sir Isaac Pitman and Hall Caine. Shanklin attracted many literary visitors and had its own devotees. Keats paid a visit in 1817 and returned to stay for a time two years later, George Eliot in 1863 and Longfellow in 1868. In 1880 the French writer Paul Bourget spent a holiday in Shanklin and has left an amusing and charming account of a typical English Sunday, which amazed him on account of the restrictions he found — he was not allowed to buy beer, nor even to swim. He also went to a cricket match, which completely mystified him, from the white "uniforms" worn by the men and the bright colours of the ladies' dresses to the weird and incomprehensible nature of the game itself. But he loved the beauty of his surroundings, and the simplicity and honesty of the inhabitants.

> "A typically English picture, in its smallest details; where else can one find this never ending avenue of comfortable gardens? where else this scene of open air life or this extraordinary taste in dress? where else these athletically minded men and in what other land can one find a sea-side resort with the obvious absence of the underworld which so often would attempt to destroy the elegance and charm of the scene?"

Cricket is still played in Shanklin, and the cricket ground is still the same beautiful and restful place, but sadly the resort itself, due to inevitable commercialisation and the competition of Mediterranean holidays, has changed, though one can at least buy beer now on a Sunday, and swim. The change is perhaps even greater in Sandown which has become a miniature Margate in a desperate attempt to attract the masses. The popularity of both resorts is directly related to the published sunshine figures, and also to the ability of Heathrow and Gatwick Airports to handle the vast numbers of holiday-makers wishing to fly south to the sun. The longer the waiting time at the Airports, the more people will decide to have holidays at home. Sad, but true.

Of course, the only real and lasting solution to this problem is to make our holiday resorts more attractive than those of the *"Costa Espana"*, and this implies not only an imaginative, determined, and indeed revolutionary, approach to the task, but a massive injection of capital. At the time of writing Developers are clamouring to invest money in the Isle of Wight and it seems a pity that their desires and energies cannot be channelled into providing the Island with some of the things it really needs. One of the most urgent of these is first class, up-market holiday towns, with all weather sunshine. This is a large, and maybe controversial, subject, but with goodwill and determination these facilities could be provided, *and* profits made for the Developer.

Sandown Zoo (with peacock). Originally a Fort built to repel visitors, but now designed to attract them.

131

XXI — *Island Towns: Ventnor*

One hesitates to use the word "unique" when describing a place, but really there is no other word which does full justice to Ventnor, which is so different to anywhere else in the Isle of Wight. The only other town that could possibly be compared to it is Yarmouth, though at first sight there would appear to be no similarities. But Ventnor and Yarmouth do have one thing in common — they are both self-contained, aloof, and slightly withdrawn. Geography has much to do with this, Yarmouth being built on a peninsula, surrounded on three sides by water and marshes, which insulate it from the outside world, while Ventnor is surrounded by the steepest hills in the Island, and until roads were tarmacadamed it was completely cut off in bad weather. Even today one feels that it should be possible to hold the Pass at Lowtherville at one end, and at Bonchurch Shute at the other, with a handful of men against an army. Perhaps it is this feeling of being protected, and living in a defensible area, that at one time caused the natives of both towns to regard everyone else as foreigners.

To pursue the comparison one stage further, this attitude to the outside world contributes in no small measure to the charm and character of each town, for an attitude that regards anyone born elsewhere as slightly unfortunate naturally makes a place very attractive to a "foreigner". To be accepted ultimately into their midst is hence a prize worth the possessing — though some do say that the probationary period may be as long as 25 years.

Ventnor is built on a hillside. From Pier Street down to the Esplanade the gardens are a delight.

As far as Ventnor is concerned, its name is of comparatively modern origin, the first mention being in 1617. Before that date the area was known as Holewey, or Holloway, part of the ancient parish of Bonchurch, which itself was part of Newchurch. In the 14th century when the Militia was reorganised, each local commander was given a second-in-command who was called a Lieutenant, or *Vintener*, the latter name meaning one who was in charge of 20 men. Kokeritz suggests that one such Vintener may have lived in Holloway, and that his farm subsequently became known as the Vintener's farm, from which it is a very small change to "Ventnor". Alternatively, the man could have been a vintner by trade, leading to a similar name derivation.

Until the 19th century Ventnor remained a very small village consisting of a few fishermen's cottages, a mill, and an inn, a delightful and totally secluded place, hemmed in by steep hills that crowded almost to the water's edge, a place that no one visited. Then came the explosion. In 1830 a distinguished doctor, Sir James Clark, visited Ventnor and the whole of the Undercliff, which at that time was a wild and relatively unknown area, and he was immediately impressed by the extraordinary climate enjoyed by this south facing stretch of the coast, all of which was completely protected from the north by high ground. He subsequently published a treatise expatiating on the value of this mild and equable climate, particularly in the treatment of pulmonary diseases, and specifying Ventnor as being one of the healthiest places on the south coast.

This pronouncement did for Ventnor what the discovery of gold did for the Klondyke, it gave rise to a veritable stampede. Victorian society decided that this was where one should have one's summer residence, and there was a sudden flurry of building activity. In spite of the difficulties of the terrain — for there was hardly a level plot in the whole area, large houses began to shoot up. Speculative builders moved in, realising that there were rich pickings to be made, and houses of all shapes, sizes and styles were crammed into every available ledge on the hillside. Alpine type roads were built, one of them even called the Zig Zag Road, enabling the hills to be climbed, and almost overnight the town of Ventnor appeared, the speed with which this occurred being shown by the astonishing growth of population. In 1838 the number of inhabitants was 350, and in less than 30 years this had increased to 5000.

No other town in the Island was ever conceived and born in such a short space of time, and in such an improbable location. Access from the rest of the Island was poor, and indeed at one time it was claimed that it was easier to reach Ventnor by sea than by land. But the miracle was that in spite of the lack of planning, in spite of the indecent haste with which the town was thrown together, in spite of all this feverish activity which should have resulted in a chaotic jumble of ill-assorted buildings, Ventnor turned out to be one of the most charming, dignified, and characterful towns in the whole of the Isle of Wight.

And so it has remained. Changes have inevitably occurred over the years, and its own popularity has to some extent destroyed the seclusion

and exclusivity that attracted its first Victorian settlers, but there are still holiday-makers who would rather spend their time in Ventnor than anywhere else in Europe. Perhaps today people come to Ventnor more for a seaside holiday than to recoup their health, but in the mid-19th century the reverse was the case, for the first Victorians came principally from London and other cities, and they came for the health-giving properties of the climate.

In 1868, between Ventnor and St. Lawrence the National Hospital for Diseases of the Chest was founded, tuberculosis being at this time one of the principal killer diseases in the United Kingdom. The Hospital was a strange building, a quarter of a mile long, and the wards were all small, not more than three beds in each, and they all faced south and had a balcony. The treatment was somewhat strange too, being based on a plentiful supply of fresh, cold air. There was no heating in the wards, and patients were put out on their balconies daily whatever the weather. Today, of course, we believe in fresh air, but in those days it tended to be shunned. Outdoor exercise, within the patient's capability, was also part of the cure, but many patients were too ill for exercise, and many died.

The development of anti-biotics revolutionised the treatment of this type of disease, and happily and hopefully "T.B." or "Consumption" is now a thing of the past. In 1964 the Hospital closed and for some years the buildings lay neglected and forlorn, while authority tried to make up its mind what to do with them. The ultimate decision was a good one; it was

When the Royal National Hospital for Diseases of the Chest was demolished, the grounds were turned into the Ventnor Botanic Gardens, and the site of the buildings became their huge, but attractive, car park. Some say the area is still haunted.

A rough sea in Ventnor Bay.

134

to turn the 22 acres of grounds into a Botanic Garden, taking advantage of the fact that the climate was exceptionally mild. The Gardens thrived and flourished, growing plants that would not survive in the open anywhere else in England. Until the winter of 1986 the lowest temperature recorded there was 4 degrees Celsius, but in that winter a series of vicious frosts killed off many of their prize plants. In October of the following year a freak hurricane hit the south of England and the Gardens lost 200 trees. These two disasters left a nasty scar, but the dedication and hard work of the resident staff soon put the Gardens back on the road to success, and to their position as one of Ventnor's most popular tourist attractions.

Sadly, the elegant Victorian town which was once so fashionable is now looking a little tired, and in common with other Island holiday resorts needs a fresh injection of capital to revive it and take it into the 21st century. In the early 1980s a plan was put forward which would have transformed the eastern end of the sea front and would have given Ventnor the face lift is so much deserves and so urgently needs. The "Cascades" plan was imaginative and innovative, and many saw in it the beginning of an exciting new life for the town. But five years later nothing seems to have happened. What went wrong? Was it perhaps too bold, too revolutionary in concept? Or was it that the developers could not see a big enough return on their investment, and took their money elsewhere? The people of Ventnor, as in other parts of the Island, will have to fight for the improvements they know to be necessary.

XXII — *Island Towns: Cowes*

Cowes Parade, looking towards the Royal Yacht Squadron.

The town and port of Cowes is today world famous as the home and international centre of yacht racing, but up until the 16th century it was virtually unknown, and had not even been given its present name. However, within the next hundred years its growth as a port had begun in earnest. Sir John Oglander, to whom we owe most of our knowledge of life in the Isle of Wight in the 16th and early 17th centuries, writing in 1627, said this of the town – -

> "I knew when there was not above three or four houses in Cowes, and I was and am persuaded that if our wars and troubles had not unfortunately happened, it would have grown as famous as Newport. For it was by all the Eastern parts of the world much approved as a place fit for them to victual, and to make a *rendezvous*, where I have seen 300 ships at anchor. And if the country had but so much discretion as to make good use of that harbour, as first to have an honest man to be Captain there, to build storehouses, to have by a joint stock a magazine of all provisions, to deal with the Dutch, and to have that their *rendezvous*, and to victual there, they need no other market or means to make the Island happy and fortunate."

Sir John, who was born in 1585, was referring to the prosperous days at the end of Queen Elizabeth's reign when the Isle of Wight, freed from the fear of the Spanish Armada, was experiencing an unprecedented boom in trade, much of which was due to this small port at the mouth of the Medina River.

The popularity of Cowes was due entirely to its geographical position, for in Cowes Roads the sailing ships of the day could find deep and sheltered water, ideal as a *"rendezvous"* at the beginning or the end of a long and dangerous voyage to the far places of the world. The Dutch, who were Europe's leading traders at this time, regularly used Cowes for this purpose on their voyages to and from their possessions in West Africa and the East Indies, and their huge East Indiamen, the finest sailing ships in the world, were a familiar sight in the Roads, and brought much trade to the Island. Incidentally, 300 sail at anchor off Cowes must have been a spectacular sight.

The first recorded use of the name "Cows" was in 1413, but this referred to two sandbanks lying off the mouth of the river — known as the East and West Cows. There was nothing unusual in this, sandbanks with rounded humps frequently being called "Cows" or "Horses", but ultimately, and possibly in Elizabethan times, the names were transferred to the land, and the two small settlements on either side of the river mouth became known as West Cowes and East Cowes.

But whatever happened to the two original "Cows"? A study of the chart shows no sign of any small sandbanks off the mouth of the Medina. The only shallow patch in the immediate vicinity is the Prince Consort Shoal, which is just outside the entrance and which is obviously a Victorian name. It can hardly be called a "Cow" as it has over three fathoms of water on it at low water springs. To the north of this shoal is the well known and extensive Brambles Bank, part of which dries at low water. To the east of the Brambles is a shoal called East Knoll, and to the west another called Thorn Knoll — could these have been the two original Cows?

Of the two land settlements East Cowes was the older and larger, having been in the 14th century one of the three recognised Island ports under the name of Shamblord, or Shamlord. (See Chapter 7 page 43). It was not until 1825 when the Yacht Club, later the Royal Yacht Squadron, moved from London and established its headquarters on the other bank of the river that West Cowes began to grow and ultimately outstripped its neighbour.

In 1272 there is a record of 90 acres of land at East Shamlord being granted by Jordan de Kingston and his wife Margery to the Abbey of Beaulieu, and of course these names are still remembered to this day, for there is a Kingston Farm in East Cowes, and a Shamblers Copse on one side of the river and a Little Shamblers Copse on the other side.

In 1518 the Abbey of Beaulieu leased its grange at Estshamlorde to a Peter Morren for a rent of 106 shillings and 8 pence per annum, plus 20 brace of rabbits at Christmas. The rent is interesting; 100 shillings is £5, and it looks very much as if the Abbot was charging that sum for the actual rent of the land, and that the six shillings and eightpence was the legal fee for drawing up the lease. 6/8d is one third of a pound, and for centuries — and indeed within living memory — this was a standard charge made by a lawyer for this sort of service. Only in the last 50 years or so have legal charges escalated — as have so many other charges unfortunately. Incidentally, the 20 brace of rabbits to be given at Chrtistmas were no doubt for the Beaulieu monks' Christmas dinner!

At the time when this lease was granted there was such a fear of invasion from the French that King Henry VIII had two forts built to protect the river mouth. These forts were built in 1539, stone from the recently suppressed Abbeys of Quarr and Beaulieu being used. The one on the East Cowes side has long since disappeared, but the West Cowes Castle, as it was called, survives in part, having been incorporated into the headquarters of the Royal Yacht Squadron. These forts seldom fired a shot in anger, but no doubt they acted as a deterrent to the French, and were an important part of the general defences of the island. 300 years later a much larger castle was built in East Cowes by John Nash, the architect, not as a defensive measure but as his residence, but like a lot of Nash's work this too has now disappeared.

One of the problems confronting the Isle of Wight over the centuries has been the amount of smuggling carried on, and for many years East Cowes contained the port's Customs House, the headquarters of the preventive men who were engaged in the never ending battle with the smugglers. A peak was reached in the second half of the 18th century, when not only was smuggling at its height but many of the Customs officials were acting in collusion with the smugglers. In 1777 a new and energetic Collector of Customs was appointed. This was William Arnold, who in the 23 years he held the position made a name for himself, and apart from the sterling work he did in reducing the amount of smuggling, and controlling corruption within his own organisation, wrote himself into the histoy books as the father of Dr. Thomas Arnold, famous headmaster of Rugby School, and as the grandfather of Matthew Arnold, the poet. *(For more information about smuggling in the Isle of Wight see Chapter 38, page 217).*

Because of its geographic position, and adequate depth of water, it was logical that Cowes should develop as a centre of shipbuilding, and firms such as J. Samuel White, and Saunders Roe brought prosperity to the town, as well as fame, through the development of high speed craft, sea-planes, flying boats, and ultimately the hovercraft, which was born and

In the centre of East Cowes is this circular seat around a tree, a welcome spot on a hot day.

The link between West Cowes and East Cowes is the Floating Bridge, an old-fashioned but reliable chain ferry.

A Red Funnel Ferry leaving for Southampton. (Netley Castle).

bred in Cowes. (See Chapter 13 page 88).

Another man who brought prosperity into the town was George Ward, who at the end of the 18th century bought the manor of Northwood. Later, in 1838, his son built Northwood House, the largest house in West Cowes. It is possible that Northwood was designed by John Nash, or by his architectural successor, Sir James Pennethorne, though it was not built until three years after Nash's death. But it has all the marks of a Nash building, and when new and a private house must have been tremendously impressive. By the middle of the 19th century the whole area of Cowes, on both sides of the river, was acquiring a number of large and prestigious houses — Northwood, John Nash's East Cowes Castle, Norris Castle — and finally the Queen herself bought the Osborne Estate and Barton Manor and made East Cowes her home. Society had arrived.

Not that either George Ward or John Nash had blue blood in their veins, though Nash had valuable connections with Royalty, since his wife

was George IV's mistress. George Ward was a London merchant who made a fortune in the City, and he and his descendants rapidly built up a property empire in the Island. The family were great benefactors, not only to Cowes but to other parts of the Island, and for example George Henry Ward, the son of George Ward, provided several thousand tons of stone for the building of the breakwater in Yarmouth. In Cowes Week Northwood House became the centre of fashionable society, many famous people stayed there, and the Wards acquired a reputation for the lavishness of their entertaining.

Those spacious and fashionable Victorian days have long since gone, but Cowes Week has survived and is still a glittering occasion, graced by Royalty and by yachtsmen from all parts of the world. The size of some of the yachts may have decreased, and there are now no longer races for the huge "J" Class with their professional crews, nor are there the large and opulent steam yachts at anchor in the Roads, but there are instead thousands of smaller yachts, racing, with just as much enthusiasm and skill, so that the activity and excitement generated is just as great, if not greater.

As long as this continues to be repeated, year by year, while off-shore the Royal Yacht rides at anchor, guarded by her Royal Navy escort, Cowes Week will continue to exercise its charismatic hold over landsmen as well as yachtsmen, and this little Island town will continue to hold the world stage.

140

XXIII — *Island Towns: Brading*

From the arch under the church tower, one of the oldest houses in the Island.

When Vespasian's 2nd Legion sailed into Brading Haven in A.D.43 and added the Isle of Wight to the Roman Empire, they found a large expanse of land-locked tidal water and few signs of human habitation. But no doubt that some members of the invading Legion noted the beauty as well as the utility of this wild natural harbour, for in the fullness of time some influential Roman decided to build himself a house here, on the hillside overlooking the water. It has even been suggested that it might have been Vespasian himself.

This Roman may not have been the first person to live in Brading, for there were possibly fisher-folk here before him, but he was certainly the first to bring civilisation to this lonely part of the Island, and the history of Brading can be said to date from this event. The Villa was probably built about the middle of the 2nd century A.D. (which may rule out the Vespasian theory, for he died in the year 79) but there are signs that it was altered and enlarged on several occasions. From its size, and the quality of the mosaic floors that have survived, it obviously belonged to someone of note who was accustomed to a high standard of living.

Once the Romans had departed in A.D.410 the Villa was abandoned and became derelict, the ruins gradually becoming covered and buried, and it was in fact almost one thousand five hundred years before it was found and excavated. During this period the village of Brading had become established and grown, in spite of the hostile presence of successive waves of invaders — Jutes, Saxons, and Vikings. Life in Brading naturally centred round the Haven, and in A.D.897 it was the scene of a memorable battle between a Viking invasion force in their long boats, and King Alfred the Great.

King Alfred had been fighting the Norwegians and Danes for many years, and had realised that to deal with their fast and powerful long boats it was necessary to build even faster ships. The Anglo-Saxon Chronicle describes what happened, and it is believed that the battle that ensued was fought in Brading Haven —

> "Then King Alfred ordered warships to be built to meet the Danish ships; they were about twice as long as the others, some had 60 oars, some more; they were both swifter, steadier, and with more freeboard than the others.
>
> Then on one occasion the same year (A.D.897) came six ships to the Isle of Wight and did much harm there . . . Then the King ordered nine of the new ships to put out, and they blockaded the entrance from the open sea against their escape. Then the Danes sailed out with three ships against them, and three of their ships were beached at the upper end of the harbour, and the crews had gone off inland. Then the English seized two of the three ships at the entrance to the estuary, and slew the men, but the other escaped; in her also all but five were slain; and they escaped because the ships of the others were aground, they were also very awkwardly aground . . . so that none of them could reach the others.
>
> But when the tide had ebbed many furlongs from the ships, the Danes went from the three ships to the other three which were stranded on their side, and then there they fought. There were slain 62 of the English and 120 of the Danes."

When the tide came in the Danish ships floated before the English and they were able to row out of the harbour. But they were so badly crippled that they only got as far as Selsey Bill, where two of them were driven ashore and the crews captured and sent to Winchester, where they were hanged. And so ended the battle of Brading Haven, an exciting episode in English history.

At the time when King Alfred was having trouble with the Danes, Brading was already an established and thriving village, and had possibly had its own church for well over 100·years. It is believed that one of the earliest Christian communities in the Island was centred here, and that it was from Brading that some of the first missionaries set out to convert the Island in A.D.686.

The name of the village at that time was spelt *"Brerdinge"*, though in the Domesday Survey it is listed as *"Beradinz"*, and is said to be one of the manors belonging to William FitzAzor. Two hundred years later ownership had passed into the hands of the King, and in 1280 Edward I awarded it a Charter as a town, and from then on it was referred to as "The King's Town of Brading". The conferring of this honour brought it increased prosperity, but the history of Brading is very much tied to the story of the Haven. As long as the latter was capable of accepting sea-going ships, so Brading flourished, but alas the harbour gradually silted up, and it was inevitable that sooner or later men, greedy for land, would want to reclaim some of the Haven from the sea.

The first "inning" of the Haven was carried out in 1338 by Sir William Russell of Yaverland, and was a simple and completely successful operation. Up to this time the sea had always been able to enter the Haven from two different directions, from St. Helens on the eastern side, and also from Sandown Bay to the south. This meant that the high ground on which Yaverland and Bembridge now stand was in effect a tidal island, and all that Sir William Russell did was to connect this island with the mainland by building a causeway and a bridge, and this effectively stopped the tide from rushing through the gap in which the river Yar ran. This bridge is still called "Yarbridge", and the land on the far side of it was termed *"Within bridge"* which soon became corrupted to *"Binbridge"* and ultimately *"Bembridge"*. Similarly *"Overland"* which in time became *"Yaverland"*.

The first real attempt to reclaim land from the Haven was made on the north marsh which belonged to the Oglander family of Nunwell, and was carried out jointly by George Oglander and Jermyn Richards in 1562. Jermyn Richards was a brewer in Brading who had made a fortune through selling beer to the many ships that visited the Haven. He lived in the house immediately to the south of the church, which is now occupied by the Osborn-Smith Wax Museum, and in 1553 he bought Yaverland Manor, which was in a dilapidated state, and rebuilt it. The reconstruction was completed by his son Edward, and between them they were responsible for the magnificent house which is still there today. Their initials can be seen over the arch to the staircase they installed, with the date 1620.

Edward Richards reclaimed more land from the Haven in 1594, this time in the south-west corner between Yarbridge and the sluice he had already built. The great earth walls he erected are still there and make a very pleasant walk from Brading church across the marsh to Centurion's Copse and Bembridge.

The next attempt was made in 1620 and was very much more ambitious since it involved reclaiming the whole of the Haven by building an embankment from St. Helens to Bembridge. An *entrepreneur* named Sir Bevis Thelwall managed to acquire the right to carry out the work in a rather subtle way. He had first purchased for himself the position of one of the pages of the bedchamber at the Court of James I. This gave him the ear of the King, who was talked into supporting the project as a trial scheme for the ultimate reclaiming of the fens in Lincolnshire. Needless to say, there was active opposition from the landowners whose property adjoined the Haven, and who disputed Thelwall's rights in the matter.

Nevertheless it went ahead, and Sir Bevis engaged the services of Sir Hugh Myddleton, a celebrated and experienced Civil Engineer, who

The Bull Ring, a relic of the cruel custom of baiting bulls before they were slaughtered.

brought in workmen from the Low Countries to carry out the work. All went well, and the Haven was satisfactorily drained, although the cost was high, and the reclaimed land was not found to be as fruitful as had been expected, but for 8 years crops were grown, rape being found the most satisfactory. Sir Hugh Myddleton, who had been persuaded to put money into the project, sold out his shares to Sir Bevis, leaving the latter the sole proprietor.

Whether Sir Hugh suspected that all was not as it should be is not known, but in 1630 the embankment developed a leak during the March spring tides, and before anything could be done the wall was breached, and within a short time it was beyond repair. As soon as he saw that the situation was serious and the Haven was flooding again, Sir Bevis requested Lady Frances Worsley — on whose land the breached wall stood — to have it repaired forthwith, and quite naturally and rightly she declined, whereupon Sir Bevis began legal proceedings against her. The lawyers had a field day, for there were claims and counter claims, but in the end Sir Bevis was the loser and was left with nothing, the whole project having cost him about £7,000, an appreciable sum in those days. It is doubtful whether anyone in the Island had much sympathy for Sir Bevis who, from the evidence we have, appears to have been a rather tricky character.

Lady Frances Worsley was a most interesting — and beautiful — woman, the widow of Sir Richard Worsley who died in 1621. She was still in her 30s, and her story is fully told in the chapter on Appuldurcombe in *"The Manor Houses of the Isle of Wight"*, but see also the chapter on the Worsley family in this present volume. (Chapter 25 page 148).

It was not until 1878, another 248 years later, that Brading Haven was once more "inned", this time by the railway company, and though the railway they built has since been dismantled, their embankment has survived and has stood firm now for 111 years, the small part of the Haven that was

Brading Church, one of the many beautiful medieval churches in the Isle of Wight.

left outside this embankment now being known as Bembridge Harbour.

With the demise of the Haven, so the importance of Brading declined, but this does not mean to say that the town is any the less interesting historically. There are many fascinating old houses — the Wax Museum is based in one of them — and near the Roman Villa is Morton Manor, which itself dates back to 1249. There is plenty for the visitor to see. In the High Street is the Bull Ring, to which bulls were tethered in the old days to be baited, there is the Lilliput Museum of Antique Dolls to which people come from all over the world, there is the old Town Hall containing records of the town, and also the Stocks and Whipping Post.

And last but not least there is the church of St. Mary, one of the oldest and most beautiful churches in the Island. This contains the tomb of "Little Jane" Squibb, who died in 1799, and was immortalised by the Curate-in-Charge at the time, the Rev. Legh Richmond, who wrote about her in his *"Annals of the Poor"*, possibly the world's first best-seller. The cottage where she lived is not far from the church.

One of the most attractive features in the church is the Oglander Chapel, for the Oglander family lived at nearby Nunwell House ever since the 11th century, and their Chapel contains several family tombs, including that of Sir John, the most famous of them all, friend of Charles I and Deputy Governor of the Isle of Wight. The Oglander story is told in Chapter 27 page 164).

Haven or no Haven, the King's Town of Brading is one of the Isle of Wight's most interesting places.

XXIV — *Island Families:*

Sir Henry Oglander, 7th and last baronet of this distinguished Island family.

Introduction

The old joke about the man who had a bicycle, and was therefore able to father children in the surrounding villages as well as in his own, at least points to the fact that when travel is easy the young and virile male has a wider sphere of activity. Conversely, when travel is difficult, courting has to be carried out nearer to home, with the result that inter-marriage between local families is normal, and frequent.

On an island such as the Isle of Wight where, until comparatively recent times, travel to the mainland was very difficult, this effect is most notice-able, and it is not surprising to find that in the past inter-marriage activity in the Island has been very high. Records do not exist for any but the so called gentry, but a flip through the modern telephone directory will produce many Island surnames that have been around for centuries, some going back to Norman times and beyond.

Where records do exist we find that all the families that have played a significant part in the continuing history of the Isle of Wight have inter-married, producing some fascinating mixtures, and though there have been several injections of fresh blood from the mainland, the Island community has developed in a very different way to an average English county.

The first family to stamp its authority on the Isle of Wight was the Norman family of de Redvers, who came from the little village of Reviers,

146

which is equidistant from Bayeux and Caen. Richard de Redvers was given the Isle of Wight by Henry I in 1102, and he and his many descendants were Lords of the Island until 1293, when the last of their line, Isabella de Fortibus, sold the Island to Edward I.

It is true that a previous Norman, William FitzOsbern, was Lord of the Island in 1066, when it was given to him by his cousin, William the Conqueror, but he and his son, Roger de Breteuil, were only in possession for nine years, after which the Island reverted to the Crown following Roger's abortive rebellion against the King.

Around the year 1100 another name became associated with the Isle of Wight, that of Oglander, and when Richard de Redvers entered into his new Lordship in 1102, one Peter Oglander was his Chaplain. Another Oglander, Roger, may even have been in the Island before Peter, for there are records of him owning land at Nunwell at this time. And of course the name of Oglander is still alive in the Isle of Wight today, a fantastic record of nearly 900 years' residence.

Other families, such as the Worsleys, Leighs, Holmes, and in more recent times the Seelys, have left their mark on the Island, and the next few chapters give brief information about the contribution some of these families have made to Island history. Unfortunately, it is not possible to pay tribute to more than a few, and it must be remembered that there are many more that are really worthy of inclusion. The list is very long indeed.

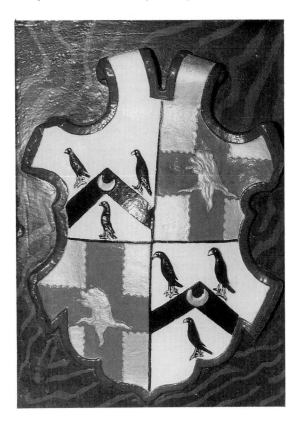

The Worsley Coat of Arms.

XXV — Island Families: Worsley

Sir James and Lady Worsley's tomb in Godshill church.

The village of Worsley, from which this family took its name, lies a few miles from Manchester, in the heart of industrial Lancashire. But it is a very old village and manor, and in Norman times the countryside was far from being commercialised. Worsleys were Lords of the Manor until the reign of Richard II (1377—1399) but as the family grew and expanded it was inevitable that members should find their way to other parts of the country. One young Worsley, for example, "emigrated" at the beginning of the 14th century to Hovingham in Yorkshire and settled there, and the branch of the family he set up then is still in a very flourishing state today.

The first Worsleys to reach the Isle of Wight were Giles, who settled in the manor of Ashey in the 15th century, and James, who came to Appuldurcombe from London where he was employed at Court. The family of Giles Worsley never really became established, and within a hundred years of his arrival none of them were left. James on the other hand took root and flourished, and the family he founded turned out to be the wealthiest and most influential the Isle of Wight had ever seen.

As a boy James Worsley was a page at the Court of Henry VII, and it chanced that he was the same age as Prince Henry, who later became Henry VIII. Now, in those days there was a law that made it a criminal offence to strike a royal prince, and this meant that if Prince Henry did anything wrong, for which a normal boy would receive a good hiding, he could not be touched. It was appreciated that this was not a good thing, but the law was the law, and to get round the problem a rather quaint custom was established of electing a "whipping boy", the same age as the Prince, who could then receive any physical punishment on his behalf.

As described in Chaper 9 page 55, James Worsley was elected whipping boy for Prince Henry, and though it may have been uncomfortable at times, it really did him no harm at all, and when he grew up it brought him definite rewards, for Prince Henry, on becoming King, knighted James Worsley, made him Keeper of the Wardrobe, and appointed him Captain of the Isle of Wight.

His pay as Captain was 6 shillings and 9 pence (33p) per day, plus 2 shillings (10p) for a Deputy, and he was allowed 6 pence (2½p) for each of 13 servants. This may not sound very much today, but at the current value of money at that time it was quite a generous salary. Also there were fringe benefits, as witness an entry in his account book, which reads —

30 December 1525   Given to James Worsley by the King's grace a coat of black velvet with two guards of black satin furred with black coney.

In the Isle of Wight Sir James Worsley met and married an heiress, Anne Leigh, and when her father, Sir John Leigh, died James Worsley found himself the owner of the Appuldurcombe estate, and the richest man in the Island. When he himself died in 1538 his eldest son Richard succeeded him, not only as master of Appuldurcombe, but ultimately too as Captain of the Isle of Wight. Sir James is buried in Godshill Church, where later his wife joined him, and their memorial shows them kneeling at two *prie-dieux*, Lady Anne being decorously a few paces behind her husband, as was the custom of the times.

Richard Worsley turned out to be one of the great characters in the Worsley family, and as Captain of the Isle of Wight contributed much to the defences of the Island at a time when threats from France were ever present. He was one of three members of the family to be given the name of Richard, and to distinguish him from the other two could well be nicknamed "The Fortifier", for at the instigation of his royal master, Henry VIII, he built forts at Sandown, West and East Cowes, and a smaller fortification to the west of Yarmouth, which became known as Worsley's Tower.

He gave the Militia an injection of energy, and equipped them with firearms, which was regarded as a very bold and progressive step, but perhaps the biggest innovation was to insist on each parish owning its own cannon, to be kept in the church and taken out regualrly for practice. This was done, prizes were awarded for profiency, and a high standard was achieved. After the *"Mary Rose"* disaster in 1545 he built Yarmouth Castle, and this marked the end of French raids on the Island, though the threat remained for some considerable time.

Besides being a born leader and full of energy, Richard Worsley exhibited other characteristics which often go hand-in-hand. He was aggressive, hot-tempered, and headstrong, and had an eye for the ladies. As a youngish man he fell desperately in love with Mabel Dingley of Wolverton Manor, whose father was Deputy Lieutenant of the Island, and when she spurned him in favour of William More of Losely in Surrey, his great friend, he thought for a time that his heart was broken. Ultimately he married Ursula St. Barbe, who came from Somerset, and they had two children, John and George. He also fathered an illegitimate son, Thomas, whose mother was his dairymaid, but to his credit he looked after the boy, educated him at Winchester, and later set him up in a farm at Chale.

At the time of the Dissolution of the Monasteries Richard was appointed one of the King's Commissioners and was involved in the closing of Quarr Abbey, his relationship with King Henry VIII proving sufficiently amicable for the latter to visit Appuldurcombe in 1541. The visit was not an unqualified success though, for the hunting was poor and the King was upset, not being renowned for patience.

When Mary Tudor came to the throne in 1553 and vigorously re-introduced the Roman Catholic religion to the country, Richard felt it was politic to resign his Captaincy of the Island, in case his previous activities as a King's Commissioner might be remembered and result in retribution. For five years he kept a very low profile, but was reinstated as Captain by Elizabeth in 1558, and held the position until his death in 1565. Two years later his two fatherless boys, aged 8 and 9, were killed in a tragic accident in the Gatehouse at Appuldurcombe when a barrel of gunpowder exploded. His widow also re-married, her second husband being Sir Francis Walsingham, Secretary of State to Queen Elizabeth.

An inventory of the contents of Appuldurcombe House was taken at the time of Richard Worsley's death, and this is reproduced below, its interest to us today lying, not in the extent of the material comforts the house contained, but in the astonishingly spartan nature of the furnishings.

Inventory of Appuldurcombe House. 1565

Hall:	2 long trestle tables, 2 forms	6/8d	(34p)
	15 tablecloths, canvas	16/-	(80p)
	15 tablecloths, white canvas	22/-	(£1.10)
Little Parlour	1 trestle table, 1 form	6/8d	(34p)
	1 chair	8d	(3½p)
	a side cupboard	16d	(7p)
Great Parlour	1 trestle table, 8'3" long and 4 forms	10/-	(50p)
	1 sideboard	4/-	(20p)
	1 chair, and 1 woman's chair	3/4d	(17p)
	12 stools	6/6d	(33p)
	12 cushions	10/-	(50p)
	2 stools for women	12d	(5p)
	2 other tables	3/6d	(18p)
	fire irons (shovel, tongs, bellows, dogs)	2/-	(10p)

Also listed were —

Kitchen, Brewhouse, Malthouse, Dairy, etc.

6 Principal bedrooms, 2 with inner chambers, most with 2 or more beds, all four posters,, and all richly furnished. Rooms were named — "Paradise", "The Broad", "St. John's", "Porch", "Mr. Richard Worsley's", "My Lady's Chamber".

5 Secondary rooms, also named — "Chapel", "The Maidens", "The Green", "Mrs. Bramshott's Chamber".

In the middle of the 16th century, when this Inventory was taken, it was still customary for several people to sleep in one room, this being a relic of the days when there *was* only one room, i.e. the Hall, and few houses at this time had spare bedrooms. Visitors very often had beds made up for them on the floor, the rooms being furnished barely. Sanitation, even in the largest houses, was primitive, and people did not wash.

A glance at the family tree of the Appuldurcombe Worsleys on page 155 will show that the second Richard Worsley was not a direct descendant of the first, but was the grandson of his brother, John, who had inherited Appuldurcombe when Richard the Fortifier's two children had been killed in the explosion. Richard the second, whom perhaps it is permissible to nickname "the One-Eyed Dick", since he had lost the sight of one eye when he was 12, was born in 1588, the Armada year, and inherited Appuldurcombe at the age of 15, in 1604. He lost his eye as a schoolboy in Winchester when following a hunt one day, through having the misfortune to run into a hazel twig, but his great friend, Sir John Oglander, later said that it was hardly noticeable.

At 20 he met, fell in love with, and married Frances Neville, the daughter of Sir Henry Neville of Berkshire, and Sir John Oglander described her as one of the handsomest women in the kingdom, but said she did not bring with her much dowry. However, there were other compensations, for in 1610 her father acquired for Richard a knighthood, and a year later a baronetcy, so really Richard, who was already rich, had no complaints. This Worsley baronetcy lived for 214 years, but became extinct in 1825 with the death of the 9th baronet, Sir Leonard Worsley-Holmes.

Sir Richard, the first baronet, was not a typical Worsley in that he was more gentle than most and not addicted to outdoor sports. His favourite exercise was to assemble a few friends and indulge in the pastime of flinging cushions at each other, but ultimately had to give even this up, for on one occasion at Gatcombe House, the home of his brother John, his friend, Sir John Oglander, hit him in his good eye with a cushion, and thought for a moment that he had blinded him.

He died in 1621 at the early age of 32, and a certain amount of mystery surrounds his death. The Oglander Memoirs state that he died of smallpox, but there is a document in the Public Record Office that claims he died in a sword fight outside the Bugle Inn at Newport as the result of a quarrel with one of his tenants over a new lease.

Sir Richard was succeeded by the eldest of his seven children, Henry,

'Life gets tedious, don't it?'
Cherub guarding the memorial in
Godshill church to Sir Robert
Worsley and his brother, Henry.

Right. *Sir Richard Worsley*
as a young man.

who was a minor but became the second baronet. His mother, the Lady Frances, within a few years of Sir Richard's death was involved in the legal argument over the inundation of Brading Haven, which had recently been drained, (see Chapter 23 page 144) but proved quite capable of looking after herself. When first widowed she vowed she would never marry again, but nevertheless fell in love with a Sir Charles Bartlett and was expecting to marry him, but unfortunately he went and married someone else. She survived this disappointment however and ultimately married a Colonel Jeremy Brett, a rough soldier, Captain of Southsea Castle. This match amazed her friends who thought him most unsuitable for her, but it apparently turned out well.

Right. *Sir Richard after*
years of trouble.

In 1690 the Worsley estates passed to Sir Robert, the fourth baronet, a young man who married a daughter of Viscount Weymouth of Longleat, and the young couple decided that the old Elizabethan Appuldurcombe House had to be replaced. They therefore demolished it, the replacement being the magnificent Palladian mansion which still survives today, albeit in a partly ruined condition. Actually Sir Robert and his Lady never finished the building of the new house, this being left to the last Worsley to live at Appuldurcombe, the third and final Sir Richard.

This Sir Richard was an art connoisseur, with the wealth necessary to indulge his sophisticated tastes, and he filled his house with beautiful things, even going to the extent of chartering his own ship for an expedition to the Mediterranean, from which he returned loaded with works of art.

One of the beautiful things he installed in his house was his wife, Seymour, the daughter of Sir John Fleming. He married her in 1775 when she was only 17, and she brought him a dowry of £80,000. She also brought him a load of trouble for she was a nymphomaniac and could not leave the men alone. Sir Richard condoned many of her outrageous *affaires* — for he himself could well have been nickamed "the Rake" — but when she eloped with one of her numerous lovers he felt constrained to take action. After all, he was Governor of the Isle of Wight, and head of the most important Island family, and now his friends were beginning to laugh at him. So he sued her paramour for £20,000, and in the subsequent High Court action a considerable amount of dirty linen was washed in public. The outcome was that Lady Worsley had to admit to having had 27 lovers, judgement was given in favour of Sir Richard, and he was awarded damages. Not the £20,000 he had requested, but the Judge's estimate of the value of his beautiful wife — one shilling.

The scandal effectively ruined Sir Richard's career, and he left the Island. And though he did return to visit it from time to time he never lived

The cause of the trouble, his wife, Lady Seymour Worsley.

153

at Appuldurcombe again. When he died in 1805 his wealth and estates passed to his sister's daughter. She married the Honourable Charles Pelham, who later became the first Lord Yarborough, and is remembered in the Island for having founded the Royal Yacht Squadron. Pelham was so grateful for the sudden wealth that had dropped into his lap that he felt in duty bound to erect a memorial in Godshill Church to Sir Richard. Sadly, the design for this monument leaves more than something to be desired, for it is a massive and monstrous sarcophagus mounted on a huge plinth, and is undeniably hideous. Originally sited in the south transept, a subseqent and sensitive Vicar could at last stand the sight of it no more, so had it moved, and it is now tucked behind the organ where it no longer clashes with the many other, and more artistic, Worsley memorials.

So ended the Worsley occupation of Appuldurcombe, and the great house they had built gradually slipped downhill. It became in turn an hotel, a school, a priory, and a billet for troops. The *coup de grace* came towards the end of the second World War when a flying bomb removed its roof and its windows, leaving it an empty shell open to the weather. Happily, in the 1980s, after many vicissitudes, English Heritage took it over and began a programme of restoration, and hopefully this will one day be completed and one of the Island's finest buildings will again be habitable.

But the Worsley family owned many other manors in the Isle of Wight besides Appuldurcombe, one of the principal of these being Gatcombe. Here, John Worsley, younger brother of the one-eyed Sir Richard, founded his own dynasty which produced its own crop of characters. Foremost amongst these was John himself, an obstinate and self-willed man, who resolutely refused to pay his taxes. One such tax was called ship money, levied by the King in 1637, and as Sir John Oglander was High Sheriff of Hampshire at this time, to him fell the task of trying to extract payment from the man who was his personal friend. Another payment that John obstinately withheld was his Church Rate, and as he was the principal rate-payer in Gatcombe parish the church fell into serious disrepair. John ultimately paid up of course, but not until the power and might of the Archbishop of Canterbury had been brought to bear on him by his churchwardens.

John's eldest son, Edward, who was born in 1621, was the devoted follower of Charles I who did so much to try and help the King escape from his imprisonment in Carisbrooke Castle. The King gave him his watch as a keepsake, and though Edward failed in his attempts to free him, his reward came in 1665, when in Carisbrooke Castle he was knighted by Charles II.

The two family trees with this chapter list just a very few members of this illustrious family who lived at Appuldurcombe, Gatcombe, and at several other manors. They dominated the Isle of Wight for nearly four centuries; four of them were Captains or Governors of the Island, and they inter-married with all the other leading families, so that their influence was widespread and was felt in every corner and in every sphere of Island life. They were ubiquitous.

THE WORSLEYS OF APPULDURCOMBE

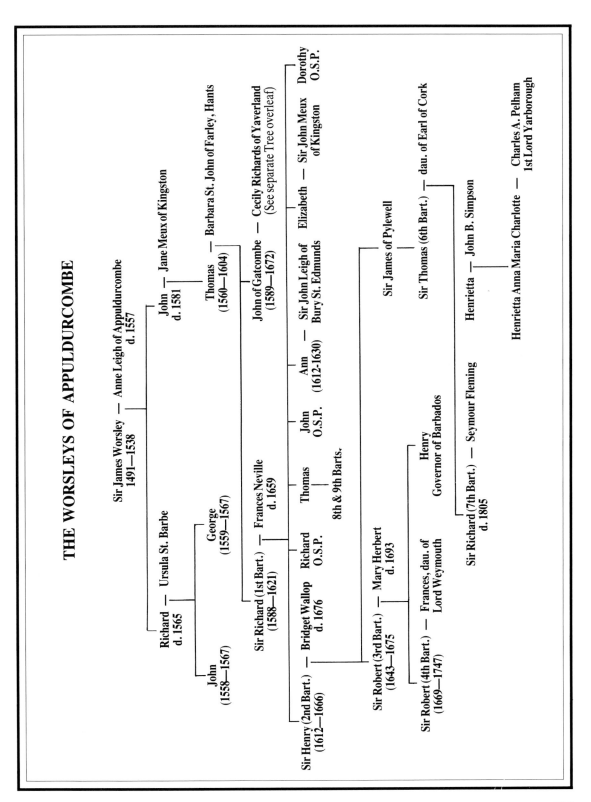

Sir James Worsley — Anne Leigh of Appuldurcombe
1491—1538   d. 1557

Richard — Ursula St. Barbe
d. 1565

John
(1558—1567)

George
(1559—1567)

John — Jane Meux of Kingston
d. 1581

Thomas — Barbara St. John of Farley, Hants
(1560—1604)

Sir Richard (1st Bart.) — Frances Neville
(1588—1621)   d. 1659

John of Gatcombe — Cecily Richards of Yaverland
(1589—1672)   (See separate Tree overleaf)

Elizabeth — Sir John Meux
                of Kingston

Dorothy
O.S.P.

Sir Henry (2nd Bart.) — Bridget Wallop
(1612—1666)   d. 1676

Richard
O.S.P.

Thomas

8th & 9th Barts.

John
O.S.P.

Ann
(1612-1630)

— Sir John Leigh of
   Bury St. Edmunds

Sir James of Pylewell

Sir Robert (3rd Bart.) — Mary Herbert
(1643—1675)   d. 1693

Sir Robert (4th Bart.) — Frances, dau. of
(1669—1747)   Lord Weymouth

Henry
Governor of Barbados

Sir Richard (7th Bart.) — Seymour Fleming
d. 1805

Sir Thomas (6th Bart.) — dau. of Earl of Cork

Henrietta — John B. Simpson

Henrietta Anna Maria Charlotte — Charles A. Pelham
                                                1st Lord Yarborough

155

THE WORSLEYS OF GATCOMBE

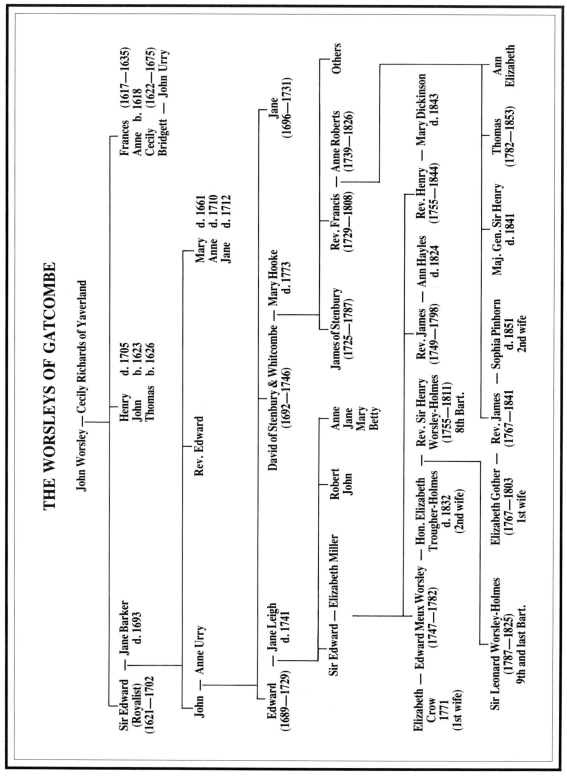

John Worsley — Cecily Richards of Yaverland

Sir Edward — Jane Barker
(Royalist)   d. 1693
(1621—1702)

Henry   d. 1705
John   b. 1623
Thomas   b. 1626

Frances   (1617—1635)
Anne   b. 1618
Cecily   (1622—1675)
Bridgett — John Urry

John — Anne Urry

Rev. Edward

Mary   d. 1661
Anne   d. 1710
Jane   d. 1712

Edward — Jane Leigh
(1689—1729)   d. 1741

David of Stenbury & Whitcombe — Mary Hooke
(1692—1746)   d. 1773

Jane
(1696—1731)

Sir Edward — Elizabeth Miller

Robert
John

Anne
Jane
Mary
Betty

James of Stenbury
(1725—1787)

Rev. Francis — Anne Roberts
(1729—1808)   (1739—1826)

Others

Elizabeth — Edward Meux Worsley
Crow   (1747—1782)
1771
(1st wife)

Hon. Elizabeth
Trougher-Holmes
d. 1832
(2nd wife)

Rev. Sir Henry
Worsley-Holmes
(1755—1811)
8th Bart.

Rev. James — Ann Hayles
(1749—1798)   d. 1824

Rev. Henry — Mary Dickinson
(1755—1844)   d. 1843

Elizabeth Gother — Rev. James
(1767—1803)   (1767—1841)
1st wife

Sophia Pinhorn
d. 1851
2nd wife

Maj. Gen. Sir Henry
d. 1841

Thomas
(1782—1853)

Ann
Elizabeth

Sir Leonard Worsley-Holmes
(1787—1825)
9th and last Bart.

156

XXVI — *Island Families: Leigh*

Arreton Manor, once the Leigh's home.

In the Isle of Wight the Leigh family are second only to the Worsleys in importance during the 16th and 17th centuries, and indeed the Leighs were here first, in the person of a Sir John Leigh from Flamston in Wiltshire who married a rich widow, Agnes Fry. She was living at Appuldurcombe, which at the end of the 15th century belonged to the Convent of St. Clare-without-Aldgate in London. In 1498 Sir John negotiated a 35 year lease of the Appuldurcombe estate with the Nuns, and began to acquire other Island property, which together with his own not inconsiderable wealth made him the richest man in the Island. When he died in 1523 the fortune he had amassed went to his daughter, Anne, who married Sir James Worsley, and this young couple were the founders of the Worsley "empire" in the Isle of Wight.

Sir John Leigh died through being thrown from his horse, which stumbled over a wild boar, and on his tomb in Godshill Church (the most splendid tomb in the Island) is an alabaster effigy of the knight, together with his wife, who joined him later. In this effigy his feet are resting on a boar, who is looking round at him as much as to say "I didn't do it on purpose — it was a complete accident!" The soles of Sir John's feet are carved in the likeness of two monks telling their beads, who are indeed known as "the bedesmen", the whole concept being a sort of medieval joke, for they are praying for his soul.

A nephew of his, another John, but of Godshill, took a lease of Arreton Manor in 1523 for 70 years, and there is a record of him in 1543 living once again in Godshill, so he must have surrendered the Arreton lease to his eldest son (yet another John Leigh) who was farming the manor when he himself died in 1540. The Leighs are a very confusing family since so many of them are called John, and every generation seems also to have a Barnabas or Barnaby, but a study of the family tree will help to separate them out.

John Leigh of Arreton, who died in 1540, had four brothers and a sister, and in his Will he left his lease in the manor to his wife, and after her death to his brother, Barnaby. There were several other bequests to members of his family, and to "my master Richard Worsley", indicating that by this time, just after the suppression of Quarr Abbey, Arreton Manor was being administered by Richard Worsley, who was the King's Commissioner. But two names were conspicuous by their absence in the Will — his two brothers Thomas and James — and there is a legend attached to Arreton which claims that these two had quarrelled over money, had drawn their swords and fought, whereby Thomas was killed outright and James received wounds from which he died three days later.

In 1541 Barnaby inherited the manor lease on his mother's death, and when he too was dying in 1560 further melodrama was enacted. Barnaby had four children, John, Anthony, Anne, and Barnaby, the latter being born on the day his Will was made. His eldest son, John, who was due to inherit, was 13 years old in 1560, and the story goes that being impatient that his father was dying too slowly, John decided to assist him, and smothered him with a pillow. While he was performing this kindness his young sister, Anne, came into the room and saw what he was about, so that he felt obliged to deal with her too, and this he did by throwing her from a top window.

Whether this story is true or not is open to question, for John Leigh went on to become Deputy Lieutenant of the Island, was knighted by James I in 1606, and according to Sir John Oglander, led a blameless and domestically happy life, dying in 1630 at the age of 83 full of years and honours. In fact his great age suggests a possible flaw in the story told about him when he was 13. One of his sons was, by tradition, called Barnaby, and was born when his father was in his early 20s, so that by the time John was in his 80s, Barnaby was around 60 years old. Barnaby was impatient to succeed hs father, whom he thought had lived long enough, and was known to have said — possibly in jest — "I wish I could say the bginning of the Lord's Prayer!" And it may be that in the telling and re-telling of this story over the years, confusion has arisen between this John and Barnaby and the previous Barnaby and John.

Sir John Oglander had quite a lot to say in his Memoirs about Sir John Leigh, for they were good friends. He describes how John Leigh, when he was a young and handsome man, was elected to be Lord of a Summerpole one year in the village of Shorwell, a Summerpole being a popular type of village Fête held at Whitsuntide. The lady elected to rule over the festivities with him was Elizabeth Dingley, the 16 year old daughter of John Dingley of Wolverton Manor, who was later Deputy Lieutenant to the Captain of the Island, Sir George Carey. A romance developed between John Leigh and Elizabeth Dingley and they married, and for many years they lived happily in Wolverton Manor with her parents. John was able to help his father-in-law with his duties as Deputy Lieutenant, and became more and more proficient as an administrator, so much so that when John Dingley died, John Leigh took his place as Deputy Lieutenant of the Island.

While still in his 30s John Leigh suffered a stroke and was paralysed all down his right side, but he refused to let this disability inconvenience him and continued to lead an active life. Considering his physical problems his activity was quite extraordinary, and there is a record that in 1587 he supervised the extensive work being carried out on the Island's fortifications, an attack by the Spanish being believed to be imminent, and he later travelled to London to collect 1000 Marks (approximately £670), the sum allowed for this work. Today a cheque for this amount would have been put in the post, but John Leigh had to go all the way to London to collect it, in bulk, and it took 6 men 12 days to effect this and get it back to the Island safely. His total expenses for this trip were £4.

About this time John Leigh bought the dilapidated Elizabethan manor house of North Court, a mile or so from Wolverton, and proceeded to build the mansion that has survived to this day. The date over the porch, together with the Leigh coat of arms, is 1615.

John's youngest brother, Barnaby, followed his brother's example and married Elizabeth Dingley's younger sister, Mabel, and they settled in Thorley, establishing an important branch of the Leigh family in this part of the West Wight. Barnaby served as Mayor of Yarmouth on three occasions, and several of his descendants followed suit; one in particular, Benjamin Leigh, who was Mayor in 1763, has left his name on the front of the Town Hall which was re-built in that year by Thomas Lord Holmes.

The family trees attached to this chapter show some of the members of this prolific family, enough perhaps to demonstrate that they have played a major role in the life of the Isle of Wight during several centuries. They married into all the other leading families — Worsleys, Oglanders, Urrys, etc, and their record is one of dignified and sustained service. When Sir John Leigh died in 1630 his friend, Sir John Oglander, wrote his epitaph, that could well apply to many more of them. He said —

"He lived well and died well. God send us do the like."

Tomb of Sir John Leigh of Northcourt (with his great grandson) in Shorwell church.

160

THE LEIGHS

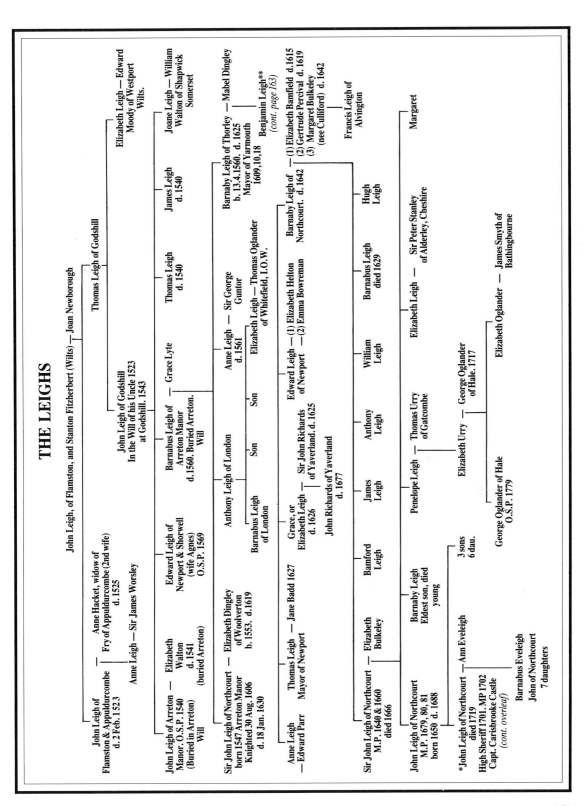

John Leigh, of Flamston, and Stanton Fitzherbert (Wilts) — Joan Newborough

Thomas Leigh of Godshill

Elizabeth Leigh — Edward Moody of Westport Wilts.

Joane Leigh — William Walton of Shapwick Somerset

James Leigh d. 1540

Barnaby Leigh of Thorley — Mabel Dingley b. 13.4.1560. d. 1625 Mayor of Yarmouth 1609,10,18

Benjamin Leigh** *(cont. page 163)*

John Leigh of Godshill In the Will of his Uncle 1523 at Godshill. 1543

Anne Hacket, widow of Fry of Appuldurcombe (2nd wife) d. 1525

Anne Leigh — Sir James Worsley

John Leigh of Flamston & Appuldurcombe d. 2 Feb. 1523

Barnabus Leigh of Arreton Manor d. 1560. Buried Arreton. Will

Thomas Leigh d. 1540

Anne Leigh — Sir George d. 1561 Guntor

Francis Leigh of Alvington

Edward Leigh of Newport & Shorwell (wife Agnes) O.S.P. 1569

Grace Lyte

Elizabeth Leigh — Thomas Oglander of Whitefield, I.O.W.

Barnaby Leigh of Northcourt. d. 1642

Hugh Leigh

John Leigh of Arreton Manor. O.S.P. 1540 (Buried in Arreton) Will

Elizabeth Walton d. 1541 (buried Arreton)

Anthony Leigh of London

Son

Son

Edward Leigh — (1) Elizabeth Helton of Newport — (2) Emma Bowreman

Barnabus Leigh died 1629

Elizabeth Leigh — Sir Peter Stanley of Alderley, Cheshire

Margaret

Sir John Leigh of Northcourt born 1547 Arreton Manor Knighted 30 Aug. 1606 d. 18 Jan. 1630

Elizabeth Dingley of Woolverton b. 1553. d.1619

Barnabus Leigh of London

William Leigh

(1) Elizabeth Bamfield d.1615
(2) Gertrude Percival d. 1619
(3) Margaret Bulkeley (nee Culliford) d. 1642

Anne Leigh — Edward Parr

Thomas Leigh — Jane Badd 1627 Mayor of Newport

Grace, or Elizabeth Leigh d. 1626

Sir John Richards of Yaverland. d. 1625

John Richards of Yaverland d. 1677

James Leigh

Anthony Leigh

Penelope Leigh — Thomas Urry of Gatcombe

Elizabeth Oglander — James Smyth of Bathingbourne

Elizabeth Bulkeley

Bamford Leigh

Barnaby Leigh Eldest son, died young

Elizabeth Urry — George Oglander of Hale. 1717

Sir John Leigh of Northcourt M.P. 1640 & 1660 died 1666

John Leigh of Northcourt M.P. 1679, 80, 81 born 1650 d. 1688

3 sons 6 dau.

George Oglander of Hale O.S.P. 1779

*John Leigh of Northcourt died 1719 High Sheriff 1701. MP 1702 Capt. Carisbrooke Castle *(cont. overleaf)*

Ann Eveleigh

Barnabus Eveleigh John of Northcourt 7 daughters

THE LEIGHS

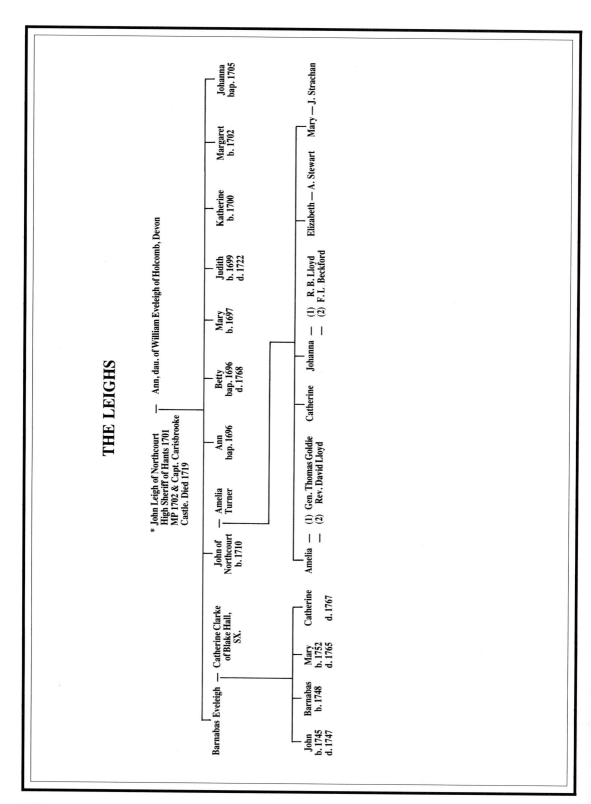

* John Leigh of Northcourt
High Sheriff of Hants 1701
MP 1702 & Capt. Carisbrooke
Castle. Died 1719

— Ann, dau. of William Eveleigh of Holcomb, Devon

Barnabas Eveleigh — Catherine Clarke of Blake Hall, SX.

John of Northcourt b. 1710 — Amelia Turner

Ann bap. 1696

Betty bap. 1696 d. 1768

Mary b. 1697

Judith b. 1699 d. 1722

Katherine b. 1700

Margaret b. 1702

Johanna bap. 1705

John b. 1745 d. 1747

Barnabas b. 1748

Mary b. 1752 d. 1765

Catherine d. 1767

Amelia — (1) Gen. Thomas Goldie
— (2) Rev. David Lloyd

Catherine

Johanna — (1) R. B. Lloyd
— (2) F. L. Beckford

Elizabeth — A. Stewart

Mary — J. Strachan

162

THE LEIGHS OF THORLEY AND YARMOUTH

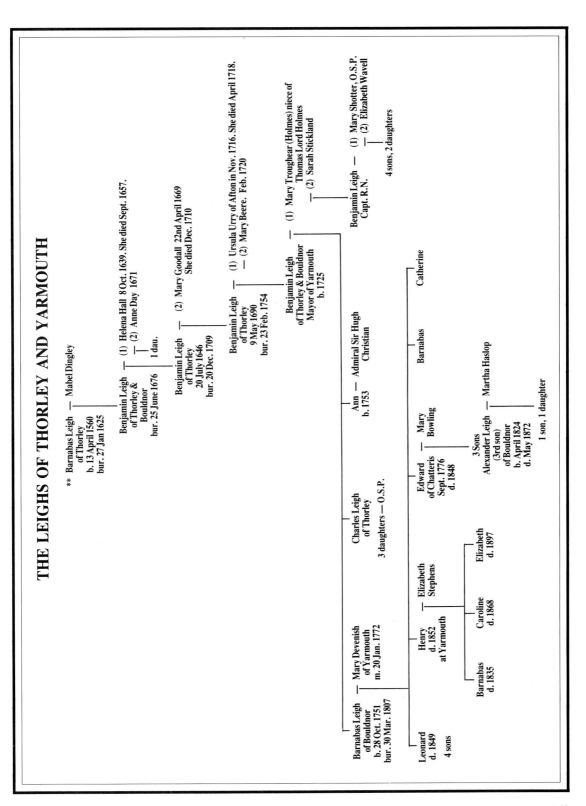

** Barnabas Leigh
of Thorley
b. 13 April 1560
bur. 27 Jan 1625

— Mabel Dingley

Benjamin Leigh
of Thorley &
Bouldnor
bur. 25 June 1676

— (1) Helena Hall 8 Oct. 1639. She died Sept. 1657.
— (2) Anne Day 1671
        1 dau.

Benjamin Leigh
of Thorley
20 July 1646
bur. 20 Dec. 1709

— (2) Mary Goodall 22nd April 1669
        She died Dec. 1710

Benjamin Leigh
of Thorley
9 May 1690
bur. 23 Feb. 1754

— (1) Ursula Urry of Afton in Nov. 1716. She died April 1718.
— (2) Mary Beere. Feb. 1720

Benjamin Leigh
of Thorley & Bouldnor
Mayor of Yarmouth
b. 1725

— (1) Mary Troughear (Holmes) niece of
        Thomas Lord Holmes
— (2) Sarah Stickland

Benjamin Leigh
Capt. R.N.

— (1) Mary Shotter, O.S.P.
— (2) Elizabeth Wavell
        4 sons, 2 daughters

Ann — Admiral Sir Hugh
b. 1753   Christian

Charles Leigh
of Thorley

3 daughters — O.S.P.

Barnabas Leigh
of Bouldnor
b. 28 Oct. 1751
bur. 30 Mar. 1807

— Mary Devenish
   of Yarmouth
   m. 20 Jan. 1772

Edward
of Chatteris
Sept. 1776
d. 1848

— Mary
   Bowling

Barnabas

Catherine

3 Sons
Alexander Leigh
(3rd son)
of Bouldnor
b. April 1824
d. May 1872

— Martha Haslop

1 son, 1 daughter

Henry
d. 1852
at Yarmouth

— Elizabeth
   Stephens

Leonard
d. 1849

4 sons

Barnabas
d. 1835

Caroline
d. 1868

Elizabeth
d. 1897

163

XXVII — *Island Families: Oglander*

A view of Nunwell from the west showing the oldest, Jacobean, part of the house.

Historians differ about the coming of the Oglanders to England. Some say they came over with William the Conqueror in 1066, others say they did not arrive till later. But the question is of little importance. The astonishing fact is that this Norman family, that originated in the village of Orglandes in the Cherbourg peninsula, was established in Nunwell, in the Isle of Wight, round about the year 1100, and until the male line failed with the death of Sir Henry Oglander, the 7th baronet, in 1874, they were there continuously, a period of very nearly 800 years. Even then the name did not die out, and Oglanders continued to live in this same house for another 100 years and more, a record which many of the great names in the English aristocracy may find it difficult not to envy.

The first one to be recorded at Nunwell is Roger Doglandre, whose younger brother, Peter, was Chaplain to the Lord of the Island, Richard de Redvers. Two generations later Roger's grandson, another Roger, inherited Nunwell c.1190, and indeed, Roger was a popular family name up until the end of the 15th century. Other favourite names were Robert, Henry, George, William and John, and apart from Robert, all the others appeared regularly until the 19th century

In many ways the history of the Oglander family followed the same pattern as that of other leading families in the Isle of Wight, and there is a fairly regular record of inter-marrying. The Roger Oglander who was living at Nunwell in 1190 married Maud de Gorges, the de Gorges being another family that was becoming established in the Island, and within the next hundred years was to inherit the manor of Knighton, which consequently became known as Knighton Gorges. In the 13th century a Robert Oglander married the daughter of Sir John Russell of Yaverland,

Sir John Oglander of Nunwell, to whom we owe much of our knowledge of life in the Island during the early 17th century.

and his son Henry married Jane, daughter of Sir John Clamorgan of Brook.

Henry, incidentally, went on one of the Crusades in 1270 with Prince Edward, who was later to become Edward I, and Henry's son, another Henry, fought with distinction at Crecy in 1346, and was knighted on the field of battle for his valour. Sir Henry also married into a well known family, his wife being Mary de Lisle, who was a great-great-grand-daughter of Edward I.

Other important marriages were to follow, with the Dingleys of Wolverton, the Urrys of Standen, the Chekes of Mottistone and Merston, and the Dillingtons of Knighton Gorges. Ann Dillington of the latter family married Sir William Oglander in 1574 and their marriage, which was a love-match and against his father's wishes, since the lady had no dowry worth mentioning, produced the greatest Oglander of them all, Sir John, who was born in 1585.

Sir John Oglander — he was knighted by James I when he was 21 — was a truly extraordinary man, and differed from any of his forbears in that he contracted the habit of making notes about anything that interested him. He was not, in the strictest sense of the word, a diarist, though many of his notes were made in large notebooks, but he also scribbled on any odd piece of paper that happened to be handy.

We are told that this habit of recording anything and everything that happened around him was acquired when he was a young man during bouts of periodic headaches which prevented him temporarily from active pursuits, but his writing came to have a much deeper motive than just whiling away the time. He was intensely proud of the long history of the Oglander family and of their occupation of Nunwell, and had a very firm eye on the future. He was, in fact, writing for posterity —

> "I so well affect my successors and the advancement of the name of the Oglanders, that I hereby wish there may come some from me in time that may over-top and outgo me, both in wealth, wit, wisdom and honour . . . "

To further this aim he collected and collated all documents relating to the previous history of the family, and carefully kept all letters. When he died he left behind him such a large and impressive collection of papers that his descendants had the sense not to throw it away, nor to disturb it in any way, and in fact to add to it. With the result that today it comprises a priceless record of the life and times in which he lived, and also, of course, it gives us a character study of the man himself.

Sir John Oglander did not have an easy life. Along with his great family pride went an equal love of the Isle of Wight and a devotion to public service, a devotion which in his later years caused him much trouble and expense, and never brought him the reward he deserved. He held many high offices of authority, Lieutenant Governor of Portsmouth, High Sheriff of Hampshire, Deputy Lieutenant of the Isle of Wight, amongst them. He was a Member of Parliament, and a personal friend of Charles I. Indeed, it was this latter connection that brought him so much trouble, for he was a staunch and outspoken Royalist at a time when the King was in disgrace, and Sir John's occasional outbursts and incautious remarks brought him several terms of imprisonment and large fines, and made him very unpopular in the Island. It is believed that Charles I, when making his way from Hampton Court to the Isle of Wight in 1647, really thought that Sir John would be able to hide him and help him, but this was a sad miscalculation, for by this time Sir John had lost all the authority he once had.

To anyone interested in the social history of the Isle of Wight, and particularly in this stirring period in the first half of the 17th century, three books are available and are compulsive and essential reading. Two are edited extracts from some of Sir John's writings — *"The Oglander Memoirs"* edited by W. H. Long, and *"A Royalist's Notebook"* edited by Francis Bamford. The third is an affectionate history of the Oglander family entitled *"Nunwell Symphony"* by Cecil Aspinall-Oglander.

In 1639 Sir John was invited by the Mayor and Burgesses of Yarmouth to represent the Borough in Parliament — there were no elections in those days — and he readily agreed, having already represented the town in a previous Parliament. But at the last moment he asked to be excused, and suggested they should elect his son, William, in his place. This was not a popular suggestion to the Mayor and his colleagues, who tried hard to turn the idea down, but Sir John was rather upset and argued vehemently in favour of his son, so that in the end they reluctantly agreed to elect William, the Mayor and Burgesses being quite over-awed by Sir John. But after the two Oglanders had left Yarmouth the Mayor and his friends had second thoughts, and a few days later, feeling much braver, they solemnly dismissed William and chose someone else.

The incident is well documented and shows how frightened the simple Burgesses of Yarmouth were of Sir John and the authority he represented. In a statement later to the High Sheriff the Mayor explains in rather quaint language how William came to be elected —

> ". . . the said Sir John . . . still labored thatt his sonne might bee the man the said maior & the most of his company weareto by the many p'swasions of the s'd Sir John beeinge overborne by his powerfullnes some with silence others by sparing speech most of them unwillingly gave consent . . . "

After they had changed their minds the quarrel developed and William rode over to Yarmouth where he visited the inn owned by William Hyde, a leading member of the Corporation. Mr. Hyde was not at home, but William spoke to Mrs. Hyde and a friend of hers, Mrs. Burley, wife of the Captain of Yarmouth Castle. Apparently he used rather rude words about the Mayor and Burgesses, for both these ladies later made statements claiming that he called the Corporation a company of fools and loggerheads. It appears that he lost his temper for when he had gone his man came back and apologised, begging the ladies not to report what his master had said.

William Oglander, who was 29 at the time, in 1640, did not lose very much through being rejected, for the parliament was one of the shortest on record, lasting only three weeks. Seven years later he was involved in the first attempt to rescue Charles I from Carisbrooke Castle, and though this failed he managed to cover his tracks so well that he got away with it and was never arrested. Captain Burley, however, who was also implicated, was caught and subsequently executed. Charles II, on making his first official visit to the Island in 1665, not only knighted William Oglander but created him a baronet, this being a reward for the part he played in the rescue attempt, and also an appreciation of the friendship that had existed between his father, Sr John, and the King's father, Charles I.

The third baronet (1680—1734), also called William, married at the early age of 19, having succeeded to the title when he was three years old. His wife, Elizabeth, was the daughter of an extremely rich man, Sir John Strode of Parnham, the owner of 16,000 acres in Dorset and Somerset. Elizabeth was the youngest of 13 children, nine of whom were male, and hence her chances of inheriting much of the Strode fortune were slim, but in the event the other 12 all died before her, leaving her the sole heiress. This caused a huge, and very welcome, injection of wealth into the Oglander family and enabled a number of building alterations and improvements to be made to Nunwell House, including the covering of the south front in the latest technological innovation, red mathematical tiles.

The fifth baronet (1733—1806), yet another William, and his very progressive wife, Sukey, also carried out further alterations to the house, re-building and re-aligning the east front and creating the beautiful Georgian facade, which is such a feature of the house today. They also produced a family of eleven, large families being the order of the day.

Sir William, the sixth baronet (1769—1852), was a character and much ahead of his time. He had a passion for hygiene and fresh air, and at this time these were not popular beliefs, it not being considered healthy to open windows and let in the outside air. His obsession caused him to be considered a crank, and he was known to ride round his estates, come to a tenant's cottage and dismount, enter the cottage, and without a word remove plants from the window-sill and open the windows wide, and then mount his horse and go on his way.

Sir William employed the architect, John Nash, to rebuild the stable and coach house at Nunwell, which Nash did in typical fashion. The architect, appreciating that Sir William was slightly eccentric, then succeeded in persuading him that the beautiful oak panelling in Nunwell, of which there was much, was unhygienic, and for the sum of £3000 Nash ripped it all out and replaced it with wallpaper. It has been suggested that he then sold the panelling to someone else and made a further profit, but this may be conjecture. In Nash's defence it must be said that oak panelling in old houses very often harboured rats, and this may have been the case at Nunwell.

The next scheme that Nash put up to Sir William was for the complete demolition of Nunwell and its replacement by an imposing neo-classical mansion, but at this point Sir William's wife stepped in and put her foot down very firmly, so that this plan came to nought.

A record has been preserved of the staff employed by Sir William in 1814, together with their wages, this being of great interest for it shows the large number of servants required to run this typical country house, and the pitifully small wages paid to them. The total number of servants employed was 24, and the annual wages bill was around £630. Many of them, of course, also got their keep, and it has to be remembered that the purchasing power of the £ was considerably higher then than it is now, but it is also true to say that the gap between the rich and the poor was very great. For more details on the subject of wages and prices see Chapter 34, page 194.

Sir William's younger brother, Henry, was also a character, and one for whom it is possible to have a great admiration. Like so many younger sons of great houses, Henry made the army his career, and he served in it continuously, most of the time abroad, until his death in 1840. He rose to the rank of Lieutenant Colonel and was given command of a regiment, but at this rank he stuck for many years during a period when the standing army was being seriously reduced in size, and chances of promotion were few.

But what made his service so praise-worthy and unusual was his care and solicitude for the welfare of his men. In this he was years ahead of his time and was regarded with suspicion by his superiors. At one point he incurred the displeasure of his Commander in Chief, the Duke of York, who commented on his "peculiar methods of discipline and eccentric system of command". He was the first officer to abolish corporal punishment in his regiment, and to set up an organisation by which his men could save money, and he is believed to have spent a considerable portion of his own private means to improve the welfare of his men's families.

But his methods triumphed in the end. Six years after the Duke of York's strictures he was complimented on the high state of discipline and efficiency obtaining in his regiment, a wonderful endorsement of the methods which had naturally endeared him to all his men. In 1837 he was promoted Major General, having been 20 years in command of his regiment.

The 7th and last baronet, Sir Henry, was born in 1811 and died leaving no heir in 1874. As a young man he was extremely good looking but was shy and withdrawn, spending much of his time sailing, to which he was addicted. His indulgent father bought him a 70 ton schooner, the *"Witch"*, and later Sir Henry bought two more boats, a 106 ton schooner, the *"Sybil"*, and a 200 ton steam yacht, the *"Firefly"*, and one or other of his boats was kept permanently in commission.

He was regarded as a confirmed bachelor, but at 35 surprised everyone by suddenly getting married. His wife was a keen yachtswoman and they spent at least three months each year cruising, visiting the Baltic, the Mediterranean, Madeira, and the Azores in turn. Alas they were unable to produce an heir, and when Henry died Nunwell passed to the son of a cousin, John Henry Oglander Glyn. He changed his name to John Henry Glyn Oglander in an attempt to continue the line, but sadly this did not work, as his only child was a girl.

A further attempt to preserve the name also failed, and in 1980 Nunwell House was sold out of the family, although Mrs. Oglander continued to live in the John Nash designed Coach House. But though the name may have gone, the spirit of the Oglanders lives on, and will continue to do so, for the record they established will never be forgotten in the Island, which was their home for so many centuries.

Effigy of Sir John Oglander's tomb in Brading church. Bought in France, he kept it at home until he died.

XXVIII — *Island Families: Dillington*

The most mysterious of all the Dillingtons, Sir Tristram, is said to be buried here in Newchurch. But is he?

"Anthony Dyllington wase ye fyrst of that familie, he came out of Somersetshire from a place called Dyllington."

So wrote Sir John Oglander, our principal source of information about this distinguished family. Anthony Dillington bought the manor of Knighton Gorges in 1563, and he and his descendants lived there for nearly 200 years, the last of the line being Mary Dillington, who died a spinster in 1749.

Sir John Oglander was well qualified to write about the Dillingtons, for Ann, the eldest daughter of Anthony Dillington, was his mother. She married Sir William Oglander, this being very much a love match, and one that did not particularly please the Oglander family, for Ann brought a very small dowry with her. Nevertheless, she and William were very happy together.

Her elder brother, Robert, inherited Knighton Gorges when his father died in 1584, but four years later he was in trouble with Sir George Carey, the self-styled Governor of the Isle of Wight. 1588 was the Spanish Armada year, and Sir George, who was a notorious autocrat, took very forceful action to improve the Island's defences, and also adopted the title of "Governor". Robert Dillington injudiciously opposed Sir George's high-handed attitude, and as a result was committed to prison, from which however he was later released, following a petition signed by most of the gentlemen of the Island.

Robert became Sir Robert in 1599 but died in 1608 without leaving any children. Sir John Oglander wrote the following glowing tribute to him:

> "If I may speak without partiality, I verily believe that the Island never bred so fine a gentleman as Sir Robert Dillington. He was as handsome and well-complexioned as you could wish. He was a good, not great, traveller and scholar; he had his Latin, French, Spanish and Italian tongues. He was very honest, stout, and valiant, but above all was his sweet, noble carriage, as full of conceits without offence, and very liberal so that all men loved his company, great lords and others."

As Sir Robert had no children, the manor of Knighton Gorges passed to his brother Tristram's son, another Robert, but according to Sir John Oglander this Robert was a very different sort of man to his uncle, being thrifty to the point of meanness.

> "His mother was a base woman, after whose base and miserable condition he much took, insomuch as his uncle, Sir Robert, could hardly endure him. After his uncle had left him the land, and marrying with a woman like himself, he grew so miserably base that, in one instance for all, when any came to his house with horses, he hath been often found in the manger rack taking away the hay."

His carefulness paid off, however, and he grew rich, acquiring several other Island manors. In 1623 he bought Mottistone, and also Westover and Budbridge. In 1628 he also bought himself a baronetcy, one of 40 which the all-powerful Duke of Buckingham gave away to his followers in lieu of money, with permission to sell them for what they would fetch. The going rate was between £150 and £200, and as can be imagined, Robert Dillington did not enhance his popularity with the gentlemen of the Island by suddenly becoming a baronet and climbing several places in the social scale, taking precedence over many of his acquaintances. Sir John Oglander's summing up of his character says it all —

> "Base, proud and miserable, he cares not for any but those by whom he may gain. In all his actions he hath relation to his own ends, doing a courtesy no farther than may stand with his own profit. One that would seem wise, yet a fool in all things — gain excepted."

When Sir Robert died he was succeeded by his grandson, another Robert, who became the second baronet. When this boy grew up he married Jane Freke, of Dorset, and they had a total of eleven children, the last one killing his mother when he was born in 1674. There is some mystery about the last resting place of Lady Jane Dillington, for both New-church and Mottistone churches claim to have her grave. According to the Newchurch memorial plaque she died on 9th February 1674, aged 35, and was buried there with five of her numerous children.

Another mysterious death in the Dillington family occurred in 1721 when the last male survivor, Sir Tristram Dillington, died at Knighton Gorges. There are several versions of how he came to meet his end. One is that his wife and four, or possibly five, children all died rather suddenly of fever, and that heart-broken, Sir Tristram committed suicide, either by

shooting or drowning himself in the lake. His butler is said to have covered up the suicide by burying the body in the orchard near the house, a skeleton having been found there many years later, but this skeleton could well have been of much earlier date, for in the 13th century the orchard was the private burying ground of the De Gorges family.

Perhaps this story of Sir Tristram's wife being buried with five of her children is confusing her with Lady Jane Dillington mentioned above, who died 47 years previously, with five of *her* children. Another version of the Sir Tristram story is that he was a bachelor and never had any children at all, and that he was buried normally in the Dillington mortuary chapel in All Saints Church, Newchurch, where there is a black marble grave slab bearing his name. In support of the suicide theory followed by burial in the orchard it is even claimed that his grave in the Dillington chapel is empty.

All these stories have their adherents, and the mystery accords well with the sinister reputation of Knighton Gorges, which ever since the murder of Thomas a'Becket in 1170 by its owner, Hugh de Morville and his accomplices, has left a record of evil and sadness, right up until its final demolition by its last, demented, owner, George Maurice Bisset.

Sir Tristram was the last male Dillington to own Knighton Gorges, and on his death the manor passed to his two sisters, Mary and Hannah. Hannah died intestate in 1739 and Mary, unmarried, died ten years later in 1749, leaving the estate jointly to her nephew, Maurice Bocland and her niece, Jane, wife of John Eyre.

And here is another intriguing little mystery — though strictly speaking nothing to do with the Dillingtons, but rather with Mrs. Eyre, one of the two joint owners mentioned above. It has been suggested that Charlotte Bronte was familiar with Knighton Gorges and used it as a model for the country house "Thornfield" in one of her novels. The name of the novel? *"Jane Eyre".*

Above left. Tomb of Lady Dillington in Mottistone church, wife of Sir Robert, who died in 1674. But is she really buried here?

Above. *This memorial plaque in All Saints church, Newchurch, says Lady Dillington is buried here, along with five of her eleven children. She was only 34 when she died.*

XXIX — *Island Families: Urry*

Thorley old churchyard, where Thomas Urry, who died in 1631, lies buried.

Urry is a good old Island name. It is mentioned as far back as 1255, when the death of one Ivo Urry was being investigated, and there have been Urrys in the Island ever since. In the current Telephone Directory there are 20 listed — as compared with 10 Leighs, 4 Worsleys, 2 Oglanders, and no Dillingtons.

In the early years of the 14th century, although well established, the family suffered a temporary eclipse when Robert Urry of Little Budbridge killed Nicholas de Bosco and was imprisoned in Winchester, his lands being forfeit. He was released three years later and from then on the family seemed to prosper and keep out of trouble. Robert seems to have been a favourite family name, and there is also a record of the daughter of a Robert, called Roberta, marrying Reginald Oglander of Nunwell in the 14th century. Another favourite, and delightful female name was Petronilla, for Robert Urry of Little Budbridge married a girl of this name, and a Petronilla Urry is recorded at East Standen in 1375.

The Urry family were also established in the West Wight from an early age, there being a record in the 14th century of a property known as *"Urry's Place"* in the manor of Alvington near Carisbrooke. Also in Carisbrooke one of the many rabbit warrens in the Island was known as *"Urry's Grove"*, and at one time Gatcombe Mill was called *"Urry's Mill"*. Another unusual and little known record of the family name occurs in the ruined columbarium or dovecote in the grounds of Shalcombe manor. Shalcombe was a grange of the Abbey of Quarr, and the monks were great pigeon breeders. After the columbarium had falllen into disrepair it was obviously used as a children's playroom and the chalk walls inside contain a variety of carved graffiti, one of the clearest and boldest being the one word "URRY".

There were several branches of the family living in this part of the Island in the 16th and 17th centuries — John Urry at Shalfleet, David at Afton Manor, Thomas at Thorley, a Captain John at Yarmouth, and a Thomas Urry who built Sheat Manor at Gatcombe.

The latter married a kinswoman of Sir William Oglander of Nunwell, Jane Day, and built Sheat for her as their marital home. Behind the huge open fireplace in what is now the dining room he incorporated a priest's hole (or could it have been a smuggler's hide?) approached through the false back of a cupbord in the bedroom above. There is a story attached to this house that this is where the Roman Catholics of the day, who were being persecuted, met secretly to celebrte Mass, and this story is told in the Chapter on Sheat Manor in *"The Manor Houses of the Isle of Wight"*. ·

There is a record of a "young" Thomas Urry of Gatcombe who in 1627 brought the smallpox down from London, as a result of which 2,000 people in the Island caught it and many hundreds died. Outbreaks of this sort, often simply referred to as "the plague", were frequent in cities on the mainland, but the isolation of the Island normally protected its inhabitants from such visitations.

"Old" Thomas Urry of Thorley died on Christmas Day 1631, and a tablet erected to his memory in the church at Thorley contained the following verse —

"The poore man's comfort, and ye stranger's friend,
A man of godlie life — then judge his end.
This stone can tell what care he had to goe
Unto his mother earth, and father too.
His aged years almost were twelve times seven,
He's called to keep his Christmas nowe in heaven."

Not a bad epitaph, to be described as "the poor man's comfort and the stranger's friend", one that any man could be proud of. He was buried on 3rd January in the middle of Thorley Church, and Sir John Oglander says there was a great funeral with Sir William Lisle, Sir Robert Dillington, and Sir John Leigh present, amongst many others. This was, of course, the old church at Thorley, only a small portion of which still remains, alongside the manor house of which it was originally the private chapel.

Three months later Sir John Oglander, in his capacity as Deputy Lieutenant of the Isle of Wight, had occasion to visit Yarmouth Castle and he took the opportunity of staying the night at Thorley, together with the various friends who went with him. From the following account, which he wrote, it is apparent that it was quite possible to combine business with pleasure in those days — and also that hospitality was generous —

"On Wednesday 14th March, I having occasion to go to Yarmouth . . . and I willing to carry my wife and daughters with me as never having seen that town, a great many of my good friends would needs accompany us thither, to wit: Sir Robert Dillington, Mr. Barnaby Leigh and his wife, Sir John leigh and his lady, Mr. Worsley and his wife, Mr. Edward Leigh and his wife, with many more. I bespoke an Ordinary at Yarmouth, where we had the Mayor, and were exceeding merry so that many had much ado to go to Thorley that night, where we lay, and at Captain Urry's, my cousin, we were kindly entertained. I caused Billinghurst, the Steward of Yarmouth, to be there, where we met Sir Robert Dillington, Mr. Barnaby Leigh, Sir John Leigh, Mr. Edward Leigh and others, where the wine came in so fast and they so merrily disposed that Sir Robert and some others, with the noise of the ordinance and fume of the wine, lost all their senses. We carried a musician with us and danced most part of the night at Thorley, insomuch as the next day many could not regain their lost senses, but to conclude we had a merry journey of it."

It is interesting to note that Sir John's wife and daughters had never previously been to Yarmouth, a matter of only 17 miles or so from Nunwell, but an indication of how limited travelling was in those days when there were very few decent roads.

Noteworthy too are the "good friends" that Sir John Oglander took with him. Sir Robert Dillington it was who had purchased a baronetcy three years before and about whom Sir John wrote rather scathingly in his Memoirs, (see Chapter 28, page 171). Barnaby Leigh was the owner of Northcourt and the son of Sir John Leigh who had died in 1630 (see the Leigh family tree on page 161). Barnaby's wife was the third of his three and had been born Margaret Culliford, a name still well known in the Isle

Captain John Urry of Yarmouth, who was noted for his hospitality.

of Wight. Sir John Leigh was Barnaby's son by his first wife, Elizabeth Bamfield, and Edward Leigh was Barnaby's elder brother, who lived in Newport. The Mr. Worsley mentioned was probably John Worsley of Gatcombe (see Worsley family tree on pages 155 and 156), and for the record, the Mayor of Yarmouth in the Spring of 1632 was William Barker.

The "Ordinary" referred to was a meal for a party of people at an inn, and the mention of "the noise of the ordinance" refers to the custom of accompanying the drinking of toasts by firing off blank cartridges.

In November 1647 Captain John Urry and his wife, Alice, had the honour of entertaining King Charles I to dinner at Thorley. The King had only recently arrived in the Island, where he expected to find sanctuary, and during his first week or so was allowed freedom to travel and visit his friends. When he visited Yarmouth the town hosted his followers, but the King himself dined with the Urrys.

A hundred and twenty years later another Captain John Urry was living in Yarmouth at a house which at that time was called the Refuge (see Chapter 16, page 107), but later became "The Towers". He retired from the Royal navy to live in Yarmouth — as so many other senior Naval officers have subsequently done — and his house overlooked the Solent so he was never out of touch with the sea. Whenever a naval ship anchored in the Roads he would send off his four-oared gig with its crew in uniform to invite the Skipper to dine with him, and his hospitality became well known throughout the Navy; so well known in fact that Captains of ships went out of their way to call on him, and the departure of ships from Yarmouth was frequently delayed. This happened so often that the Commander-in-Chief, Portsmouth, finally had to complain and ask him to desist.

Captain John Urry had the wherewithal to enable him to live in almost regal state at the Refuge, some of his money deriving from the Alum Bay sand works which he owned, for at this time, and up to 1851, the fine sand found in Alum Bay was in great demand for the manufacture of glass and porcelain. Captain John was also something of a character, and had imitation gun ports painted on the sea-facing wall of his garden to frighten off would-be invaders.

His life in Yarmouth was not without a whiff of scandal, for there was a serious disagreement at one time with the Churchwardens over the burial of a baby in the Urry vault. The Churchwardens refused to have the vault opened, presumably because the baby was illegitimate, and Captain Urry was said never to have gone to church again. The mystery also involved his daughter Mary, his father, who was Captain of the Governor's yacht, and a Miss Elizabeth Morgan, a lady who is still remembered since she was later buried in Yarmouth church, reputedly wearing a valuable string of pearls and in the same grave as Captain Urry's father! All the ingredients here of a first class scandal, but one that was hushed up and quietly forgotten, and one that should not be allowed to detract from the value and prestige of this fine old Island family. Life would be very dull if there were no skeletons in cupboards.

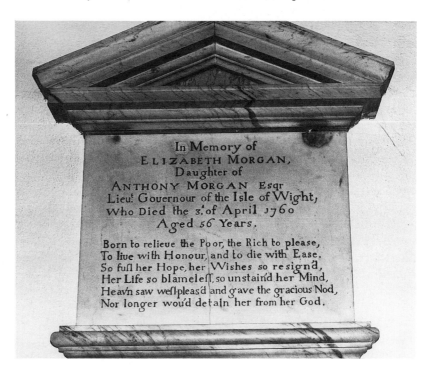

Tablet in Yarmouth church to Elizabeth Morgan, who was a friend of the Urrys.

XXX — *Island Families: Lisle*

Wootton Creek, one of the most delightful yacht anchorages in the Isle of Wight. The wooded west bank, seen here, was once the home of the Lisles.

At the Norman Conquest the Isle of Wight was given to Willam Fitz-Osbern, the Conqueror's cousin, as his reward for successfully planning the invasion. FitzOsbern himself had to reward his own followers, and there were three men in particular who received generous gifts of lands in the Island. These were William FitzStur, William FitzAzor and his brother Gozelin FitzAzor, the appellation *"Fitz"* meaning "the son of".

It was probably the latter family, the FitzAzors, who being pleased with their new Island possessions, decided to settle down here and, to identify themselves with their new home, changed their name. It was common practice at that time to be known as either "the son of" your father, or after the place where you lived, and after a comparatively short time the Fitz-Azors were proudly using the name *"de Insula"* which is Latin for "of the Island". Latin was the language of the Church and the legal profession at the time, though the Normans spoke French, the French version of *"de Insula"* being *"de L'Isle"*. From this it is a very short step to the English name *Lisle*. In the middle ages, when spelling did not seem to matter, this name was frequently spelt "Lislie" or even "Lesley".

By the middle of the 12th century the de Insulas were popping up all over the Island, not only as landowners, but also in the Church. A Geoffrey de Insula was Vicar of Shanklin c. 1150, and a little later Jocelyn

178

de Insula was recorded as Vicar of Newchurch. A John de Insula was Rector of Shalfleet in 1275 and of Arreton in 1283. There were so many de Insulas about that they began to be identified more explicitly by the name of the village in which they lived, as for example William de Insula de Sorewell (Shorwell) and John de Insula de Gatcombe.

Their principal seat was from early times at Wootton, where they owned all the land on the west bank of the Creek, but they were soon established at West Court, Shorwell, and at Thorley, Gatcombe, Whitwell and Calbourne. By the end of the 14th century their empire also included Shanklin, Bonchurch, Blackpan, Briddlesford, Mottistone, the Undercliff, Bathingbourne, Roud, and several other manors.

After the Isle of Wight had been sold to the Crown by Isabella de Fortibus in 1293 the King appointed a Warden, or Governor, of the Island, and in 1302 Sir John de Insula de Bosco, who lived at Wootton, achieved this position. He held this for five years but was then replaced by his brother, Nicholas. Edward II, who came to the throne in 1307, appointed his favourite courtier, Piers Gaveston, as Warden of the Island, and Nicholas de Insula de Bosco was ordered to surrender the Island to him. But there was such an outcry about this appointment that Gaveston never took over and Nicholas continued as Warden. However, in 1308 Nicholas was killed in a private quarrel with Robert Urry of Little Budbridge (see Chapter 29, page 173), and Sir John de Insula was re-appointed.

In 1339, when invasion scares in the Isle of Wight were at their height, Bartholomew de Insula was one of the wealthy landowners who evacuated themselves and their families to the mainland for safety, and as he was the man in charge of the beacon warning system in the Island he was severely reprimanded by the King. Later he was obviously forgiven for in 1341 he was appointed as one of three Wardens, and his appointment was confirmed two years later.

Another de Insula, Thomas, the Vicar of Shanklin, was also in a little trouble in 1340 when the French actually mounted an armed raid on the Island. In view of the emergency an attempt had been made by the Civil Power to mobilise the Clergy against the French, and this brought about a stern rebuke from the Bishop of Winchester, who said that he would decide if and when the Clergy were to be involved. Thomas de Insula was suspected of having organised a protest, and having persuaded his fellow clerics not to obey the call to arms.

During this turbulent period of the Island's history when we were almost continuously at war with France, Edward III decided it was time to abolish French as the official language of this country, and establish English in its place. And it was at about this same time that the names de Insula and de L'Isle ceased to be used, being replaced by the English version, Lisle.

In the early years of the 16th century Sir John Lisle of Wootton was one of the biggest landowners in the Isle of Wight, and was anxious that when he died his estates and the name of Lisle should be preserved. But alas, he had no son, only one daughter. He married her to Sir Roger Kingston,

who was a Courtier, but they also were unable to produce a male heir, and had but one daughter.

Both Sir Roger and his wife died before Sir John Lisle, and the latter then conceived the idea of marrying off his grand-daughter, Marie, to a distant relative, one Thomas Lisle, thus cleverly preserving the name, and incidentally, giving Thomas the opportunity of becoming an extremely rich man, for Marie was heir to the Kingston as well as the Lisle wealth. But not only had the male genes deserted the Lisle family, but the female too, for Thomas and Marie had no children at all. Sir John Oglander commented that Marie was "fair, but weak and silly", but it seems unkind to put all the blame on to her.

Nevertheless, the Lisle estates were ultimately split up, Wootton going to Thomas Lisle's brother, Lancelot. West Court passed to the family of Dennis, a Sir Edward Dennis becoming Deputy Lieutenant of the Island together with Sir John Oglander.

The great grandson of Lancelot Lisle was Sir William Lisle, who was a great friend of Sir John Oglander, and who, incidentally, is mentioned by him as being at the funeral of Thomas Urry of Thorley in January 1632. (See Chapter 29, page 175). Sir William was godfather to Sir John Oglander's eldest son, George, who died tragically of smallpox in France in 1632, and himself had two children who married in that same year, 1632.

His eldest son, John, who was the godson of Sir John Oglander, was married in February 1632 to Elizabeth, the daughter of Sir Henry Hobart,

Lord Chief Justice of the Common Pleas. She brought him a dowry of £4,000, the largest ever known in the Isle of Wight at that time, and Sir John commented wryly that perhaps it was some compensation for the fact that she was not very beautiful to look at. Almost exactly a year later she died in giving birth to a son. Sir William Lisle's other child was a daughter, Bridget, and Sir John has this to say about her —

> "On 24th September 1632 Mistress Bridget Lisle, daughter to Sir William, a rude girl and ill brought up, her parents letting her have her way in all things, ran away with one Mr. Jennings, an ironmonger's second son. She was a handsome gentlewoman, aged 20 years."

John Lisle, Sir William's eldest son, was a curious character who has gone down to posterity bearing the label "The Regicide", for he was a staunch Parliamentarian during the Civil War, and was involved in the organisation of Charles I's trial and execution. According to Sir John Oglander, he was not a very dutiful son, and treated his father extremely badly —

> "Sir William died privately at Wootton in a nasty chamber (being all his son would allow him for his men, horses, dogs, provisions and for the cooking of them). He would suffer no man to come to him during his sickness — no, not his wife and children — but would bid them be gone since their company would kill him. Neither did I hear of any divine with him to give him spiritual physic, nor scarce any physician for corporal.
>
> Sir William was, while he enjoyed his estate, a very good housekeeper, indeed one of the best in our Island, but after a homely, slovenly way because there were differences between him and his wife, so that she looked not to anything and he looked to all things himself. But, after that way, he was very free and bountiful, and his cellar always full of good beer. As his entertainment, so was his person slovenly; you would take him for a farmer rather than a knight. At last his son got all his estate from him and confined him to £150 and one chamber. Truly I may say he was a good neighbour for, if he had anything worth the sending, I should be sure to have part."

Poor Sir William! He seems to have had a lonely and uncomfortable end.

Sir John Lisle married again, his second wife being Alice, the daughter of Sir White Beckenshaw. At the Restoration in 1660 he thought it prudent to leave the country in view of his active participation in the execution of Charles I, and he fled to Lausanne. But fate caught up with him, in the person of Sir James FitzEdmond Cotter, a fanatical Irishman and ardent Royalist, who sought him out and murdered him.

His widow, Dame Alice Lisle, lived on for another 25 years and ran foul of authority during the Monmouth rebellion of 1685. She was arrested and accused of harbouring two of Monmouth's supporters, and had the misfortune to be arraigned before Judge Jeffreys at the so-called *"Bloody Assizes"*. He condemned her to be burnt at the stake, but in view of her age — she was 72 — the form of execution was commuted, and she was beheaded in Winchester later that year.

So ended the story of the man who tried so hard to get rid of his King. But there is a corollary which is of interest. Sir John Lisle had a younger brother, William, who worked equally hard to rescue the King from Carisbrooke Castle, and was involved in the two escape attempts in March and May 1648. Edward Worsley was the prime mover in these attempts, and when they failed he had to go into hiding. He took shelter in the woods near Wootton Creek and for several days William Lisle looked after him there and ultimately found him a boat to take him to the Continent.

Life in the Lisle household at this time can only be imagined, with Sir William dying in squalor, his heir, Sir John, a fanatical parliamentarian, and his son, William, actively and secretly helping Edward Worsley to escape.

At the Restoration, when Sir John fled to Switzerland, he was specifically excluded from the Act of Oblivion which pardoned most of the late King's enemies. All his estates in the Island, including Wootton, Briddlesford, Woodhouse in Whippingham, and Chillerton were confiscated by Charles II, who granted most of them to his brother, the Duke of York. The Duke disposed of this property, but retained for his own use part of the manor house of Wootton.

In December 1661 the King granted William Lisle the manor of Appleford and two others on the mainland as a reward for his loyalty to the late King. In 1663 William was appointed Recorder of Newport, and was knighted in 1665. But he died the same year of fever, leaving a posthumous son, born in 1666, and christened, significantly, Edward.

The Lisle "empire" in the Isle of Wight had lasted for 500 years, and in extent had even rivalled that of the Worsleys, but like all the works of man it ultimately crumbled away, leaving only the barest record of those who had built it up, men and women who had been proud to identify themselves with this beautiful part of the kingdom by calling themselves "Lisle".

West Court, Shorwell, part of which was built in 1519 by Sir John Lisle.

XXXI — *Island Families: Cheke*

Mottistone Manor, a beautiful and gracious Island manor house, was built by the Chekes, the eastern part, on the right of the picture, dating back to the 15th century.

Whippingham is one of the more curious places in the Isle of Wight. Its name — possibly a Jutish *"-ingham"* name — suggests that it was at one time the home, or the river meadow, belonging to Whippa's people, and its position on the east bank of the Medina River supports this explanation. It covers a large and hilly area, and the medieval parish of Whippingham was huge, including Wootton and extending southwards as far as Coppins Bridge in Newport. But it is not a typical medieval village, with a manor house, church, inn, and thatched cottages clustered round a village green. Whippingham is well spread out, and though it certainly has a church, and a very famous one too, traces of the original settlement, or of a medieval village, are bewilderingly absent.

One of the first families to be recorded as living in Whippingham were the Chekes, or as they were apparently first called, *Chekes-on-the-hill*, later abbreviated to *Chekehill*, and then *Cheke*. They were well established there in the first half of the 13th century, and were prospering and extending to other parts of the Island. At the beginning of the 14th century Thomas Cheke bought the manor of Mottistone from the Clamorgans, and the family lived there for the next 300 years, being responsible for building the present glorious house. Another branch of the family was established at about this time at Merston Manor.

It was Robert Cheke, who died in 1500, who first re-built the old Saxon manor house of Mottistone, the present east wing containing much of his original work, but it was his grandson, Sir Thomas Cheke, who completed the house by building the great west wing, the date of completion being 1569. Mottistone is thus not only one of the most beautiful, but one of the oldest houses in the Isle of Wight.

Robert Cheke's younger son, feeling that there was no future for him in the Island since his elder brother would succeed his father in due course, left home and emigrated to the mainland. He settled in Cambridge, married, and fathered Sir John Cheke, who turned out to be the most famous of all the Cheke family. John Cheke was well known as a scholar and professor of Greek at Cambridge. He was highly thought of by Henry VIII, and became tutor to Prince Edward, later King Edward VI. He was appointed Secretary of State, was knighted, and his career seemed to be "set fair", but as a Protestant he later fell foul of Queen Mary Tudor. He was involved in the attempt to put Lady Jane Grey on the throne, and when this plot failed he lost all.

After a year in prison he was exiled, but never managed to escape from the clutches of the Government for he was brought back to England and imprisoned in the Tower. Here he was subjected to a long and harrowing ordeal of brain-washing which ultimately destroyed him, and he died a broken man, though right at the end he summoned up enough strength of spirit to denounce Roman Catholicism.

Sir Thomas Cheke, who completed the building of Mottistone, though living a quieter life than Sir John, also had his problems. One of his daughters upset him by making a runaway and unfortunate marriage to Robert Goter, innkeeper at the Bugle in Newport High Street, and his only son, Thomas, was also a disappointment to him. Sir John Oglander calls the latter the "lewd son of a discreet father" and describes him as an "idle, cock-witted fellow, taking no good course after his father's death". He seemed quite unable to manage the family estate, and in 1623 sold Mottistone to Robert Dillington.

Sir Thomas Cheke's own life was honourable and successful. He was a local Justice of the Peace, and became Recorder of Southampton. His first wife died and he married again, but his death was, to say the least, unpleasant. Sir John Oglander describes it as follows —

> "He was much troubled with the stone in the bladder and was cut for it, but marrying a second wife and being too busy with her, he caused the rupture of his old sore, which killed him."

Contemporary with Thomas Cheke of Mottistone was Edward Cheke of Merston, who married as his second wife Eleanor, the eldest sister of Sir John Oglander. Sir John records that the present Merston manor house was built by Edward Cheke, and that he himself gave Edward most of the timber for it. Some of the enormous oak beams used in the construction of the house are still in good condition today, 350 years later.

Right. Merston Manor, originally built in 1615 by Edward Cheke, but partly re-built in brick later.

Edward Cheke died at the age of 80 in October 1648, a few days before Sir William Lisle. (See Chapter 30, page 181). Both of these gentlemen were friends of Sir John Oglander, and he could not resist writing about, and comparing, the nature of their last days on earth. For whereas Sir William Lisle died in unhappy circumstances, Edward Cheke died surrounded by his friends and sympathisers. But in a sense they both marked the end of their respective families in the Isle of Wight. Sir John, who always refers to Edward Cheke as his "brother", has as usual an interesting comment to make —

"My brother was buried at 2 in the aftrnoon with a great assembly of the gentry and all the town (Newport), and gloves and ribbons given to all. Sir William's son John caused his father to be buried privately in the evening, and I hear not of any gentlemen that were invited. I hope Sir William's soul (as I am confident my brother's is) is in Heaven, whither myself, being the next in course, hope shortly to follow them."

However, the name of Cheke did not completely die out in the Isle of Wight, though nowadays it is usually spelt Cheek. The name is still well known, and will remain so, as a perpetual reminder of one of the oldest and most important of Island families.

XXXII — *Island Families: Seely*

Charles Seely came to live in the Isle of Wight in 1861, and from then on he and his descendants exercised an ever increasing influence on Island affairs. They proved to have a greater impact on life here than any other family in modern times, and the Island has good reason to be grateful to them.

Brook House, first home of the Seelys in the Isle of Wight.

The Seelys originated in Lincolnshire where at one time they were flour millers. By the middle of the 19th century they were large landowners in that county and in neighbouring Nottinghamshire, where their wealth was based on the rich seams of coal found underneath their land.

Charles Seely was not only rich, he was also politically active and was for many years a Member of Parliament, representing the City of Lincoln. In the Island he bought Brook House as his retirement home, and gradually acquired more and more land until he and his family were the biggest landowners in the Isle of Wight. He continued his political activities until he was 81, being the oldest member of the House of Commons, and in 1864 he invited to England, and to Brook House, the popular Italian hero, Garibaldi, an act which is said to have displeased Queen Victoria. The two men planted an oak tree outside Brook House to commemorate the visit, and styled it "The Tree of Liberty", and after leaving Brook, Garibaldi went on to stay with Tennyson at Farringford, where he planted a similar tree.

In his 25 years in the Isle of Wight Charles Seely became a well known and respected figure, spending much of his time riding round his estates, and when he died in 1887 at the age of 84 it must have seemed that an era was ending. But in truth this was really only the beginning, for his son, Charles, who followed him, was a worthy successor, enhancing the family prestige, and becoming the Island's greatest benefactor.

Sir Charles — for he became a knight and a baronet — will always be remembered in the Isle of Wight for his energy and initiative in two directions, the first of which was organisation of the Lifeboat service. The south coast of the Island had acquired, over the centuries, a sinister reputation for the number of ships it had wrecked, particularly along the stretch from Brook through Atherfield Bay to Blackgang, and the establishment of lifeboats at Brook and Brighstone, which was largely the work of Sir Charles Seely, was instrumental in saving hundreds of lives.

The other Island organisation attributable to Sir Charles is the County Library Service, which was set up as a direct result of his drive and enthusiasm and financial help. Starting in a small way by establishing a Reading Room in the village of Brook, he ultimately persuaded the County Council to build in Newport a combined Library and centre for technical education. This prospered and grew, and from this beginning developed the Islandwide Library service that bears his name, and also the Isle of Wight College of Arts and Technology. A benefaction indeed.

Seely House in Newport, the original home of the County Library Service, set up by Sir Charles Seely.

Sir Charles Seely continued the political tradition begun by his father, and was a Liberal member of Parliament from 1865 to 1869, and he also maintained his links with Nottinghamshire through the Seely family home, Sherwood Lodge. When he died his son, Charles, became the second baronet and continued to live at Sherwood Lodge, and in the Island at Gatcombe House. During the first World War the second baronet's eldest son, Charles Grant Seely, was killed as a young man at Gaza, and a beautiful monument was erected to him in Gatcombe Church. The second son, Hugh Seely, inherited the baronetcy, and later became Lord Sherwood.

The first Sir Charles Seely had two other sons, his second son, Frank, living in the Island at another large house built by his father, Brook Hill House. This house later became the home of J. B. Priestley, who had for 25 years owned Billingham Manor, near Kingston. But it was the third son, Jack, that became the most celebrated of the Seelys and a great Island character.

Jack Seely was born and lived as a boy in Nottinghamshire but spent many of his school holidays in the Island, where he acquired a love of the sea and the open air life. He was never happier than when riding or sailing in the Island, and at the early age of 17 he obtained a place in the Brook Lifeboat, a place he retained for many years in spite of an extremely busy career in the Army and in politics. The Lifeboat was proud and honoured

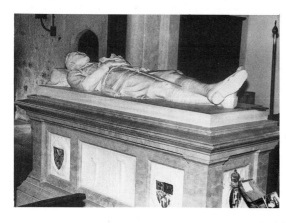

Fine memorial in Gatcombe church to young Charles Grant Seely, killed in the first World War.

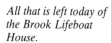

All that is left today of the Brook Lifeboat House.

to have him as a crew member, for his courage and leadership were out-standing, and for some years he was Coxswain of the boat.

His army career was equally meritorious. He achieved the rank of Major-General and on the way won a D.S.O. In the first World War he commanded a Canadian Cavalry Brigade with great dash, and he and his horse, 'Warrior', became a legend. He was both wounded and gassed, and was mentioned in Despatches five times.

In the political field he was originally a Unionist M.P. but became increasingly critical of the Conservative Government's military policy. In 1904, together with his great friend Winston Churchill and other critics, he crossed the floor of the House and joined the Opposition. In the 1906 election he fought as a Liberal and won, and two years later he was Under Secretary of State for the Colonies. In 1912 he became Secretary of State for War, and helped to prepare the country for the approaching conflict. In 1919 he resumed his political career as Secretary of State for Air, and in 1923 fought his last election, winning the Isle of Wight once more for the Liberals.

General Jack's first wife died in 1913, and in 1917 he married the widow of his former private secretary, Captain George Nicholson, who had been tragically killed in the war, while serving in the Royal Flying Corps. He continued to live at Brook House until 1926, when his friend, Sir Edward Lutyens, encouraged him to restore Mottistone manor house, the east wing of which had remained buried up to the eaves since a landslide in 1706. The restoration was carried out by his eldest son, John, who was finding fame as an architect, and it was a huge success.

In 1918 General Jack was appointed Lord Lieutenant of Hampshire and the Isle of Wight, a position he held for almost 30 years, and he continued to play a leading part in both local and national affairs. He also found time, in spite of his very busy public life, to write several books — *"Launch"*, *"Fear and Be Slain"*, and *My Horse Warrior* amongst them. In 1933 he became the first Lord Mottistone, an honour which was a fitting reward for his years of energetic and successful service to his country. When he died his son John became the second Lord Mottistone and continued the tradition of service started by his father and grandfather.

General Jack's stepson, Sir John Nicholson, was also out of the same mould and for many years was Lord Lieutenant of the Isle of Wight, retiring only when he reached the age of 75. He was succeeded by his younger brother, David, the 4th and present Lord Mottistone.

Since Charles Seely first came to the Isle of Wight in 1861 the family have established a record of service which is unsurpassed by any other family in the Island's long history; it is a record of which they can feel justly proud, and all Islanders can feel grateful. Over the porch at Mottistone is a Latin inscription written by Lord Birkenhead when the restoration was complete. In it he compares John Seely, the architect responsible, with John Cheke, the most illustrious member of the family who built the house in the 15th century. This is an apt comparison, and one that will keep the memory of both families alive for many future generations.

XXXIII — *The Island Economy*

The moonscape appearance of an old disused chalk pit. There are many such pits in the Island, a legacy of the days when liming the land was found to be essential.

The successive waves of invaders who have come to this country and have made it their home have each brought their own life style and culture, and each has contributed something to what we now call the English way of life. The result is unique, is far from static, and will continue to change as it is continually being influenced by economic and technological developments, the growth of population, and even the changing weather pattern.

In the Isle of Wight, in Roman times, the population numbered only a few hundred, and though in the 400 years of the Occupation a few of the inhabitants may have achieved parity with the Romans, the majority were little better than slaves. The North German and Scandinavian tribes that followed the Romans created the nucleus of the English race, and by the time of the Norman Conquest the Island had a population of just over 1000. The Normans, who were great colonisers and administrators, in due course made their peace with the Islanders and were absorbed and integrated into their community. They brought peace with them, and had harsh but just laws, so that the country prospered.

Gradually the English became a nation in their own right, their language superseded French as the official language of the country, and under the Norman feudal system, which demanded that every man should

190

give service in exchange for his right to live, the nation went from strength to strength. In an agricultural community such as the Isle of Wight life for the majority was harsh and primitive, the lord of the manor ruling his domain like a prince, and in his manorial court dispensing justice to all those who were bound to him. The system worked tolerably well, quaint though it may seem to us today. A typical example of a service contract between a lord and a villein is the following, which comes from the year 1278 —

> Adam Underwood held of his lord one yard of land (a yard varied from 15 to 40 acres) paying for the same 7 bushels of oats yearly and a hen, and agreeing to work for the lord from the feast of St. Michael the Archangel (September 29th) to Lammas (August 1st) every other day except Saturday, mowing as long as that time should last, for which he was to have as much grass as he could carry away with his scythe, and at the end of the hay harvest he and his fellow mowers were to have the lord's best mutton, except one, or 16/- (80p) in money; with the best cheese, saving one, or 6d (2½p) in money; and the cheese vat wherein the said cheese was made full of salt."

The importance of salt is emphasised by the above, for salt provided the only means known of preserving meat. Later the manor house would probably have an ice house — a building, possibly underground, in which blocks of ice were stored in winter for use later in the year — but the use of ice was not possible for the peasant.

Gradually, over the years, it began to be realised that the feudal system was cumbersome and inefficient, service was not given willingly, and increasingly lords of manors found it more satisfactory to commute the service to which they were entitled, and for which they paid in kind, to a straight cash transaction. In this way the villein and the serf (who was literally a slave with no rights of his own) slowly achieved emancipation and became paid labourers.

Pay was poor, and living conditions continued to be primitive in the extreme, the gap between the rich and the poor being tremendous and apparently unbridgeable. Principal crops grown were wheat, barley and oats, the latter on the poorer clay soils. Beans, peas, and turnips were also cultivated, and later on potatoes, though for some time potatoes were expensive and a luxury only eaten by the gentry. Sheep were reared on the Downs, the quality of Isle of Wight sheep becoming well known. By the 18th century there were estimated to be over 40,000 in the Island, and there is a record that in 1793 a total of 5,000 lambs were sold to London butchers.

Manufacturing industries included stone, the quarries of Binstead and Bembridge being particularly well-known, though they were largely worked out by the 16th century. There were many small brickworks, clay being plentiful, and though none of these has survived, their sites may still be traced in such places as Hamstead, Newtown, Werrar, and Rookley, a recent survey listing about 60. Chalk has been dug in the Island from a very early age, and sand for glass-making became popular in the 18th century.

The principal source of this sand was Alum Bay in the West Wight, but the business collapsed dramatically in 1851, when a superior French sand was introduced to the Great Exhibition in Hyde Park.

The monks of Quarr Abbey established a grange at Haseley, and here they manufactured woollen cloth for their habits, introducing into the Island the strengthening process of fulling. Another process introduced by the monks was the tanning of hides and skins to produce leather. In the 19th century Isle of Wight lace became temporarily famous when it was admired and used by Queen Victoria. Nunn's Lace Factory, employing 700 people, was established in Newport at Broadlands, the building later having been converted to offices and housing the Island branch of the Department of Health and Social Security.

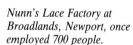

The Sand House at Yarmouth, now a thriving boatyard, but originally a storehouse for Alum Bay sand.

Nunn's Lace Factory at Broadlands, Newport, once employed 700 people.

As mentioned above salt was of great importance as a preservative and extensive salterns, where sea water was evaporated and boiled, were laid down at Newtown and in Wootton Creek, the latter being owned by Quarr Abbey. The monks of Quarr were also energetic fish farmers and breeders of pigeons for their table, oysters being cultivated at Fishbourne and in the Medina River at Claybrook, where the Romans had also farmed oysters a thousand years previously. (See page 104). Traces of the dovecotes, or columbaria, operated by Quarr can still be found on the sites of their granges, as for example at Arreton and Shalcombe. With regard to fishing, this has, of course, always been an important part of the Island economy from the very earliest days, and from the 18th century its concomitant smuggling became of equal, and much more spectacular, importance. (See Chapter 38, page 217).

For centuries the economy of the Isle of Wight developed along traditional and conventional lines until that day in the summer of 1831 when the Duchess of Kent brought her 12 year old daughter, Victoria, to spend a holiday at Norris Castle. This holiday was the beginning of the biggest revolution the Island had ever experienced, for when the young Victoria became Queen she came to live here, and where Victoria went the world followed. Within 50 years the population of the Island leapt from 35,000 to 74,000, and within the next 100 years it doubled again. Keeping pace with this huge increase in population was the number of visitors, who discovered — like Victoria — that the Isle of Wight has much to offer in the way of peace and tranquility.

After centuries of invasions and intended invasions from the continent of Europe, the 19th and 20th centuries have seen the biggest annual invasion of all — from England — and the Island economy has changed, inevitably and irrevocably. For better or for worse, for richer, for poorer, the Isle of Wight is now wedded to Tourism, and this is a marriage that must be made successful, for there is no divorce.

Tourist beaches are not all crowded and noisy. This is Monks Bay, Bonchurch, a delightfully restful spot.

193

XXXIV — *Wages and Prices*

After the harvest. A typical Island scene.

Even the most superficial study of the relationship between wages and prices over the centuries indicates the deficiencies and inequalities of a system under which the price of essential commodities, such as food, can fluctuate wildly while wages do not. Under such a system the poor inevitably suffer more than the rich, and to alleviate hardship in the severest cases it has been found necessary to apply palliatives in the form of subsidies. Unfortunately, in spite of progress in many technological ways during the last 2,000 years, society has not found it possible to develop a system which will ensure an equitable distribution of food, and we are faced with the baffling situation in which there are "mountains" of butter, grain, and other essentials, while three quarters of the world is starving.

Some statistics do exist for the Isle of Wight showing the relationship between wages and the price of food and other commodities, though these are not very complete. It is, of course, necessary to consider wages and prices together, on account of the continual reduction in the value of money, which makes a true comparison difficult, and even so all figures quoted should be accepted with caution.

The principal commodity affecting the lives of the poor was for many centuries wheat, for wheat bread was the main ingredient of the Island diet. In the 13th century the average price of wheat was a shade under 6/- (30p) per quarter of 28 lbs. and at this time an agricultural labourer was paid, on average, 1/- (5p) per week. The average price of wheat did not change significantly for about 300 years until the reign of Henry VIII, but it fluctuated wildly, the lowest price recorded being 2/10½d (14.4p) in the year 1287 when there was a glut, and the highest 16/- (80p) a quarter when a series of poor harvests led to a condition officially described as famine.

During the 13th, 14th, and 15th centuries wages gradually increased and by the beginning of the 16th century the labourer's pay had doubled to 2/- (10p) per week. As a matter of general interest, a woman was usually paid at half the rate of a man, and a boy at approximately a quarter the rate. That is to say, in the 13th century a woman would be paid 6d (2½p) per week, and a boy 3d (1¼p) per week. In the 14th century some interesting additional figures are given for military personnel, namely, an archer was paid 1/6 (7½p) per week, a man-at-arms 6/- (30p) per week, an Esquire (the son of a knight) 6/- per week, and a Knight 12/- (60p).

In 1348 the plague called the Black Death, which killed off many able-bodied young men in the Isle of Wight, created a shortage of labour, particularly at harvest time, and this had the effect of keeping agricultural wage rates up, but growth was very slow, and even at the end of the 15th century the labourer's wage was under 3/- (15p) per week. Certain skilled trades, such as plumber and mason, earned 3/- for they were specialists and there were not many of them. If food was supplied to a workman then 6d to 8d a week was deducted, and board and lodging was charged at 1/- (5p) per week. In those days men sometimes walked a considerable distance to work, so that occasionally board and lodging was necessary. An example is quoted (in the 19th century) where a Niton carpenter walked 18 miles to his work in Freshwater on a Monday morning, stayed the week, and walked home on Saturday.

In Henry VIII's reign two major changes took place, both of which affected prices and wages, sending them up and initiating a shock wave of inflation which was never totally expunged from the system. These changes accelerated, if they did not actually begin, the wages-prices spiral which is such a bugbear of our lives today in the 20th century.

One change was the Dissolution of the Monasteries in 1536, which threw more burden on the parishes for the care of their poor, and the other was the debasing of the currency by reducing the weight of silver in the coinage, replacing this with base metal. Economists maintain that by consistently using less and less silver in the coinage Henry practiced a great fraud on his people, and though 20 years later his daughter, Queen Elizabeth, returned to the old standard, it was too late to correct the damage that had already been done.

After 1540, when the effect of these changes was beginning to be felt, wheat prices rose to about 13/- (65p) a quarter, and they continued to rise, a peak of 32/- (£1.60) being reached in the last decade of the century, when there were two consecutive years — 1596 and 1597 — of extreme famine. A labourer's wage rose to 4/- (20p) a week, and a skilled man, such as bricklayer, tyler, or sawyer, to 5/- (25p), but as the price of wheat had more than doubled, everyone was worse off — except for the King, who had acquired all the possessions of the Monasteries, and had saved a considerable sum in the minting of the country's money.

Other interesting figures for the 16th century come from the new Castle at Yarmouth, where pickaxes were charged at 3d (1¼p) each, spades at 6d, and hatchets at 1/4d (6.7p). A porter at the Castle was paid 4/- (20p) per week, and a sailmaker (for making windmill sails) 1/8d (8.3p) per *day*.

Prices continued to rise in the 17th century and a situation was reached where it was found necessary to have prices and wages regulated by the local Justices. But in spite of their efforts the price of wheat increased and at times gave every appearance of being out of control. A few typical years in the first half of the century clearly demonstrate the situation.

Year	Price per Quarter		
1607	36/8d	(£1.83)	
1608	55/8d	(£2.78)	A period of scarcity
1613	48/8d	(£2.43)	
1620	16/-	(80p)	Best Wheat fetched 20/-
1630	64/-	(£3.20)	Poor Harvest
1631	68/-	(£3.40)	Famine
1648	80/-	(£4.00)	A particularly wet summer

1648, incidentally, was the summer of Charles I's imprisonment in Carisbrooke Castle, though whether anything can be read into this is doubtful. Some other food prices quoted at this time seem very reasonable and include bread at 2d (.83p) for a 4 lb loaf, pigeons at 3 for 1d, and beef at 1½d — 4d (.63 — 1.67p) per lb. Wine was available at 3 quarts for 1/- (5p). The only costly item was potatoes at 2/- (10p) per lb.

Agricultural labourers worked a standard week of 48 hours in winter, for which they were paid 3/6d (17½p). In summer their week was 58 hours for a wage of 4/- (20p), but at harvest time the rate was sometimes advanced when labour was short. Mowers were paid 5/- (25p) to 6/- (30p), reapers 9/- (45p). The Clerk of the Works at Sandown Castle, which was being built at this time, was paid 12/- (60p) per week.

Other miscellaneous 17th century prices include barley and malt, which varied from 10/8 (53p) to 40/- (£2) a quarter, hay at £88.14 per ton, a mare, bridle and saddle for 32/- (£1.60), and 7 horses and their harnesses for £23. Roofing laths 1/6d (7½p) per 1000, and nails 3d (1.3p) to 4d (1.67p) per 100.

In the 18th century wages continued to rise slowly but steadily, a labourer's pay reaching 6/- (30p) per week. Wheat prices stabilised somewhat at around 48/- (£2.40) per quarter until the end of the century, but in 1795, due to a deficient harvest, the price rose to a new high of 104/- (£5.20p) per quarter and stayed there for about a year. The hardship that this caused to families on a low and static or slowly moving wage may be imagined.

When wheat was 48/- a quarter, ground flour was 66/8d (£3.33p), the milling thus costing 18/8d (93.3p). A 4 lb loaf now cost 5d (1/-). Other prices include chickens at 8d (3.34p) each, and butter at 1/4 (5.17p) per lb. Coal was 8/- (40p) per quarter, or £32 a ton, a blanket cost 6/- (30p), a sheet 4/6d (22.5p), and 2 skirts 6/- (30p). 200 bricks cost 2/4 (11.7p), and laying them 1/8d (8.34p). In Yarmouth Castle the Captain was paid £3 per week, his gunners were paid 6/- (30p), and the master gunner 12/- (60p). William Arnold, the highly successful Collector of Customs in Cowes, was paid £3 a week, out of which he had to pay for his clerk, but he was allowed another 9/- (45p) a week for a second clerk.

The 19th century opened with war being waged by England against both France and Spain, and with a growing struggle at home between

196

capital and labour. This struggle was accelerated by the effects of the Industrial Revolution, the continual rise in the price of food, and the equally persistent efforts of the employers to keep profits up by keeping wages down. War with France was concluded in 1815 but unrest at home steadily worsened, and by 1831, when the Reform Bill was having a stormy passage through Parliament, riots were breaking out all over England.

The Isle of Wight escaped the worst of these troubles, but there was much poverty, and regrettable complacency on the part of the gentry, who under pressure had increased a labourer's wage to 9/- (45p). But this was still an appallingly low level, the price of bread was high, and the gap between rich and poor ever widening. An interesting example of this gap, and the poor wages paid to domestic servants, comes from *"Nunwell Symphony"* by C. Aspinall-Oglander, in which the author lists the staff employed by Sir William Oglander in 1814 to run this typical country house.

Mrs. Golding, Housekeeper	£45 p.a.
Thomas Harris, Butler	60 Guineas p.a.
William Lord, Under Butler	30 Guineas p.a. and all clothes.
James White, my wife's Footman	25 Guineas p.a., all clothes, and 1 Guinea p.a. for hair powder.
Robert Turner, Footman	24 Guineas p.a., all clothes, and 1 Guinea for hair powder.
George Green, Footman	24 Guineas p.a., all clothes, and 1 Guinea for hair powder.
Mary Bowditch, Upper Housemaid	12 Guineas p.a. and she finds her own tea.
Elizabeth Loveless, Under Housemaid	9 Guineas, and she finds her own tea.
Jane Pusey, Under Housemaid	7 Guineas, and she finds her own tea.
Elizabeth Biles, Nurse	18 Guineas, now raised to 22 Guineas, and tea found her.
Jane Phillips, Nurserymaid	8 Guineas, and tea found her.
Eliza Switch, Under Nursemaid	6 Guineas, and tea found her.
Mary Rumbell, Cook	20 Guineas, and finds her own tea.
Charlotte Peachet, Kitchenmaid	12 Guineas, and finds her own tea.
Sarah Grub, Scullerymaid	5 Guineas and a rise of 1 Guinea if she stays a year. Finds her own tea.
Martha Jones, Laundrymaid	18 Guineas, and finds her own tea.
Hannah Wills, Under Laundrymaid	7 Guineas, and finds her own tea.
Charles Ford, Coachman	40 Guineas plus £10 for boots, breeches, stable waistcoats and overalls.
2 Grooms	At 35 Guineas each.
G. Gallop, Coachman's Lad	13 Guineas, all his clothes and one pair of boots.
Head Gardener	40 Guineas
John Lilly, Head Keeper	£60 plus £3 for wood and vermin.
John Harvey, Woodman	£30 p.a.

The total salary bill for the 24 staff employed comes to just over £632 per annum, plus of course their keep. Incidentally, Sarah Grub, the Scullerymaid, did stay for a year and did get her rise of a guinea per annum.

Several more 19th century examples of wages and prices could be given, but perhaps instead it is permissible to quote an advertisement from an Island paper at the end of the century. This advertises Eldridge Pope & Company's Dorchester Ales, and is a good example of how prices have changed since then. It says their Ales are —

> ". . . as supplied to H.R.H. the Prince of Wales Yacht, the Royal Yacht *"Osborne"*. In casks at 1/- (5p) per gallon and in half pint screw top bottles at 2/6 (12½p) per dozen."

One other advertisement from the same paper cannot be resisted. It says simply —

> "Champion's mustard is the best,
> Try a plaster on your chest."

And so to the 20th century, and another great confidence trick played on the long suffering British public — the decimalisation of the currency. There were no doubt very strong arguments for doing this, but its effect was to send prices sky-rocketing overnight, followed naturally and inevitably by more and more demands for higher wages. After experiencing two world wars in the first half of the century with their attendant trade recessions, this was more than the country's economy could stand, and no Government appeared to know how to control the ensuing inflation and unemployment, never name have the courage to make the drastic changes necessary to bring prosperity back to the country.

Examples of what has happened are commonplace, and distressing, but perhaps the following are worth recording.

1. Not so many years ago it was possible to send a letter for 1½d (.625p), with a very strong possibility of it being delivered within 24 hours. Today (1990), for a much inferior service, we pay 4/0d (20p).

2. Just over 40 years ago a typical 3-star hotel charged as below. Compare this with today's prices.

	Then		*Now*
Bed and Breakfast	10/6	(52p)	£45
Dinner	5/-	(25p)	from £13.50
Early Morning Tea	6d	(2½p)	£1

3. An ordinary 3 bedroom, semi-detached house, built in 1939 and sold new at £750, is now valued — 50 years later — at over £100,000.

4. An 800 gram loaf of bread today costs between 56p and 65p. If it was a 4 lb loaf it would cost £1.27 to £1.45. In 1750 a 4 lb loaf cost 5d (2½p), in 1642 it cost 2d (.83p), and in 1495 it cost ½d (.21p).

In order to afford the above scale of prices wages have had to be drastically increased, and the labourer who 50 years ago was earning £3 a week, and 150 years ago was earning 9/- (45p), is now earning over £200. The wages-prices spiral is still spinning away, and no one seems to be able to stop it. We may have learned many things over the centuries, but we have unfortunately not learned how to control the economy of this country.

198

Yarmouth Mill, built in 1793 by William Porter. Now a holiday home.

Thatching is still a thriving industry in the Isle of Wight.

XXXV — *Ancient Highways*

One of the most fascinating studies in the story of this wonderful island is to try and discover the routes by which men moved about in the old days. The Isle of Wight is covered with a maze of footpaths, tracks, bridleways, ancient highways, lanes, and roads, some of which are fairly recent, some old, and some very old. Every succeeding generation has, however, altered and improved the pattern of routes that it found, so that after several thousand years of this process, culminating in the 20th century with the invention of the bulldozer and the transformation of quite simple tracks into smooth, straight roads suitable for the motor car, it is really quite surprising that any evidence at all has survived.

A study of this ancient network is, therefore, not only exciting, but also frustrating, since so much has been covered up and obliterated. Nevertheless, there are still — astonishingly — traces of ancient highways used by the inhabitants of this Island over 2,000 years ago. To discover such a trace, tantalising though it may be in the brevity and lack of clarity of this glimpse into the past, is rewarding indeed.

To carry out an exploration of this nature necessitates a considerable amount of work, both theoretical, with maps and books, and practical, on the ground, but it is work that anyone can carry out. The younger and more active you are the easier this may be, but no one should be deterred

These old bridleways are very well signposted, and provide a varity of fascinating walks.

from having a go, for even an arm chair exploration can be fun. The tools necessary are simply a set of maps, a love of the Isle of Wight, and if you go walking — suitable shoes or boots.

The maps are no problem. The 1″ to one mile Ordnance Survey map is a good basis, for this gives on one sheet a complete picture of the whole Island, and shows its network of current major and minor roads and some footpaths. Supplement this with the 2½″ to the mile Ordnance Survey *"Pathfinder"* Series which cover the Island with four maps (SZ28/38, SZ47/57, SZ49/59, and SZ58/68). These maps are easy to read and give considerable detail, including public footpaths and bridleways.

Armed with the above it is possible to learn much about the island and its old — and new — highways without ever leaving one's chair, though the real excitement comes from being able to identify on the ground features you have found on the map. This is very much a personal exercise, and the more you study your maps the more interesting festures you will spot, and the more rewarding the exercise will turn out to be. The following notes are intended as guidelines, to help you in your exploration, and must be regarded as such, and as only a scratching of the surface. The deeper you dig, the more treasure you will find.

As an example let us consider just one ancient highway, one that runs from west to east, starting on West High Down near the Needles, and even today being traceable for many, many miles. This was an old road when the Romans were in the island, a thousand years before the Normans. No one knows exactly how old it is, but high up on what is now Tennyson Down is a Neolithic mortuary enclosure in which the dead were kept until the flesh had rotted away, and a little further east on Afton Down is a long barrow in which it is believed the bones were ultimately buried. Between these two sites this ancient track passes through what is now Freshwater Bay, which in those remote days was an inlet from the sea penetrating about a mile inland.

Ancient east-to-west highway through Brighstone Forest.

Part of the 'Tennyson Trail' in the forest.

From the Bay the road climbs up on to Afton Down and goes steadily eastwards over East Afton Down, Tapnell Down, Wellow Down and Brook Down to Five Barrows. Here are a number of Bronze Age barrows, and not far away, in the centre of a maze of ancient tracks, is Dunsbury, a Saxon name meaning 'the fortified place on the Downs'. Several of these old tracks converge on the ancient highway, and cross the road from Brook to Shalcombe and Chessell at map reference 396851. Near Chessell there is a Jutish cemetery. Immediately after this crossing, the road climbs up on to Pay Down and shortly afterwards forks, one branch going through the forest to Calbourne Bottom (420848), and another proceeding in a southeasterly direction to Mottistone Common and the Long Stone (407848). The road itself runs through Harboro (406847) where in much later times (16th century) there was a beacon. Harboro was also a *rendezvous* for the Militia in times of invasion.

At 421846 the old road crosses Lynch Lane which runs from Calbourne to Brighstone, and at this point there is a strategically placed National Trust Car Park, near which lie the remains of the Roman Villa at Rock. Walking from the Car Park in either direction along the old road is thoroughly to be recommended, the going underfoot is excellent and the views to the south and east are stupendous. Three quarters of a mile further to the east the old road bends to the left, through a gate, and enters one of the most interesting areas in the whole Island (432842).

This area is one of lost ancient villages, *tumuli*, and above all, trees, for

202

some years ago the Forestry Commission planted the whole area, mainly with conifers, which effectively hide most of the archaeological remains. Soon after entering the forest the old road is crossed by another bridleway connecting Calbourne with Limerston and Shorwell, and indeed there is a web of old bridleways here which once were an important part of Island communications. Unfortunately, at this point the hurricane of October 1987 struck the forest with ferocious fury, destroying hundreds of trees in a wide swathe. The majority of these have now been cleared and the area re-planted, but it will be many years before the forest recovers.

Half a mile further on the old road forks, the left hand bridleway striking off due north via Rowridge and Ashengrove to Swainston and Newtown. The old highway itself continues in a north-easterly direction, skirting Gallibury fields and Bunkers Bottom, Idleborough and Row-borough Downs, to Bowcombe Down, where it passes an Anglo Saxon Burial Ground and ultimately descends from the Down into Carisbrooke. If you are feeling particularly tired and thirsty by the time you reach the Anglo Saxon burial ground, fork left along a bridleway which will bring you down to the Middle Road (Newport to Calbourne) immediately opposite the very welcome sight of the Blacksmiths Arms, (465879).

The above is a description of only one ancient Island highway, and one that is easy to follow on the map and on the ground. There are many more, waiting for you to discover them. Dig first in the southwestern quarter of the Island for here are the most interesting and rewarding finds.

Bridleway on Idlecombe Down, where you may get away from it all.

XXXVI — *Island Buildings*

Saxon design used as a house — Bagwich Farm.

When the Saxons arrived in Britain in the 5th century they brought with them the design of a building. It was a very basic design, much simpler than the buildings the Romans had erected, and it consisted of a plain rectangular structure, very approximately twice as long as it was wide, usually two stories in height, and with a steeply pitched roof. It was a multi-purpose building that could be adapted to one of three different purposes — it could be used as a house, or as a barn, or as a church.

And when you come to think of it, these are the three essential needs of human beings in these northern latitudes. We have to have shelter — we cannot live out in the open like the animals for we do not have their built-in fur coats. So we have to have a building in which to live. We have to have food — which means in basic terms that we must grow it or rear it. So we have to have barns in which to store it. And last, but by no means least — every single one of us has to have some form of spiritual sustenance, we cannot live by bread alone. So we need to have churches.

In the Isle of Wight, perhaps because we are an island where development has been a little slower than on the mainland, there are still many examples of this original Saxon design of building, some being used as houses, some as barns, and some as churches. The following are just a few old houses which, though perhaps not dating back to Saxon times, are of this basic design. In the West Wight the farmhouses of Rowborough (461830), Lower Watchingwell (445894), Limerstone (441826), Chilton (414825), Compton (376851), and Coombe (429837). In the east of the Island, Kern (579867) and Eddington (632893), and in the centre Bagwich (517822), Bridgecourt (521815), and the east wing of Arreton Manor (533868), the oldest part of this house, originally built by the monks of Quarr in the 14th century.

THE SAXON BUILDING

HOUSE?

BARN?

or CHURCH?

As for barns, every farm has one, and it is only necessary to keep your eyes open as you go round the Island to see many fine examples of this type of building. Look out particularly for the barns at West Court (452827), Wolverton (453824), Chale (485778) and Lessland (542828).

The Saxons built many churches in this little Island and in some of them — as for example in Arreton and Freshwater — traces of the original Saxon masonry can still be seen. A number of our older churches too still retain the original basic Saxon design shape, though most of them have been re-built, some more than once. Good examples are St. Edmund's, Wootton (542927), St. Lawrence Old Church (536766), Yaverland (614859), St. Nicholas-in-the-Castle (in Carisbrooke Castle 485877), Binstead (575928), and Bonchurch Old Church (577781). Binstead, Bonchurch, and St. Lawrence have all been lengthened by the addition of a Chancel, but the Naves are still the original Saxon shape. For further information see *"Village Churches of the Isle of Wight"*.

Note the steeply pitched roofs of all these buildings, for they were all originally thatched, and with a thatched roof you need a steep pitch to encourage rain water to run off before it has time to seep through. Notice also how at the gable ends the coping stones stand proud of the roof, this being done to prevent the wind blowing under the thatch and lifting it.

Above. *Saxon design used as a church — St. Nicholas-in-the-Castle.*

Left. *Saxon design used as a barn — Wolverton Manor.*

This Saxon multi-purpose building was in many cases found to be too small and had to be extended. Houses had wings added to them, lean-to's, extensions, and the original building was soon barely recognisable, but it still retained the core of the house, the "hall", in which for many centuries the whole of the family would live. Churches also were extended, as at Binstead, Bonchurch and St. Lawrence, but this type of extension was often inadequate and additional buildings of the same shape had to be added. Look at Arreton, Brading, Brighstone, Shorwell, and a dozen others to see how they have grown.

Right, Top. *The first method of extending a church — Binstead.*

Right, bottom. *The great medieval barn at Wolverton.*

206

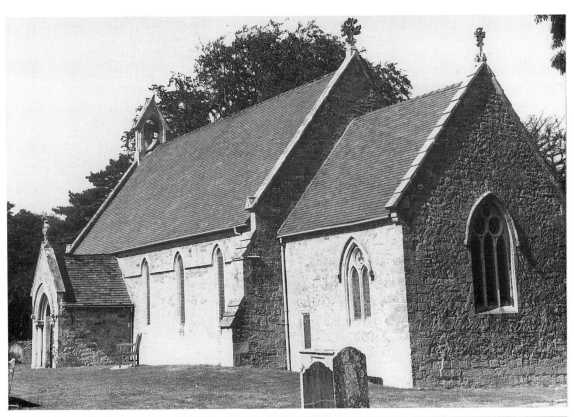

By the Middle Ages, though the better off were living in larger houses, living conditions were still very crude. The poor lived in cottages which were of the most primitive kind containing one, or at best, two rooms. There was no privacy and no sanitation. Large families were produced and it is not surprising that infant mortality was high.

Even the "hall" houses of the well-to-do were crude and basic, consisting, as mentioned above, of a central hall in which the whole household lived, ate and slept. There was a dais at one end for the lord of the household and his lady, and a room behind the dais in which his lady slept. Everyone else slept on the floor in the hall. At the other end of the hall was a screen behind which was a cross passage with outside doors at each end, and on the far side of this passage the service rooms — the pantry (from the French *"painterie"*, a bread store), and the buttery (from *"boutaillerie"*, a bottle store). The kitchen was usually in a completely separate building on account of the fire risk.

The floor of the hall was of earth, and in the better class houses this would be strewn with rushes. The scholar Eramus, who visited England in 1530, wrote —

> "The floors are commonly of clay, strewed with rushes, under which lies unmolested an ancient collection of beer, grease, fragments, bones, spittle, excrement of dogs and cats, and everything that is nasty."

The fire was built in the centre of the hall, most of the smoke finding its way out through a hole in the roof. Wall fireplaces were invented in the 12th century but were still unknown in farmhouses and cottages before the middle of the 16th century. Glazed windows began to be fitted in the 13th century but were not in general use till the 16th. Cottages were still unglazed in the 18th.

There was a tremendous gap between the rich and the poor, but all people lived under these crude conditions, and when it is remembered that no one, either rich or poor, ever washed, some idea of the appalling nature of life can be gathered. The "hall" house gradually disappeared in the 16th/17th century as people felt a growing need for more privacy, and the hall was split up into smaller rooms. The name has, however, survived, though in modern houses it is now no more than a lobby inside the front door.

At the beginning of the 16th century there were only two truly great buildings in the Isle of Wight, the first of these being the Norman Castle of Carisbrooke, which was first built in Island stone by Baldwin de Redvers in the 12th century. It remained impregnable until the invention of gunpowder, and in 1647 served as a royal prison for Charles I until November 1648. Later it became the official residence of the Governor of the Isle of Wight, and though now partly in ruins, it still houses a valuable museum. It is a place that everyone should visit.

The second great building was also built by Baldwin de Redvers, and was the Abbey he founded at Quarr in 1132. This huge complex of buildings has now almost entirely disappeared, having been closed down in

A medieval castle? No. A 19th century farm, at Norris, East Cowes.

1536 by Henry VIII, and demolished for its building stone. Only a few ruins and farm buildings are left (566928), and of the great Abbey Church, which was nearly 200 feet long, not a vestige remains. The fine new Abbey of Quarr, built in brick in the early years of this century, is hard by.

The greatest building the Isle of Wight now possesses is possibly Osborne House. This is not the most beautiful house in the Island, but as the home of Queen Victoria for many years it is the biggest tourist attraction and should certainly be visited. It was built in the middle of the 19th century and its design was heavily influenced by the Prince Consort, who wanted an Italianate Villa. The house is now under the care of English Heritage, and the private apartments of the Queen and her Consort are open to the public.

In addition to Osborne House and Carisbrooke Castle, English Heritage are also responsible for Appuldurcombe House, a building of some architectural merit though now in a partly ruined condition. This house was the principal seat of the Worsley family in the Isle of Wight for several centuries and was built in 1710. The design is Palladian and the architect is believed to have been John James, who at one time worked for Sir Christopher Wren, and who was influenced by two celebrated Palladian architects, Sir John Vanbrugh and Nicholas Hawksmoor. When the Worsley occupation of Appuldurcombe came to an end in the 19th century the fortunes of the house declined (see Chapter 25, page 154), and ultimately a flying bomb in 1945 removed roof and windows. Now, under English Heritage, there is renewed hope, for they have started to re-roof it and make it weather-tight.

Two other large Island houses have avoided the fate of Appuldurcombe and are still going strong. These are Mottistone Manor, one of the most lovely houses in the Isle of Wight, built in the 15th and 16th centuries, and since 1926 the home of one branch of the Seely family (see Chapter 32, page 189), and North Court, built in 1615 by Sir John Leigh, and now divided into three separate houses, each occupied by branches of the Harrison family.

A number of Elizabethan and Jacobean manor houses survive in the Isle of Wight, all slightly different, but all E-type houses, that is to say, houses that looked at from above would resemble a capital 'E'. They were all built in the latter part of the reign of Elizabeth I, or in the reign of James I, some being re-builds of previous houses. They include Arreton (533868), Sheat (493845), Barton (519944), Merston (522855), Wolverton (453824), and Yaverland (614859).

There was much building of houses in the 18th century, starting with Appuldurcombe in the first decade. Also at this time a number of slightly smaller houses was buiilt in a style that had become popular towards the end of the previous century. This style included a symmetrical front to a square or rectangular building, with a hipped roof and cornice, and most of these were of two storeys only. If a third storey was provided the windows were allowed to break through the roof as dormers. Typical of these very pleasing houses are Afton Manor (348869), and King's Manor (348881) both in Freshwater, Thorley Manor (367891), and the George Hotel, Yarmouth (354898).

Fifty years later two other prestigious houses were re-built, one being at Gatcombe (493850) where in 1751 Sir Edward Worsley built an imposing rectangular house on severely classical lines, replacing an old E-type building, not altogether successfully. Originally it was intended to build two such rectangular 3-storied blocks, connecting them with a smaller single-storey building, but this plan was never carried out. Nor was the ornamental lake in front of the house ever constructed, though a picture was painted showing not only the lake, but a yacht sailing on it.

Gatcombe is one of several Island houses to have had a Venetian window fitted in the 18th century, when this type of window became a fashionable necessity. The Gatcombe window is a very fine one, and there are equally splendid examples at Haseley (547857), North Court (457832), and Nunwell (595874). At Gatcombe and North Court the Venetian window is used to light a particularly good "four-abreast" staircase, the effect being extremely impressive. Several other houses have this splendid type of staircase, notably Afton Manor, Billingham Manor (486819), and the George Hotel, Yarmouth. The owner of Wolverton Manor in the 18th century went so far as to build an annexe at the back of the house to take a four-abreast staircase, and he intended to light this with a Venetian window, but alas the staircase was never installed, nor was the window ever glazed.

The other prestigious house mentioned above as having been re-built in 1750 was the old Summer Palace of the Bishops of Winchester at Swainston. When this re-building was first carried out it was a fairly plain classical rectangular building, but it was subsequently added to and now has two large bow windows on the south front and a ballroom on the west side. (See Chapter 18, page 117). Swainston is one of the most historic spots in the Isle of Wight and as it is now an hotel it is open to the public and can be visited. Many other lovely old manor houses in the Island are also rich in history, and several are open to the public. The histories of these houses and the people who have lived in them are told in full in *"The Manor Houses of the Isle of Wight"*.

The following houses and gardens are open — Arreton Manor, Barton Manor (gardens and vineyards only), Appuldurcombe, Haseley Manor, Nunwell House, Swainston Manor, Osborne House (house only), and Carisbrooke Castle.

The beginning of the 19th century saw the arrival of another architect who had already found fame and fortune on the mainland, and who was destined to make an impact on the Isle of Wight. This was John Nash, who designed Newport's Guildhall and County Club. Much of his other work in the Island has now gone, but he will be remembered for the above two buildings. In our own times we have been blessed with a County Architect who has made his mark with several public buildings which have combined modern ideas with pleasing exteriors. Michael Rainey's designs are essentially functional, and he and the team he has built up have contributed — and are continuing to contribute — to the improvement of our Island towns. The Lord Louis Library in Newport, the Mountbatten Centre, The Gouldings Home for the Elderly in Freshwater, Glamis Court Home in East Cowes, The Adelaide Club and Adelaide Court in Ryde, and a whole fistful of schools and other public service buildings are products of the County Architect's Department of which they — and we — may feel justly proud.

Modern architecture. The Lord Louis Library, Newport, designed by Michael Rainey.

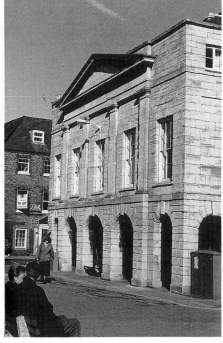

The County Club, Newport. A typical Nash building.

XXXVII — *The Church in the Isle of Wight*

In *"Village Churches of the Isle of Wight"* this author dealt with 24 mainly medieval churches in Island villages, and made a passing reference to 11 others. In *"Churches of the Isle of Wight"* the author, Margaret Green, gave valuable information about a total of 60 churches, including not only the medieval but some Victorian ones as well. The purpose of the present chapter is not to replace either of the above books, nor to deal with the many other non-Conformist or Roman Catholic churches in the Isle of Wight which have not been listed, but to say something about the development of the Church of England from the early years of the 16th century, when a tremendous wave of reforming zeal swept Europe and came into headlong collision with the Church of Rome.

Dissatisfaction with the corruption of the Church had been growing since the 13th century and had been repeatedly expressed. Many reforming movements had arisen, most of them being crushed swiftly and violently, but nevertheless the urge to introduce reforms into the established Church grew rapidly, the trigger in Europe being Martin Luther, who in 1517 came out in open revolt.

The trigger in England was the King himself, Henry VIII. He wanted a divorce from his first wife, Catherine of Aragon, so that he could marry Ann Boleyn, but this the Pope steadfastly refused to give him. The solution to this problem, suggested to the King by his Chancellor, Thomas Cromwell, was to renounce allegiance to the Pope and to become Head of the Church in England himself. The last thing Henry wanted to do was to change the religion of the country, he was a confirmed Catholic and wished to remain so, but his action in deserting the Church of Rome released and encouraged reforming forces that he was quite unable to control.

Henry's divorce, which he granted himself in 1533, was a political rather than a religious act, as was the Dissolution of the Monasteries, which Thomas Cromwell also master-minded three years later. The King was short of money and the Monasteries were rich, and though powerful they were corrupt and badly in need of reform. Due to the rise in secular education they had largely lost their role as centres of learning, but their wholesale destruction was not the reform that was needed, and it deprived the poor of the care and support that the State did not provide. No begger was ever turned away from a Monastery door empty-handed.

When Henry VIII died and was succeeded by the boy King Edward VI, the reformers gained control and events moved swiftly. The final break with Rome was made, and in 1549 the first English prayer book was issued. As so often happens when the pendulum swings, it swings too far, and a wave of destruction of church images, particularly statues of Christ and the Blessed Virgin Mary, took place. Stained glass windows were smashed,

*Godshill's Lily Cross,
painted in the 15th century.*

the priests' vestments were discarded, and the many coloured murals on church walls were white-washed over.

In Isle of Wight churches traces of these murals have been found under the whitewash, perhaps the most startling being the beautiful and unique Lily Cross in Godshill (the only one of its type in the British Isles), but there are several other murals, including one of St. Christopher on the north wall of Shorwell church, and another in the splay of an early Norman window in Arreton.

All church Roods (the Rood being a Crucifix) were destroyed at this time and the character of services was completely altered. Previously the laity had not been allowed to enter the Chancel of a church except on very special occasions; they remained standing in the nave and took little part in the service, their role being essentially to watch the clergy celebrating Communion. There was a heavy screen between nave and chancel, on top of which was the Rood, and the service was read or sung by the Cantor who sat in the Rood Loft, also on top of the screen. Services were conducted in Latin, there were several daily, and the laity could enter or leave at any time. Only the sermon was delivered in English. When services were not being held the nave of the church was used for secular purposes and fulfilled the functions of our present church hall.

The Act of 1549 changed all this. The laity were required to take part in all aspects of the service, matins and evensong were to be conducted from the chancel, and lessons were to be read in English so that all could hear. In fact, the form of service then instituted has survived the test of time and is still very much the same today.

Many other reforms were made over the years, not all of them for the good. In 1560 Elizabeth I decreed that the Ten Commandments and the Creed should be set up at the east end of the church, and these commandment boards can still be seen in many Island churches. A further decree in the following year allowed screens to be retained, but Rood Lofts were to go, and in place of the Rood the Royal Arms were to be set up. Screens have subsequently disappeared from most Island churches, but one or two Roods have returned, and traces of the old Rood stairs can still be seen in Arreton, Brighstone, Carisbrooke, Chale, Godshill, Freshwater, Newchurch, Niton, Shorwell, and Yaverland — an intriguing reminder that once upon a time we were all Roman Catholics!

A great controversy raged in the 16th century about the position of the altar, and even about its name, for at one time it had to be called "the table". Its position became flexible, the Puritans favouring lengthwise in the chancel, while some brought it down into the nave for celebration and took it back afterwards, a practice that has been re-introduced into some churches in recent years. Stone altars were condemned, for the same reasons as statuary, and the table had to be made of wood. Communion rails were introduced in 1633 — primarily to keep out dogs!

The pulpit became the centre for conducting the service, and the 3-tier pulpit was evolved, the Clerk sitting on the ground floor, the priest on the second tier, and the sermon being given from the third tier, but there are no 3-tier pulpits left in the Island. The font also waxed and waned in importance, and various positions were tried out for pulpit and font as well as for the altar. And so it went on, change after change after change, the astonishing and humbling thing being that while men continued to squabble over the minutae of how to do this and how to do that, God continued to look after us and give us the blessing of Life.

During the 17th and 18th centuries our Island churches, togther with others on the mainland, were regrettably neglected, but in the 1830s began a most remarkable wave of church restoration. On the crest of this wave was a very young and very talented architect who rejoiced in the name of Augustin Welby Northmore Pugin, and who is perhaps best known to most of us for his design of the Houses of Parliament in Westminster. Pugin was a Roman Catholic and had very strong views on church architecture, to which he devoted most of his energies.

He propounded that to be Christian, architecture had to be Pointed, and that hence only the Gothic style was acceptable. He went further, even condemning certain types of Gothic, as for example Early English, which he claimed was immature, and the Perpendicular style, which he dubbed degenerate. The only really acceptable style was that produced in the late 13th and early 14th centuries, as exemplified by the bar tracery found in Westminster Abbey. This became something of an obsession with him, and ultimately a cult which spread like a contagious disease, infecting

214

Above. *Remains of the stairs leading to the Rood loft in Brighstone church.*

Below. *The Rood Beam, Godshill.*

all who came into contact with it.

In 1839 the Camden Society was formed, its object being to revive ancient ritual and promote architecture accordingly. It attracted the leading architects of the day and became very powerful and autocratic, influencing the restoration of medieval churches, and imposing its rather narrow philosophy on the architects involved. We now know the style that was developed at this time as Victorian Gothic.

There is not a medieval church in the Isle of Wight that was not touched by this type of restoration, and as a consequence many attractive medieval features disappeared, being re-built or covered up, and many people regret that this should have been so. But before criticising the Victorian restorers too harshly, it must be remembered that many of the churches they tackled were in very poor shape, and would undoubtedly have fallen down if no restoration had been carried out.

Many of our village churches are of Saxon origin, and all have been altered and restored many times in the intervening years. They are all beautiful, and no amount of unsuitable restoration can take away from them the atmosphere that has built up over the centuries. If you are troubled in mind, in spirit, or in body, go into any of them, sit down, and be still, and you will find that the peace and tranquillity they have to offer will envelop you and bring you comfort.

Peace and tranquillity, exemplified in the nave of Mottistone village church.

XXXVIII — *Smuggling*

The cottage facing St. Helens Green where Sophie Dawes, the smuggler's daughter who became a French Baroness, was born.

No book telling the story of the Isle of Wight could be regarded as complete without at least a passing reference to Smuggling, for we are told that in the 18th and early 19th centuries this was the most popular occupation, employing up to two-thirds of the Island's population. Actually, the history of smuggling goes back very much farther than the 18th century, and 300 years earlier the trade was in the opposite direction, Isle of Wight wool being smuggled out to the continent, this long stapled wool fetching a much higher price in France than in England. There is a record that in 1394 even the Vicar of Freshwater was involved in this trade, for he was arrested one day in — of all places — the Red Lion Inn — which is next door to his church.

Every coastal village in the south of England claims to have had a smuggling problem at one time or another, and the Isle of Wight, through its geographical situation and the wildness of its southern shore, is particularly suitable for the landing of illicit cargoes from France. The principal goods involved were brandy, tea, tobacco, and silk stuffs, and at the height of the boom in the second half of the 18th century cargoes were large and frequent, and all classes of Island society, from the gentry downwards, were involved.

The writer of every book on the history of the Isle of Wight — and there are many — has dealt with this period in detail, and several have quoted statistics and given actual examples of the trade carried on. Some, indeed, have even retailed the recipe for transforming a 14/- tub of 100 proof French spirit into a 50/- cask of the best brandy.

The boats they used for ferrying the contraband from France to England are of great interest, for they were specially designed and built for the job, Samuel White's boatyard in Cowes having a particularly high reputation for the fast and powerful cutters it produced, not only for Island customers, but for other ports along the south coast. The sheer size of some of these vessels is extraordinary.

There were two types of sailing boat popular, the *cutter* and the *lugger*. Cutters were large, carried a crew of up to 100 men, and were stoutly armed with 22 guns. Their speed is reputed to have been up to 12 knots, and the largest of them could carry 2,000 tubs of spirits, each tub holding 4 gallons, plus 5 tons of tea. Luggers were, if anything, larger, from 50 to 300 tons, of shallow draught, with low masts, and equally fast. They were capable of carrying up to 3,000 of these 4 gallon half ankers of spirits, plus 12 tons of tea.

In addition to the sailing boats there were also rowing boats in use on the south coast as well as in the Island, and these could be anything from 30 to 120 feet in length, with a beam of up to 20 feet. Powered by as many as 40 oarsmen they were capable of speeds of 10 knots, and when pursued by a Revenue cutter a favourite tactic was to turn up into the eye of the wind, whither the Revenue men could not follow. In 1721 a law was passed limiting the number of oars in a boat to six, and this put a stop to that little game.

Equipped with such powerful craft the smugglers had it very much their own way for a long time and became quite brazen, openly landing their cargoes in daylight. In the Isle of Wight the appointment of William Arnold of Cowes as Collector of Customs in 1777 did much to curb their activities for he was a fearless and upright man who stamped out bribery and corruption in his own men, many of whom were quite prepared, for a consideration, to turn a blind eye to what was going on. But it was an uphill task, and it was not until 1815 that any really dramatic progress was made.

In that year the threat of invasion by Napoleon came to an end with the battle of Waterloo, and some new employment had to be found for the Royal Navy, whose fleet had been patrolling the Channel with great success. Consequently, the Navy was put in charge of the revenue cutters used in the anti-smuggling effort, and very soon the most spectacular results were being achieved. Records show that they seized 370,000 gallons of gin and brandy, 42,000 yards of silk, 36,000 packs of playing cards, 21,000 Indian silk kerchiefs, 19,000 lbs of tea, 3,000 lbs snuff, — and what was the most significant haul — 875 smuggling ships of various types and sizes.

In 1831 the Coastguard Service was formed, the Royal Navy began using their own ships, and laws were passed freeing many items from duty, the combination of all these measures having the effect of breaking the back of the smuggling problem. But smuggling did not, and probably never will, cease, it being an essential part of man's nature to want to beat the system, particularly if danger and excitement are involved and large profits are to be made.

The grave of Thomas Sivell in Binstead churchyard. Sivell was shot by Customs Officers as a suspected smuggler.

Much of the literature on the subject paints the smugglers in a sympathetic and romantic light, implying that they were the heroes and the government the villains, and there is certainly no doubt that they were brave and hardy in the extreme. Anyone who is prepared to row a small boat to Cherbourg and back on a winter's night is a man in every sense of the word, and their courage and fearless tenacity has to command our respect. But there is more to it than that; there is an evil side to smuggling that completely negates any romantic notions there may once have been. Clashes between smugglers and preventive men inevitably occurred, and unfortunately physical violence escalated, there being records of sadistic brutality that make unhappy reading. And though this may not be prevalent today, the evil attached to the trade has survived in another form, making the business more reprehensible than ever.

For smuggling today is truly a beastly business. No one minds the tourist trying to get a few extra cigarettes for his own use past the customs men, or the yachtsman hiding the odd bottle of gin in his locker, but smuggling today is big business, and in particular the smuggling of drugs. The actual act of smuggling may be peaceable enough, the evil lying in the devastation caused to the drug user, who once 'hooked' finds it almost impossible to get away. Addiction is a degrading business and is a destroyer, leading only, through despair, to death, the tragedy being heightened by the fact that many of the deaths are of young people.

Traffickers make huge profits and have no thought for the misery they are bringing into people's lives, and sadly our existing laws seem quite unable to control what is now a major social disease. Perhaps what is wanted are laws that make it easier to do what is right, and much more difficult to do what is wrong. But first and foremost, what is needed is a change of attitude in the hearts of men, and the realisation that greed as a motive is fundamentally wrong. But until those that rule us — or should it be said, those who are elected to rule us — appreciate this point and make a concerted effort to eliminate greed as man's prime motive, smuggling, and its associated evils, will continue.

Let it not be thought that the Isle of Wight is innocent of any connection with this terrible trade. Far from it. There may not be any 40-oared galleys making a night dash to Cherbourg any more, but there are other, and more sophisticated, ways of landing cargoes of contraband, and under the noses of the authorities too. An apparently innocent small yacht sailing from, say, Poole Harbour to the Island may quite easily have made a *rendez-vous* with a larger ship out of sight of land, and taken onboard a deadly cargo. This is known to happen, but it is only on the rare occasion when things go wrong that it is detected. Not long ago a dinghy was found drifting near the Needles; it contained a load of drugs with a street value of several million pounds. This was only part of a much larger consignment, some of which got through.

How many more deadly loads are passing through this beautiful and tranquil Island? And how may it be stopped? For stopped it must be!

XXXIX — *The Royal Island*

During its long history the Isle of Wight has had many contacts with Royalty, and indeed in the Middle Ages, when the threat of invasion was often in the air, the monarch frequently took more than a passing interest in the Island, for it was vulnerable to attack from across the Channel. Once these dangers receded Royal visits became less regular for a time, but the development of yachting stimulated another interest. When Queen Victoria discovered the Island and made it her home not only British but foreign Royalty began to come to the Isle of Wight, and happily a more frequent contact with members of our own Royal family has been established.

A few of the visits made by Royalty in the past are recorded below, showing how closely this little Island is linked to English history —

1013 King Ethelred, nicknamed "The Unready", spent Christmas in the Isle of Wight. He had a very trying year, for Sweyn, King of Denmark, had landed at Sandwich during the summer and had been rampaging round his kingdom, harrying, burning, and pillaging. By Christmas time Ethelred had had enough and was glad to escape to the peace and quiet of the Island. Sweyn died in February, being succeeded by his son, Canute, who turned out to be fiercer than his father, and soon had control of most of the country. Ethelred himself died in 1016, and his son Edmund, called "The Ironsides", split the kingdom between Canute and himself. But Edmund too died in 1016 and Canute became the first Danish King of all England.

1022 Canute visited the Island, but for what purpose the Anglo-Saxon Chronicle does not say. Perhaps he came to visit his father's manor of Sweynston (Swainston)?

1066 When King Edward (the Confessor) died on January 6th Earl Harold Godwin seized the throne, but he knew there were other claimants, including William of Normandy. King Harold raised an army and spent the whole summer in the Isle of Wight, waiting for William's expected invasion.

1206 On May 28th King John arrived in Yarmouth to stay for a few days. He was assembling a fleet, and sailed for La Rochelle on June 1st to try and recapture some of his lost territories. The expedition failed, for after months of ineffectual fighting, the King lost interest and came home, leaving his army to get on with it.

1214 King John was back in Yarmouth again on February 3rd. This time he was preparing to invade Poitou, along with his friends, the Count of Flanders, the Count of Boulogne, and the Emperor of Germany. Their object was to capture the whole of France and divide it up between them, but they failed.

King John (1199—1216)

220

Edward I (1272—1307)

Henry VII (1485—1509)

1215 When King John returned to England he found his barons up in arms and waiting for him, and he had to submit to their demands at Runnymead. After signing the *"Magna Carta"* he appealed to the Pope for help, and is reputed to have come back to the Island and stayed at King's Quay, sulking, while awaiting the Pope's reply.

1285 Edward I arrived from his capital at Winchester on November 5th to stay with John di Pontiserra, Bishop of Winchester, at his summer palace of Swainston. The King stayed till the 11th before going home, and later took the manor of Swainston away from the bishop. (What he was really after was Newtown Harbour). Did he ever return? In 1293 he bought the rest of the Island from Isabella de Fortibus.

1499 King Henry VII made a tour of the Island, staying at Nunwell House, and at Brook House. He was so pleased with the hospitality he received at Brook that on leaving he presented his hostess, Joan Bowerman, with his drinking horn, and a warrant for a fat buck of the season to be delivered to her annually from his forest of Carisbrooke.

1503 The Princess Cecily, daughter of King Edward IV, married an Islander, Richard Keynes, and lived at Great East Standen Manor, near Arreton. (See Chapter 8, page 40).

1538 King Henry VIII was entertained at Appuldurcombe by Richard Worsley, Captain of the Island, but the King was not quite so pleased as his father had been, for Richard took him out hunting for pheasant and partridges and they could not find any. Richard blamed the poachers, but Henry was not pleased.

Henry VIII (1509—1547)

1607 King James I made his first visit to the Isle of Wight in August this year, and according to Sir John Oglander was delighted to watch a company of boys being drilled in martial exercises. He also hunted in Parkhurst Forest and apparently had a picnic there. Prince Charles, aged 6, was with him. (Prince Charles was, of course, later King Charles I).

1609 On Wednesday, August 2nd, King James paid another visit to the Island. On this occasion he saw the Militia training in the morning, dined at the Castle, and in the afternoon went hunting, Prince Charles being with him again. According to Rev. John Baker, the Vicar of Carisbrooke, the King killed a buck.

1618 Prince Charles (now aged 17) visited the Island on Thursday August 27th, saw the Militia training, and had a tour of the Island, visiting the Castle, but dining in Newport at Cosham Manor, the home of one Andrew James. Riding through Castlehold in Newport the Prince noticed an inn sign showing a lion clawing a friar, and asked Sir John what it meant. Sir John told him that the Island served all papists and priests thus. There is no record of what the Prince thought of this rather odd and controversial remark. Why did the Prince not dine at the Castle? Perhaps because the Governor, the Earl of Southampton, was at Beaulieu Abbey, entertaining the King.

James I (1603—1625)

1627 After Prince Charles had become King Charles I he came to the Isle of Wight on Wednesday, June 20th, to inspect Sir Alexander Brett's Regiment which was billeted near Nunwell, preparing for what turned out to be an ill-fated expedition to the Isle of Rhé (La Rochelle), led by the Duke of Buckingham. Sir John Oglander met the King at Ryde and escorted him to Arreton Down where he saw the Regiment in training. With the King were over 20 noblemen, including the Duke, six Earls, and a number of lesser Lords.

1628 Another visit by King Charles, on September 1st, this time to inspect the Scottish Highland Regiment that had been giving the Island so much trouble. (See Chapter 10, page 70). They were officially on their way to La Rochelle and came for a week, but stayed a year. The King's visit speeded up their departure for they left within a few days, though their billeting money was not paid for another year, and then was only 25% of the claim. Sir John Oglander christened them "the Red Shanks".

1647 Sunday Nov. 14th. The last, and saddest, visit of King Charles I. He stayed until Nov. 30th 1648, living in Carisbrooke Castle, and gradually having his freedom taken away from him. Finally he was taken by the Army to Hurst Castle, thence to London and his execution. (See Chapter 10, page 74).

Charles I (1625—1649) saying goodbye to two of his children, Princess Elizabeth and Prince Henry.

1650   A sad sequel to the death of Charles I was the imprisonment of two of his children in Carisbrooke Castle, the Princess Elizabeth and Prince Henry, Duke of Gloucester. (See Chapter 10, page 74). Princess Elizabeth died in captivity, aged 15, only a month after arriving in the Island, but Prince Henry, aged 10, had to endure imprisonment for two years. Cromwell freed him in March 1652, and he went to live on the continent. He returned to England with his elder brother Charles, when the latter became King in 1660, but alas Henry died of smallpox very shortly after.

1665   The first official visit to the Isle of Wight by King Charles II. He landed in Brading Haven on July 31st, and the occasion is perhaps noteworthy for the fact that the King refused to see the Governor of the Island, Sir Robert Holmes, who though an old friend of his, had omitted to patch up his quarrel with the King's younger brother, the Duke of York (later James II).

1671   In the summer of this year Charles II paid another visit, this time landing at Gurnard, and being accompanied by the Duke of York and Prince Rupert. The Royal party stayed with Sir Robert Holmes in his new house in Yarmouth (now the George Hotel) so that obviously old differences had been resolved.

223

1675 Charles II landed on the other side of the Island at Puckaster after "enduring a great and dangerous storm at sea". He spent two nights recovering from his ordeal as the guest of the Rector of Niton, the Reverend Thomas Collinson.

1677 The King is believed to have visited the Island again, once more as the guest of Sir Robert Holmes.

1684 There is a bedroom in Shalcombe Manor in which Charles II is reputed to have slept on a visit towards the end of his life. He was 54 at the time, dissipated and worn out, and spending what energy he had on his various mistresses. Perhaps Sir Robert Holmes, who had similar tastes to the King, and had been his companion on many a spree, was involved in this visit?

1817 In June of this year the Prince Regent, writing from his yacht, the *Royal George*, lying off Brighton, applied for membership of the Yacht Club, subsequently the Royal Yacht Squadron, and though the Squadron did not achieve its permanent headquarters in Cowes till 1825, its races were held in Island waters, and the connection between the House of Hanover and the Isle of Wight can be regarded as starting from this date. When the Prince Regent became King George IV in 1820 he also became Commodore of the Yacht Club which then became the *Royal* Yacht Club.

1831 A very significant year in the history of the Isle of Wight, since the 12 year old daughter of the Duke of Kent, the Princess Victoria, was brought by her mother to spend the summer in Norris Castle.

1833 Yet another King, William IV, became Commodore of the Royal Yacht Squadron.

Charles II (1660—1685)

George IV (1820—1830)

Far left. *Victoria (1837—1901)*

Left. *Albert, Prince Consort*

1845 Queen Victoria and Prince Albert bought the Osborne estate and Barton Manor, thus establishing a permanent domicile in the Isle of Wight, and this was to last until Queen Victoria's death in 1901. During her long reign the Island became a *rendez-vous* for the nobility and royalty of the whole world, and this continued after her death.

1901 King Edward VII lost no time in giving Osborne to the nation, for he had unhappy memories of his childhood there, but he kept Barton Manor as a *"pied à terre"* and frequently visited the Island to race his yacht *"Britannia"*, and also to entertain his guests at Barton.

We must be grateful to King Edward for his gift of Osborne, for this has made it possible for the state rooms in the house to be opened to the public. Whippingham Church, which was designed by his father, the Prince Consort, and in which Queen Victoria worshipped, is also open at times. The church contains much Victorian memorabilia and the graves of Queen Victoria's youngest daughter, Princess Beatrice and her husband, Prince Henry of Battenberg. In the churchyard are the graves of Prince Louis of Battenberg and Princess Victoria of Hesse, parents of the late Earl Mountbatten, and grand-parents of Prince Philip, Duke of Edinburgh.

The Prince and Princess of Wales, later King George V and Queen Mary, with Prince Edward of Wales, later King Edward VIII, and Prince Allbert, later King George VI, at Barton Manor, 1909.

225

1908 Edward VII hosted a house party in honour of Czar Nicholas II of Russia and his family. This was the last state visit of the Russian royal family to this country. Also in this party were the Prince and Princess of Wales (later King George V and Queen Mary) and Prince Edward, later Edward VIII.

1910 King George V continued in his father's footsteps, racing *"Britannia"*, and playing host to numerous Kings and Emperors. The Emperor of Germany, Kaiser Wilhelm, was actually in Cowes, racing his yacht *"Meteor"* a few days before the outbreak of the 1914—1918 war.

1937 When George VI came to the throne on the abdication of his brother a new link was forged between the Isle of Wight and the Royal family, a link that has become stronger as time has passed.

1965 Queen Elizabeth II visited the Island for a very special ceremony, the investiture of her uncle, Admiral of the Fleet the Earl Mountbatten of Burma, as Governor of the Isle of Wight.

Since that date Her Majesty and members of her family have continued to visit the Island, some of them many times. Prince Philip comes to Cowes Week every year, the Prince and Princess of Wales have visited us, as have the Princess Royal, the Duke and Duchess of York, the Duke and Duchess of Kent, and other members of the family. The list is almost without end, an unparalleled record of royal visits which entirely justify the Isle of Wight regarding itself as a Royal Island.

H.M. Queen Elizabeth II at Carisbrooke in 1965, when inducting Lord Louis Mountbatten as Governor of the Isle of Wight.

XL — *As Others See Us*

Over the years much has been written about the Isle of Wight, and every shade of opinion has been expressed, ranging from the complimentary and flattering, to the frankly critical. On the basis that it does no one any harm to hear what others think of them, here are a few extracts from a variety of writers — Islanders, "Overners", and some who have never had the good fortune to live in the Island.

☆ ☆ ☆ ☆ ☆ ☆ ☆ ☆ ☆

The Reverend E. Boucher James, Vicar of Carisbrooke, writing in 1886, just over one hundred years ago, said —

> "The Isle of Wight of our ancestors in the last century was it seems, merrier and more jovial than that which we inhabit. In spite of much tribulation, people, both high and low, managed to enjoy themselves. We are a hundred years older. That age of the world that had its birth about the time of the French Revolution is advanced in years, and has outlived the illusions of its youth. A writer of our own times has laid it down that there never was a period when there seemed to be less hopefulness among mankind. However this may be, a foreboding overshadows the thoughts of many persons, that the close of the 19th century may witness a great Armageddon fight between the forces of good and evil. Our fathers and grandfathers in the last year of the last century entered upon that fight in the assured faith that good in the end must have the final victory. We, if Christians, hold to the same belief; let us act upon it as they did, and we need not be afraid."

☆ ☆ ☆ ☆ ☆ ☆ ☆ ☆ ☆

What would he have said today? The next extract is more recent — from the Introduction to the *"Isle of Wight Village Book"*, published by the Island Federation of Women's Institutes in 1974 —

> "The wonderful natural beauty of the Island is its greatest asset, and those who prize it have to fight hard against the encroachments of big business and uniformed development; but the struggle is worthwhile if we can hand on the Isle of Wight to future generations, lovely, and in the main, unspoiled."

☆ ☆ ☆ ☆ ☆ ☆ ☆ ☆ ☆

John Julius Norwich wrote this about the Isle of Wight in his book *"The Architecture of Southern England"* —

> "In the past twenty years or so, the uncontrolled growth of the tourist trade has spoilt all too much of the Isle of Wight, but, mercifully, there are still a few places where traces of the old Victorian seaside architecture survive. Of these, Ryde and above all Ventnor are the best. Even there, however, one has that feeling of constriction and confinement which pervades so much of the island — that feeling that there is simply not enough of it to go round. Too many people, too many houses. For those who go there to sail, such considerations matter little; the sea gives them all the elbow-room they need. But for us landlubbers, claustrophobia soon sets in."

K. Adlard Coles, a yachtsman, has this to say about Newtown —

"There must be few yachtsmen who, after visiting Newtown for the first time, have not returned to it again year after year. The snug anchorage, the creeks winding silently through the marshes and the unspoilt countryside, combine to give the place a character of its own. Perhaps the finger-prints of history linger on in some distant way to the present time."

☆ ☆ ☆ ☆ ☆ ☆ ☆ ☆

Sir John Oglander, to his children, wrote —

"If thou ever desirest to live plentifully, out of debt, worshipfully and with the respect of thy neighbours and the inhabitants, settle thyself to live in the Island and roam not out of it."

Later, towards the end of his life, he became disillusioned —

"This Island was beyond compare, *Anno Domini* 1630: so full of knights and gentry that I have seen 12 knights at the Ordinary at Newport. It was the Paradise of England and now, *Anno* 1647, it is just like the other parts of the Kingdom, a melancholy, dejected, sad place — no company, no resort, no neighbours seeing one of the other."

☆ ☆ ☆ ☆ ☆ ☆ ☆ ☆

On September 14th 1878, the Editor of the *"Whitehall Review"* reported as follows —

"If you ever need change of air, as indeed you must at this time of the year, take a ticket at Waterloo Station for Yarmouth, Isle of Wight, via Lymington. Neither of these towns has, it is true, much to commend it. Lymington is a dull country place, with a member of Parliament and a pretence of trade, the stronghold of the Wests, the Burrards, the Kennards and the Sartoriuses, while Yarmouth, just opposite, on the other side of the water, is as dead-alive a spot as it is possible to conceive. It is not ugly, it is not pretty — in short it is altogether mediocre. But crossing the Solent on a blazing September day, with the undulating slopes of the Island bathed in violet mists, with a mirage clipping our view of the wooded Hampshire coast on the left, while to the right Hurst Castle, white and trim, looks out with masked ferocity upon the green-blue sea, we confess that the want of social attractions in Lymington and Yarmouth trouble us as little as they do the gulls and cormorants. The scene is indeed passing fair, and has a soft beauty which in truth is far lovelier than any foreign lake, for neither Como nor Lucerne can show you the fresh green tints of yonder shores save in the very early spring. The little steamer which carries us over the streak of water does her work well in half an hour, and we are reminded of the end of our voyage by the attentions of an aged lady who has beguiled the time by sundry symphonies on that bygone instrument the harp, and by certain ditties sung in a voice whereof the freshness also belongs to a remote period. As we land on the narrow and altogether diminutive pier, we hear the toll-collector proudly informing a friend that "at the regatta yesterday we'd seventeen hundred people on us". But he did not explain how the feat was accomplished."

The next excerpt is taken from *"A Picture of the Isle of Wight"* by H. P. Wyndham, published in 1794 —

"As it may be considered an unpardonable omission, if I was not to take some notice of a voyage round the Isle of Wight, in this little work, the pleasures of which are anticipated, with raptures, by those who have not undertaken it, and who regard the tour of the Island as incomplete without it: I shall indulge my reader's curiosity, though I must take leave to premise my account of it, with a few general observations.

I have made this sailing expedition many times, and at different seasons of the year, but I never engaged in one where the party did not express more pleasure and satisfaction at its being completed, than either at the actual commencement, or in any part of its continuation. The circuit by water is about 80 miles, and it can scarcely be expected, in the most accommodating weather, to be finished in less than fourteen hours, though I have experienced its tedious duration for twenty-five. If the voyage be made in a calm and smooth sea an impatience and lassitude will certainly oppress and overwhelm the spirits of any company; and if a gale of wind should hasten the progress of the vessel, sickness and fears, though groundless, will, probably, prevent them from enjoying the variety of landscapes that the coasts of the Island offer to their view. I should therefore recommend this uncertain voyage to those ladies and gentlemen only, who may possess an uncommon degree of cheerfulness and good humour, and are proof against the convulsive operations of a sea sickness."

☆ ☆ ☆ ☆ ☆ ☆ ☆ ☆ ☆

And finally an extract from *"Fear, and be Slain"*, by the first Lord Mottistone, that great and brave man who played such a vital part in Island affairs in the first half of the present century, and was for many years a member of the crew of the Brook lifeboat —

"I have come to love very deeply these native island folk, amongst whom I have spent most of my life. They are different from any other people in the British Isles and it may well take a lifetime to understand them; but they are a great-hearted people, with a conception of loyalty to their kith and kin which carries them to every length of self-sacrifice, and though they regard all the rest of the world as *"overners"*, in moments of real emergency and danger they are prepared to hazard life itself even for these despised strangers.

They are indeed a remarkable people. Boys from elementary schools become captains of great merchant ships, or distinguish themselves in the Royal Navy, and this in numbers out of all proportion to the population; and so with the girls, who get scholarships and rise high in the teaching profession. One outstanding fact about the girls is their good looks. If anyone doubts this, let him come to see, and if anyone doubts the claim which I have made for the great virtue of courage in the men who are my neighbours on this island, let him come to any part of the South Coast on a day of south-westerly storm and watch the breaking sea. Then let him remember that for nearly a hundred years no lifeboat, when summoned, has failed to brave those seas, and he will, I am sure, concede the claim and discover why one loves these people and rejoices to live amongst them. Jacobs, Hayters, Downers, Jackmans, Joliffes, Ways, Chekes, Ratseys, of all classes and all degrees, loyal in adversity, brave in danger, respectfully I salute you."

INDEX